SCRIPTURE II

Called by the Father

Sister Mary Kathleen Glavich, S.N.D.
Sister Loretta Pastva, S.N.D.

General Editor: Sister Loretta Pastva, S.N.D.

BENZIGER
A division of Glencoe Publishing Co., Inc.
Encino, California

Consultants

Reverend John G. Crawford, M.A.
Professor of Theology, Notre Dame College of Ohio
South Euclid, Ohio

Reverend John T. Pawlikowski, O.S.M., Ph.D.
Professor, Catholic Theological Union
Commission, Bishop's Secretariat for Catholic-Jewish Relations
Chicago, Illinois

For "A Jewish Update":
Rabbi Max Roth
Temple Beth Sholom
Sarasota, Florida

Nihil Obstat

Reverend Paul J. Sciarrotta, S.T.L.
Censor Deputatus

Imprimatur

Most Reverend Anthony M. Pilla, D.D., M.A.
Bishop of Cleveland
Given at Cleveland, Ohio, July 2, 1981

The nihil obstat and imprimatur are official declarations that a book or pamphlet is free of doctrinal or moral error. No implication is contained therein that those who have granted the nihil obstat and imprimatur agree with the contents, opinions, or statements expressed.

Scripture passages are taken from *The New American Bible,* copyright © 1970 by the confraternity of Christian Doctrine, Washington, D.C. All rights reserved.

Benziger
A division of Glencoe Publishing Co., Inc.
17337 Ventura Boulevard
Encino, California 91316
Collier Macmillan Canada, Ltd.

Printed in the United States of America

ISBN 0-02-655860-2

Contents

Adulthood and Maturity:
The Monarchy

Crisis and Growth:
Prophets, Priests, Kings

Reflection and Hope:
Theologians and Poets

Introduction

ISRAEL'S LIFE STORY AND YOU

Since the beginning of history, people have delighted in tales of courage, love, birth, and death. Maybe it is because stories mysteriously transform us: we gain wisdom without having to go through the actual experience.

The most important stories are those that center on the meaning of existence as revealed by God. Religious stories probe these haunting human questions: Where did the world originate? Where did we come from? What is the purpose of life? Why do we have violence, sickness, and death? What happens after we die?

Christians find the answers in the Scriptures, and especially the Gospels. But besides the twenty-seven books of the New Testament, the Christian Bible contains the Hebrew Scriptures, forty-six books tracing the faith history of the Jewish people. Why are these stories of the Hebrews part of our heritage?

God did not wait until the time of Christ to give himself to the world. From the first moment of creation he began unfolding himself to all who faithfully followed their conscience. Just as your parents may drop hints about a gift they intend to give you, God prepared the world for the gift of his Son by gradually revealing his plan to the Hebrews.

Matthew 5:17
1 Peter 1:10

Although God's speaking through his Son brought a new dimension to the ongoing process of revelation, Israel's stories remain valid. Jesus himself loved and taught the Jewish Scriptures as the Word of his Father. "I have come, not to abolish [the law and the prophets], but to fulfill them," he said. And the Letter of Peter teaches that the same Spirit forms God's people now as in ancient times. The word of God never goes stale. In Israel's stories it continues to speak with a fresh and vital voice. To get the most from them, it is helpful to glimpse the Bible's overall plan and then see how each part relates to it.

■ Why do people drop hints about gifts they plan to give?

TRACING THE GROWTH

Hosea 11:1

Speaking for Yahweh, the prophet Hosea referred to Israel as God's favored son: "When Israel was a child I loved him, out of Egypt I called my son." In inviting the Jews to close relationship with himself, the Father seemed to play favorites. Actually, his gifts were for the benefit of all nations.

You might think of the Hebrew Scriptures as a biography of God's "son," the Jewish people. The folk tales of the patriarchs present the days of Israel's *birth and infancy*. Under Moses, Israel in its *youthful adolescence* found its identity as a people. Gaining independence on its own land, King David united the nation and commanded the respect of the world powers, launching Israel into adulthood.

But the story does not end there, because even in maturity adults continue to learn and grow. Israel made mistakes and, through exile, was called to purification and deepening. Suffering enlightened God's Chosen

CALLED BY THE FATHER

People, and they gained new *wisdom and hope* based not on politics but on the mercy of God. The hope of Israel was not misplaced; God continued to call. In the Spirit, the disciples recognized that Jesus, God's true Son, reconciles all God's children with the Father.

The stories of the Hebrew Scriptures are the stories of Israel's religious growth. They prepare the way for Jesus, but they also mysteriously reveal your own personal story. For, like Abraham, you are called by the Father. Like the Hebrews, in passing through baptismal waters you are freed from bondage in Egypt. In the Eucharist you are fed by manna from heaven. You have your own Promised Land and your own Exile. And all the while you draw closer to the Father. If you have eyes to see, you will find yourself among the characters and events of Israel's religious stories.

■ Which of the stages in Israel's growth can you identify with?

■ Glance at the Contents pages of this book. Which person or event attracts you most? Why?

■ What questions do you have about the Old Testament?

COVER:
   "Hear, O Israel, the Lord our God, the Lord is One." With these words of the *Shema*, the most important prayer of the Jewish faith, Jews traditionally acknowledge their faith and belief in One God, from which the Christian faith derives.
   Michel Schwartz, artist and Judaic scholar, uses the beauty and historical evolution of the Hebrew alphabet to depict the essence of Judaism and the spirit of the Old Testament.

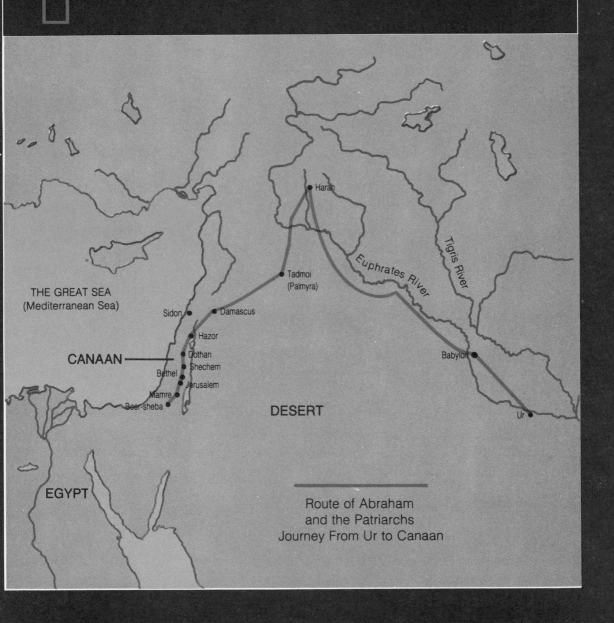

THE GREAT SEA
(Mediterranean Sea)

Haran

Tadmoi
(Palmyra)

Tigris River

Euphrates River

Sidon   Damascus

Hazor

CANAAN   Dothan
                Shechem
Bethel
        Jerusalem
    Mamre
Beer-sheba

Babylon

DESERT

Ur

EGYPT

Route of Abraham
and the Patriarchs
Journey From Ur to Canaan

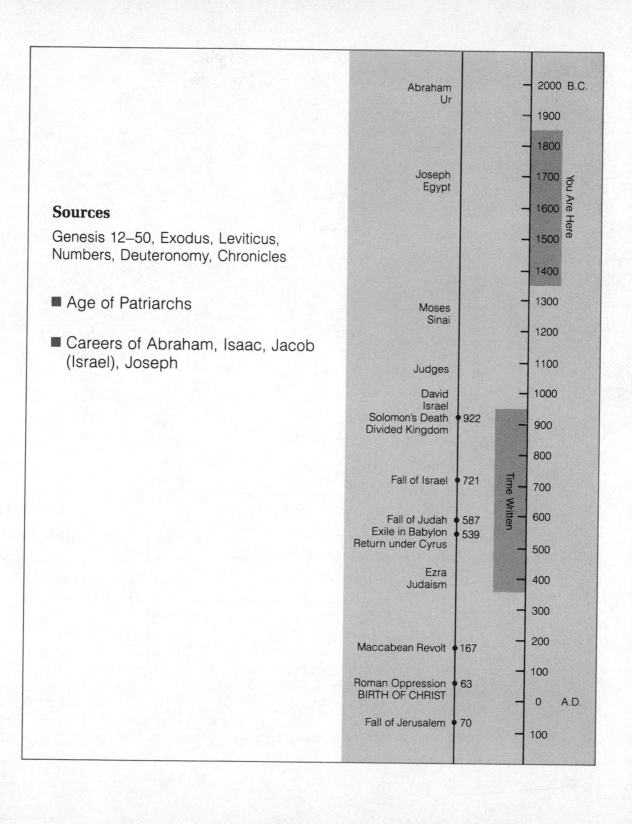

Sources

Genesis 12–50, Exodus, Leviticus, Numbers, Deuteronomy, Chronicles

■ Age of Patriarchs

■ Careers of Abraham, Isaac, Jacob (Israel), Joseph

Abraham Ur	— 2000 B.C.
	— 1900
	— 1800
Joseph Egypt	— 1700
	— 1600
	— 1500
	— 1400
	— 1300
Moses Sinai	— 1200
Judges	— 1100
David Israel	— 1000
Solomon's Death • 922 Divided Kingdom	— 900
	— 800
Fall of Israel • 721	— 700
Fall of Judah • 587 Exile in Babylon • 539 Return under Cyrus	— 600
	— 500
Ezra Judaism	— 400
	— 300
	— 200
Maccabean Revolt • 167	— 100
Roman Oppression • 63 BIRTH OF CHRIST	— 0 A.D.
Fall of Jerusalem • 70	— 100

You Are Here

Time Written

By faith man freely commits his entire self to God.

CONSTITUTION ON DIVINE REVELATION, #5

UNIT OVERVIEW

Tracing the family tree back to its roots has become a popular pastime.

- How far back can you trace your ancestors? What do you know about them?

Just as you can look back to the people who are responsible for your natural life, you can also trace the origins of your faith life. Your parents probably inherited from their parents the faith they gave you. But where did that faith start? Who was the first person to believe in the one true God that you worship?

If you are a Muslim, a Jew, or a Christian, your faith began with Abraham, the great Father of believers. A picture of Abraham and other transmitters of the faith can be pieced together from information provided by

biblical accounts, history, and modern excavations of ancient sites.

Abraham was probably the head, or patriarch, of a clan of Semitic seminomads who roamed the Fertile Crescent between 2000 B.C. and 1700 B.C. These peoples lived on the fringes of settled communities, moving from time to time in search of better pastures. According to the Bible, Abraham's father, Terah, took his family from Ur in Mesopotamia, six hundred miles north to Haran. At Terah's death, Abraham led his clan into Canaan, the Promised Land. Excavations of ancient state records of the day refer to *Hibri* and *Habiru*. These names suggest the Hebrews, the descendants of Abraham, who became the Chosen People. The biblical stories trace their gradual change from a disorganized group of food-gathering people to a pastoral or food-raising community.

Every so often a man is born who changes the earth: Columbus did it with a daring voyage, Edison with a

Semites are descendants of Noah's son Shem. They originated in southwestern Asia. A clan was a family subgroup related to a common ancestor.

Recently excavated clay tablets confirm many practices, such as working to earn a bride and exchanging birthrights, that are mentioned in the Bible.

light bulb, and Einstein with the theory of relativity. Abraham revolutionized religion by recognizing a new God.

Before Abraham, each tribe believed in fickle gods who granted prosperity or disaster according to whim. To buy their favor and ward off their displeasure, the people sacrificed the best part of their crops, their animals, and even their children. The gods were to be feared, but when a city fell, its god surrendered to the god of the conquering people. The changing fortunes of the people shaped the life of their gods.

Abraham grew up in this system of belief. Most likely he worshipped the moon god, Nanna Sin, who was venerated in Ur and had a temple in Haran. But then, in a deep religious experience, he learned of the existence of El Shaddai, the "mountain god" or "most high god." Not only was this god more powerful than the other gods, but he was also loving. He had no intention of destroying his people, but wanted to be their friend and protector.

Instead of being shaped by the people, the God of Abraham shaped a people by the bond of faith. Later, under Moses, who received greater knowledge of this unique God, they were cemented into a nation. Still later, they learned that the Lord they worshipped is the one true God. It was for Jesus, however, to fully reveal Abraham's God as our Father. To this day believers continue to grow in the knowledge of Abraham's God and his plan for drawing all people to his friendship.

It all began with the faith of Abraham. Despite pressures to adopt the local worship of Canaan, Abraham's descendants remained faithful. Through them, the true God is known and honored by half the world's population today. Nothing remains of the moon god Nanna Sin or of any of the Canaanite gods, but the God of Abraham lives on.

In the faith story that is part of your heritage, you will trace a family history, meeting Abraham's wife, Sarah; their son, Isaac; his wife, Rebekah; Isaac and Rebekah's twin sons, Esau and Jacob; Jacob's beautiful wife, Rachel; and Abraham's most important grandsons, Joseph and Benjamin. You will follow them from Canaan into Egypt, where they remained for four hundred years, eventually becoming enslaved.

The journey of the patriarchs was spiritual as well as geographical, for in finding their God they found their identity. They were models of faith to the Israelites, and they are no less models for us. God's fatherly call and care brought the Chosen People to birth with Abraham. Under the other great patriarchal sheiks, the infant Israel began its growth.

A *sheik* is an Arab family leader.

ONE

ABRAHAM AND ISAAC

Pioneers of Faith

God has created me to do Him some definite service; He has committed some work to me which He has not committed to another. I have my mission—I may never know it in this life, but I shall be told it in the next.

I am a link in a chain, a bond of connection between persons. He has not created me for naught. I shall do good. I shall do His work. I shall be an angel of peace, a preacher of truth in my own place while not intending it—if I do but keep His commandments.

CARDINAL NEWMAN

Go forth from the land of your kinsfolk and from your father's house to a land that I will show you.

GENESIS 12:1

CHAPTER PREVIEW

The world was stunned a few years ago when a section of the fifteen-mile-long Sunshine Skyway Bridge in Florida was rammed by a steamer and a busload of people plunged to their death in the ocean. Behind the bus was a car that stopped inches short of the edge.

■ If you had been in that car, to what would you attribute your being saved?

With Abraham the human race experienced a major breakthrough in religious thought. In fact, you could call Abraham God's own convert. God stepped into his life and revealed himself as someone who was interested in human welfare and directed people through the ordinary events of their lives. All he asked was trust.

Abram, as Abraham was called before the Covenant, must have wondered why he was picked to fall into God's hands. Although it was not the first time God had

Other ancient people who also received inspiration from God are symbolized by such biblical characters as Cain, Abel, and Noah.

visited his people, Abram was the first Hebrew to whom God had spoken. God's choice of Abram to light the world with the knowledge of God is a mystery, but God repeatedly calls unlikely people to special tasks. Although Abram and his descendants possessed many fine qualities, they were illiterate and rebellious. For Israel, however, greatness lay not in intelligence, talents, power, or goodness of life, but in a wholehearted response to God. Abram's trust in God led to action.

God told Abram to leave his flourishing business in Haran for a new land. The command was important for what it didn't say: it didn't say which land, and it didn't say how the new land would be acquired, or when. God expected Abram simply to follow. He only promised that Abram's descendants would become a great nation and that the earth would be blessed through him. Abram decided to risk it. At age seventy-five and still childless, he migrated to Canaan, the Land of Promise, placing his destiny in the hands of the divine caller. He let go.

Abram journeyed until he found a good location for his herds. When there were quarrels among his relatives over pasturelands and wells, he moved on, leaving the better fields to his nephew. When immorality brought the great cities of Sodom and Gomorrah to ruin, Abram

CALLED BY THE FATHER

interceded for his nephew and God saved Lot, whose family was tempted to go along with their neighbors' evil ways.

The search for grasslands took Abram as far as Egypt and back again to Canaan. His faith was rewarded when God renewed his promises and even entered into a contract, or covenant, with Abram, renaming him Abraham, father of many nations. Finally, when Abraham was ninety-nine, the promise of a son made to him and his aged wife, Sarah, was fulfilled.

The contract God made with Abraham was a covenant because its binding power was a personal relationship, not just a legal agreement.

Later Abraham faced the supreme test of his faith when God asked him to offer his son, Isaac, as a sacrifice. Abraham wondered how he could have as many descendants as the stars and the sands if he killed his only son, and he dreaded sacrificing his beloved Isaac. But he was ready for anything God asked. In order to safeguard the precious family heritage—knowledge of the true God—before his death Abraham arranged to have his son's wife chosen from within the clan. To the end, he remained a man of faith.

If you are the type of person who shoots for the moon in a card game or dives off the highest board, you have the gambling spirit of Abraham, who was ready to risk all for the chance of being a winner.

■ When you are not sure whether you should join a certain club or apply for a certain job, how can you find out which way the Lord is pointing?

Words to Know

scribes, Old Testament, sheik, patriarch, Semitic, Israelites, Mesopotamia (mes-ah-peh-**tay**-mi-eh), Ur (er), Haran (**hair**-ehn), Canaan (**kay**-nehn), Hebrews, Fertile Crescent, seminomad, tribe, clan, El Shaddai (ehl-shuh-**die**), Abraham/Abram (ay-bruhm), Terah (**tare**-eh), Sarah/Sarai (**sehr**-igh), Lot, Melchizedek (mel-**kiz**-eh-dek), Hagar (**hay**-gahr), Ishmael (**ish**-mi-ehl), Isaac (**eye**-zak), Laban (**lay**-behn), Sodom and Gomorrah (**sod**-ehm; geh-**mor**-eh), tithe, sterile, covenant, theophany, circumcision, hospitality

GOD CALLS ABRAM
(Genesis 11:27–12:9, 13:1–18, 14:11–24)

Think of three good friends. How have you grown to know them better? Do you know any of them perfectly?

No matter how long you know your friends, there will always be something to surprise you in them—and your closest friend will never understand you perfectly, either. If human beings are a mystery, God is more so. For centuries, ancient peoples recognized divine powers in nature. Neither sun, sea, earth, nor storm could make or break them. Although they had a sense of God, their knowledge of him was impersonal and vague. When God found someone ready to listen, he revealed himself more directly and personally. The Bible records this revelation in the story of Abraham's call.

As you might expect of a spiritual being, God uses his own ways to communicate: dreams, events, visions, direct words, angels. Even though God is totally present in all his revelations, human beings find it hard to be totally open to his word, which challenges even while it attracts. Abram was the kind of person who could tune in to God's wavelength. Because of his receptivity, God could begin to unfold his plan for the salvation of the human race. When Abram became a man of God, his life was transformed.

What Abram heard was an invitation to be ready for surprises. He did nothing special to bring about the offering, and in fact he didn't even know a "true God" existed. He just obeyed. His obedience led him to greatness. The Lord said to Abram, "Go forth from the land of your kinsfolk and from your father's house to a land that I will show you. I will make of you a great nation." Even though the words were full of mystery, they did contain two promises—*land* and *descendants*. In this communication Abram received his vocation to father a people favored by the knowledge of the true God. Already, in this earliest pronouncement, there was a hint that Abram was not to be blessed for his own sake, but for the sake of the whole world: "All the communities of the earth shall find blessing in you." One man,

Genesis 12:1–2

Genesis 12:3

CALLED BY THE FATHER

one word, one decision—and the earth was never to be the same again.

Read and Recall

Read Genesis 11:27–12:10, 13:1–18, and 14:11–24. This may be your first direct encounter with the Old Testament. Since it is important to learn to read the Bible, proceed in this way: (1) Read one text at a time, silently or aloud to a partner. (2) Read the question, keeping a paper over the following question and the answer to the first question, which is printed in the margin beside it. (3) Write the key words of the answer. (4) Check your answer with the answer provided. (5) If your answer is incorrect, reread the Genesis passage to find whatever you overlooked. Then move on to the next question.

1. The Call
   a. 12:1 *Who received this command?*
   b. 12:1 *What did the "Most High God" call Abram to do?*
   c. 12:2–3 *What promises did God make for Abram's sake?*
   d. 12:4 *How did Abram respond to this vague call?*
   e. 12:7 *Where did the Lord communicate further with Abram?*
   f. 12:7–8 *How did Abram worship?*
   g. 12:10 *Why did Abram move on?*
2. The Quarrel
   a. 13:1 *Why did Lot's and Abram's herdsmen quarrel when they returned from Egypt?*
   b. 13:8–13 *How was the quarrel settled?*
   c. 13:14–17 *How was Abram rewarded for his generosity?*
   d. 13:18 *How did Abram react?*

(a) Abram

(b) To leave for a land that would be shown him

(c) Land; descendants; divine help; blessing on the nations through him

(d) Abram went as the Lord directed him.

(e) Canaan

(f) Abram built the first altar to the most high God.

(g) Because of famine in Canaan

(a) Their possessions were so great that the sparse pastures couldn't support all their herds.

(b) Abram suggested that they part, giving Lot the first choice of the land.

(c) By a promise of many descendants

(d) He moved to Hebron and built another altar at Mamre.

3. The Thanksgiving Sacrifice
   a. 14:11–24 *What happened to part of the Abramite tribe as a result of the war of the Mesopotamian kings against the Canaanite rulers?*
   b. 14:15–16 *What did Abram do to counteract the situation?*
   c. 14:17, 21–24 *What offer did the King of Sodom make Abram for his victory?*
   d. 14:18–20 *Why do you think this passage is in this chapter?*
   e. 14:20 *What offering did Abram make to Melchizedek?*

(a) Lot was captured.

(b) He attacked at night and rescued Lot.

(c) To let Abram keep all his possessions if he would return the captives

(d) It shows God's direct action in favor of his Chosen People.

(e) A tithe (10 percent of one's income)

Reflect

1. What qualities did Abram need to (a) hear God's call, (b) strike out for new land, and (c) stick to the road?
2. Jews, Muslims, and Christians sometimes refer to themselves as "pilgrim people." In what ways is everyone's experience like Abram's? When are you most likely to feel like a pilgrim on the march? Like a pilgrim uncertain of the road? What practical things might make your journey smoother at these times?
3. Did God actually guide Abram's journey, or was Abram just migrating like everyone else at the time? Give reasons for your decision. Think of three ways in which God guides your journey to the promised land. Name some promised lands you look forward to reaching.
4. Melchizedek is mentioned in the first Eucharistic Prayer of the Mass. In what ways did Melchizedek foreshadow Jesus? Every priest? What does the Melchizedek incident teach about attitudes toward people outside the church?
5. How is Abram's generosity shown? What causes people to be stingy? What does it take to be generous? What are the rewards of generosity?
6. How does the word of God come to you personally?

CALLED BY THE FATHER

GOD'S PROMISES
(Genesis 15, 17:1–14)

How did you think of God in childhood? How do you think of him now? Why has there been a change?

Abram's call was more than an invitation to lead his family to Canaan. Abram also made a spiritual journey that led to a deeper knowledge of God. In Canaan, he encountered God again, to learn more about God's plans for him. Abram continued to seek God's will all his life.

■ People who like each other must show their feelings outwardly. Mention ways the following groups might do this: young children, older children, young adults, persons in business.

The God of Abram continued to favor Abram by renewing his promises, making them more specific, and entering into a formal agreement, or covenant, with the aging patriarch. As a reward for faith, God promised to be Abram's shield. But the great Father of Faith did not find faith easy. He questioned the message. "What good will your gift be," he asked, "if I remain childless and have only a servant as my heir?"

Genesis 15:2

In those days, sons alone had a right to inheritance, and the eldest received a double share of his father's property. There was no such thing as a written will or testament. Before he died, a father would give verbal instructions about the distribution of his goods. By law, a wife who could bear no children had to provide a substitute wife for her husband from among her servants. The sons of this slave-woman concubine had no share in the inheritance unless their father legally adopted them. Sarai (later Sarah), Abram's barren wife, had given Abram her serving girl Hagar, but she did not want Abram to adopt Hagar's son, Ishmael. Abram himself would have preferred his heirs to be born of Sarai.

A *concubine* is one of the women, though not a legal wife, making up a man's household in ancient times.

Israel's tradition tells us that Ishmael became the ancestor of the Arabs, while the Hebrews were the descendants of Isaac.

God did not spell out the remedy for this touchy situation. He merely made a blanket promise: "Your own son will be your heir." He led the aged patriarch outdoors. "Look up at the sky and count the stars, if

Genesis 15:4

you can. Just so, shall your descendants be." In ancient times, when there were no police, men with means of protection made contracts, or covenants, to exchange a familylike protection for service or land from a weaker party. Just as legal contracts today have standard forms, ancient covenants also had parts: (1) review of the benefits bestowed by the superior party on the lesser one, (2) a response of trust and loyalty by the lesser party, and (3) the statement of the promise by the superior party. Although they were not in order, these three parts were included in the covenant between Abram and God.

It was a confirmation and clarification of God's original promise to make Abram a great nation. Even though he didn't understand how all this would take place, Abram accepted God's word and God entered into a symbolic covenant ritual with him.

The covenant ceremony began with God's promise. After Abram's response of acceptance, God commanded him to split some animals in two and place each half opposite the other. This signified that either party vi-

CALLED BY THE FATHER

olating the pact would suffer the same fate as the animals. By staying with the carcasses, Abram kept the birds of prey away from the raw meat. This action is interpreted by some analysts to be symbolic of how Abram's faith would serve to keep anything from destroying the covenant.

Finally, God reviewed past benefits bestowed on Abram: the call out of Ur to his own land, protection on the journey, and settlement on the land. (The promise would be fully delivered only when the Israelites gained secure possession of Canaan during David's reign.) Images of a setting sun, a trance or very deep sleep, and a terrifying darkness were efforts on the part of the writer to convey the theophany, or manifestation, of God. All through the theophany God spoke as an intimate friend, a father-protector, but he was also the all-holy and mysterious "most high God." At the conclusion of the rite, a vessel containing smoking coals and a flaming torch passed between the split carcasses. In the ancient ritual, both contracting parties usually passed between the animals to symbolize their mutual cooperation. Here only God, symbolized by the burning torch, appeared to pass through to show that he took full responsiblity for the covenant himself.

Theophany: theo—"god," *phany*—"to make shine." It comes unexpectedly and, because of its frightening nature, is often introduced by the words "fear not."

Some years later God would reveal his name as El Shaddai—the "most high God"—and command: "Walk in my presence and be perfect." Abram's experience was so profound that his name was changed to signify that it had left him a new person. To seal the covenant relationship, he made the mark of circumcision upon his body. Abraham performed this ceremony on all his male descendants and servants in order to include them in the covenant relationship. After this, marriage outside the tribe would be frowned on; later in history, it was absolutely forbidden.

Circumcision is the cutting of the loose skin of the male genital organ as a sign in the flesh of blood brotherhood with God. Circumcision had been practiced by other peoples, but Abraham gave it a religious meaning.

Read and Recall

Read Genesis 15 and 17:1–14.

1. In what three ways did the God of Abram show his continuing preference for Abram?

2. Why did Abram long for an heir? In the first promise, God used the image of sand for Abram's descendants. What second image was used?
3. List the steps of the covenant ritual. Explain the meaning of the animals, the birds of prey, and deep darkness.
4. Cite the parts of the covenant God made with Abram.
5. What external sign showed that the Hebrews were covenanted to God?

Reflect

1. What did Abram learn about God in the covenant ritual? Catholic novelist Flannery O'Connor has said, "It's not theology that clears up your religious problems, but prayer." Do you agree? Why or why not? What do the Church's public rites, or liturgy, do for you?
2. Abram's theophany came in the midst of darkness. What does this suggest about growth in knowledge of God?
3. In New Testament times, baptism replaced circumcision. How are the two ceremonies related? How are they different?

Matthew 3:9

4. John the Baptizer warned the Jews that it wasn't enough to be a son of Abraham. What did he mean? What else besides baptism is necessary for the salvation of Christians?

THE VISITATION OF GOD
(Genesis 18:1–19:29)

Decide which *two* of the following qualities you would most want in a friend: humor, loyalty, neatness, generosity, responsibility, humility, honesty, intelligence.

It is said that two of the most respected qualities of our times are loyalty and honesty. Betrayal of friends, even in the underworld, is considered the lowest of actions.

In the age of the patriarchs, when travelers stepped into mortal danger whenever they left their own land, hospitality topped the list of the most-admired qualities. People regarded it as a point of honor to welcome strangers into their tents, and to refuse someone lodging was almost criminal. The head of the household was expected to assume complete responsibility for the safety and well-being of his guests. In the story of Abraham and the visitors, you see this ancient noble quality in action.

The age of the patriarchs is the time of Abraham, Isaac, Jacob, and Joseph, who are thought to have lived between 1900 and 1700 B.C.

Read and Recall

Read Genesis 18:1–19:29, and have a group dramatize or pantomime the incident in chapter 18 between the Three Men, Abraham (outside), and Sarah (inside).

In the remainder of the passage, the scene switches to Sodom. There, although Lot received the visitors as graciously as Abraham had, the citizens of Sodom intended them harm. It seems that the visitors were on their way to destroy Sodom and Gomorrah, cities of great beauty and wealth but corrupted by the immorality of the inhabitants. Abraham's compassion and goodness shone out clearly as he tried to save the cities by unashamedly bargaining with the Lord. His argu-

Sodom and Gomorrah, now thought to lie under water in the Dead Sea, are symbolic of the moral corruption of the pagan nations. *Sodomy* is an unnatural method of having sex.

To this day pillars of salt and gypsum stand guard over the Dead Sea. The Israelites turned the natural surroundings into a parable.

ment was that a few good people far outweighed the many who were evil. Find out how the visitors saved Lot and some of his family. Answer the following questions.

1. What hospitality did Abraham show the visitors?
2. What prediction was made? Why did Sarah laugh? Why did she deny laughing?
3. How is this story connected with the larger story of Abraham? What line in chapter 18 sums up the incident?
4. How did Lot's guests get rid of the attackers?
5. Why was the city destroyed?
6. Which three people accompanied Lot to safety? What happened to Lot's wife?
7. God did not save the cities, but he did listen to Abraham's prayer. How? (Refer to Genesis 19:29.)

Reflect

1. Who was the visitor? (See Genesis 18:16–22.) What truth about hospitality is implied? What other stories do you know in which the Lord appears as someone to be served?
2. Chapters 18 and 19 present two sharply contrasting scenes bridged by the prayers of Abraham. The first is highlighted by Abraham's gracious hospitality and its reward—the promise of a son and a new nation. The second presents the lust, violence, and punishment of a world ignorant of the true God. What is implied about Israel's role in the world?
3. Why did Lot and his family hesitate to leave Sodom? What connection do you see between Lot's choice of the plush Jordan valley and his near destruction?
4. What is symbolized by Lot's wife turning back? Salt is sterile and lifeless, like stone. What deeper meaning do you see in the pillar-of-salt image? How does Lot's wife tie in with Luke 9:62?
5. What does the story of Sodom say about sexual immorality? How can you, like Abraham, keep your door open to the Lord?

CALLED BY THE FATHER

6. How does the story of Sodom and Gomorrah answer the question of why there are natural disasters? While suffering and death are tied to sin, you know from Christ's death that tragedy is not limited to sinners. What are some good effects of calamities?

The story of the destruction of Sodom and Gomorrah by a rain of sulfurous fire may have been based on explosions of gases that formed around the Dead Sea, which had no outlet.

ABRAHAM'S SUPREME TRIAL
(Genesis 21:1–20, 22:1–19)

Abraham was almost a hundred years old when Sarah gave birth to a son whom they named Isaac because, in Sarah's words, "God has given me cause to laugh, and all who hear of it will laugh with me." Blessed as she was, Sarah grew jealous of Ishmael, Hagar's son, and, to Abraham's dismay, she drove them both out. Although God seemed to defend Sarah's action, he also cared tenderly for Hagar and Ishmael in the desert. Ishmael became a hunter, married a pagan Egyptian, and became the father of certain Arab desert tribes. Through this incident God revealed his saving love for all peoples of the earth, not just the Hebrews.

Several years later, Abraham's faith was put to a severe test, and through that test he made some important discoveries. If you are familiar with the story of Abraham's sacrifice of Isaac, briefly retell or act out the story, including as many details as you remember.

Genesis 21:6. *Isaac* means "he laughs" or "let God smile on the bearer (of the name)." Why was Isaac given this name?

Read

Read Genesis 22:1–19. As you read the passage, use the following commentary to guide you to a better understanding of one of the world's most moving stories.

22:1 "test"/You have the advantage of knowing that Abraham's ordeal was a test of faith, but at the time Abraham didn't understand what was going on.

22:1 "Ready!"/Judging from the early-morning departure (22:3), the call came during sleep. Abraham's usual disposition toward God's requests was readiness rather than resistance.

22:2 "your son Isaac, your only one, whom you love"/ The command stressed that Abraham was asked to destroy the source of his hope for descendants. He must withstand the greatest test—a threat to the very basis of his faith.

22:2 "on a height"/Hills and mountains represent the meeting place with God.

22:4 "On the third day"/The Bible uses three-day journeys as a signal that the theological or spiritual meaning is the focus of the story.

22:6 "wood . . . laid . . . on his son"/This offering was to be a holocaust—that is, a sacrifice that is completely destroyed by fire.

22:8 "God himself will provide the sheep for the holocaust"/Abraham was referring to Isaac, but the reader knows that God will make his statement true in a surprising and far better sense.

22:11 "the Lord's messenger"/The messenger was God himself, as the first-person pronoun "me" in verse 12 shows.

22:13 "Abraham . . . offered it . . . in place of his son"/The Canaanites among whom Abraham lived believed that sacrificing their first-born sons would persuade their god to grant them many children. Abraham,

Animal sacrifice became the central act of Hebrew worship until around Jesus's time, when the Pharisees de-emphasized it in favor of the home-meal setting of the Passover.

CALLED BY THE FATHER

whose knowledge of the "most high God" was still very limited, must have been torn between what seemed to him a self-sacrificing action and the promise of God. God revealed that he did not favor human sacrifice. There is no need to pay off God. He loves freely and he wants his people to do his will wholeheartedly. Abraham's faith made him pleasing to God.

22:14 "the Lord will see"/He would make sure that the needed item would be provided. Abraham's name for the mountain summed up what he had learned in his faith test! Trust in God guarantees God's care. Abraham didn't *have* to worship God; he *wanted* to because he recognized the goodness of "God most high."

22:15 "I swear by myself"/Abraham's faith caused God to renew his promise of descendants with a special solemnity. He swore in the most sacred way—by his own most holy Being. No more serious oath could be imagined.

God's taking an oath is only a human way of expressing the seriousness of God's promise.

22:17 "take possession of the gates of their enemies"/ A new note was added to the promise—God would help the Israelites win over their enemies in their search for a land.

Recall

Tell, act out, list, or draw the main steps of Isaac's sacrifice.

Reflect

1. How is the Ishmael episode related to the modern ecumenical movement?
2. What new truths did Abraham learn in this trial?
3. The Canaanites believed that the gods required human sacrifice. Many good people today honestly believe that such harmless things as dancing and card playing are forbidden by God's law, while others sincerely think that abortion is approved by God. The Catholic Church stands by the revelation made to Abraham concerning the sacredness of human

The *ecumenical movement* is the effort of the Christian churches to reunite according to Christ's wish expressed in Jesus's Prayer for Unity (John 17:21).

life. List all the reasons you know that are used to justify abortion. How do the reasons for abortion hold up against God's revealed word?

4. Write a letter in the style of "Dear Abby" telling of a situation in which your faith and obedience to God's word were severely tested. Describe all the pulls you felt to violate God's law. Let the class or a partner write Abby's answer.

5. What line from this section in Genesis does Paul use in Romans 8:32?

6. The Letter to the Hebrews (11:17–19) puts a Christian interpretation on Abraham's hope in offering his only son. In this letter, what does the return of Isaac to Abraham symbolize?

7. Abraham's faith was rewarded by a renewal of the promise. What are the rewards of our faith?

8. Abraham was required to make the journey and actually bind up his son. Faith needs to be expressed in action. List two specific ways to express faith in each of the following: prayer, sacraments, ordinary actions, sacrifices.

THE DEATH OF SARAH; A WIFE FOR ISAAC
(Genesis 23, 24)

Isaac grew to manhood. When his mother, Sarah, died, Abraham purchased a burial plot for her in a cave near Hebron. Fittingly, as the great mother of the Israelite family, she was the first of the Chosen People to be laid to rest there. The purchase of the plot from the pagan Hittites was Abraham's first permanent occupancy in Canaan. Abraham himself is buried there.

Although Ishmael, the slave woman's child, inter-married with a woman from a neighboring tribe, Abraham had to assure himself before he died that Isaac—the seed of the new people of God—would not marry into a Canaanite family, as this would endanger the inheritance God had promised. He commissioned his chief servant to find a wife for his son from his own

Hittites (also Hatti) were a non-Semitic people whose center was near present Ankara, Turkey, in the Near East. Their empire collapsed around 1300 B.C.

CALLED BY THE FATHER

people. However, he made his steward swear most solemnly not to take Isaac back with him to the "old country" of Aram. He knew that God's plan was to be carried out in Canaan.

Read

Read Genesis 23 and 24, and act out the beautifully told ancient story in which, once again, hospitality plays a role. Include these characters—Abraham, Rebekah, Laban, Nahor, Milcah, Isaac, senior servant, maids, and camel drivers—and use gold bracelets, gifts, jugs, and a table as props.

Recall

1. Who was behind Abraham's command to his chief steward to get Isaac a wife? Where was the servant sent? Why? (24:7)
2. How was Rebekah related to Abraham? What was the sign by which Isaac's bride-to-be would be recognized? How did Rebekah pass her test?
3. What was Laban's reaction to the visitor?
4. What favor did Rebekah's family ask of Abraham's servant? How did Rebekah resolve the issue?

Reflect

1. Why was God's guidance on Isaac's choice of a wife important? How important is God's guidance on your life decisions?
2. Land, water, and posterity were three needs of settling seminomads. This story centers around life-giving water. What symbolism do you see in Rebekah's eagerness to water Abraham's camels? What light does Rebekah's action shed on Jesus's first public miracle?
3. The obligation of hospitality to strangers is not so strong today as in Abraham's day, but making others feel welcome is Christian. Discuss ways to do it.

TRACKING YOUR JOURNEY

The life style of the patriarchs was always to be on a journey. They moved to a campsite and set up tents, and then in the spring broke camp for greener pastures. At the same time their quest was spiritual—to know God, to find their own identity, and to understand their relationship to one another and to the world. Their story is your own. Tracking your life's journey, you can receive insights into its meaning. Here are suggestions on one way to proceed.

General Directions

Choose one method under "Stepping-Stones" below to recall key situations of your life. Then follow one of the two procedures under "Digging More Deeply" to find the meaning of your stepping-stones. Third, try to find a pattern in your journey by one of the two suggested "Patterning" techniques. Finally, follow the last step as it is given under "The Road Ahead."

Stepping-Stones

Sit comfortably. Close your eyes and remember the key events of your life. Don't arrange them in order. Use the houses you lived in, your favorite clothes, books, or toys, or significant persons or places to trigger your memory. Let your memories flow. Avoid judging them. Note key phrases as they arise. When you have a fair number, identify the five most outstanding events and place them in chronological order. Label your list "Stepping-Stones of My Spiritual Journey."

Part of Abraham's list would look like this (the most important events are starred):

> Trip with father to Haran
> Marriage to Sarai
> Death of father
> *Call from God to leave Haran: the move
> Gift of better land to Lot—God's promise

Rescue of Lot—Melchizedek's blessing
*Covenant with God after vision—circumcision

Or, instead of making a list, draw a line representing your life and put in the stepping-stones at appropriate spots.

Digging More Deeply

Dig around the biggest stones with questions like these:

- What was going on in my life at the time? (Was I in a period of quiet or crisis?) What circumstances added to the meaning of the event?
- Who was important to me then (living, dead, or in writings)?
- What was my reaction to the event?
- How did I change as a result of it? What new insights did I receive? What decisions did I make?

Patterning

Share your journey with a small group you trust. Ask for feedback to help you see your story through their eyes. Listen as they read their stepping-stones and put yourself in their place. Share your reactions. What general meaning do you see?

Or, instead of discussing your journey, look over your stepping-stones and try to see if there is a thread of meaning connecting them. What overall sense does your spiritual journey make? What helps or hindrances did you meet?

The Road Ahead

Finally, glance into your future and decide where you are actually going compared with where you want to go. Think quietly. In what direction are you being called? Is it *where* you want to go? What is the next stepping-stone you see? What spiritual effect do you expect it to have on you?

Without letting your mind exert control, draw an image of what you see in your future. Use crayons, felt-tip pens, or paints, if possible.

Where will you get the "fuel" to move toward the next stepping-stone? What obstacles stand in the way? The rest of the journey is up to you.

Adapted from *How to Track Your Journey* (Columbia, Md.: Faith at Work, Inc., 1980), pp. 14–15.

CALLED BY THE FATHER

GETTING IT TOGETHER

Abraham was called to follow a new kind of God—one who offered a personal love and asked a free response of faith. Although uncomprehending, Abraham trusted. He was willing to risk everything on a promise: he could endure a far and lonely journey; he could wait a quarter of a century for an unlikely son; he could give up that son, his only hope, at a moment's notice.

One of the Bible's most appealing characters, Abraham was a man of rare gifts: generosity, obedience, humility, and gratitude. These qualities burst the limits of self-centeredness. By contrast, his nephew Lot could not reach beyond his own skin. Choosing the best fields and the easiest course, Lot shrank as a human being. Abraham never stopped growing.

What was Abraham's secret? It was faith. His faith prompted him to yield his life totally to God—not like a slave, but like a lover wanting to please the loved one. Abraham said "yes" to whatever God asked and refused to worry about the future. The faith-filled Abraham was a person of contentment. His happiness didn't depend on more and better possessions, security, independence, or an easy life; even human love came second to God. Following God on his journey, Abraham found true and lasting peace.

REVIEWING THE CHAPTER

Linking Your Ideas

Cite incidents from the Abraham stories to demonstrate three of the following themes:

1. Faith is God being *so* real to you that you entrust your whole person to him. You believe his word just because it is his.
2. God always takes the first step toward us. He reveals himself and loves, corrects, and rewards us.
3. There is a pattern in God's action: he calls each person for a special job; you are free to respond or not.
4. Hospitality, generosity, and selflessness make us attractive to God and to one another.
5. Only the large-hearted are big enough for the humility and nobleness of sincere gratitude.
6. A sincere relationship with the true God must be expressed by both an internal conviction and some visible action.
7. From the beginning, God raised up saviors for his people.
8. Obedience is never easy, but it is a pleasing worship of God and carries with it great blessings.
9. God is someone with whom we can be on the most intimate terms, and yet he is far, far beyond us in holiness and power.
10. To sin is to press the button labeled "self-destruct."
11. Extreme ease of life can lead to moral corruption.
12. God's ways are most surprising—a source of continual wonderment.
13. Worshipping the true God is more than a matter of animal or human sacrifice. It involves clean living.

Strengthening Your Grasp

Write one- to three-paragraph answers to these questions:

1. Where did Abraham's journey take him besides to another country? What could you do that is equivalent to building altars?
2. The Bible often places contrasting figures together to play up the character of a good person. What qualities do Lot and Sarah bring out in Abraham?
3. Why did Abraham's response to his call require faith? Why is faith just as necessary for you as it was for Abraham?

Expressing Your Convictions

Write a creed expressing your personal beliefs, and then list some concrete things you do to make your inner convictions visible to others.

Extending Your Interests

Hesed is a Hebrew word meaning the special family loyalty, love, and faithfulness that nomadic people, who had no protection other than their own clan, owed one another. It appears in the Bible as a recurring theme about 250 times. In the following passages, tell between whom *hesed* is shown and what words are used to express it: Genesis 21:22–24, 24:27, 24:49, 47:29.

TWO

JACOB AND JOSEPH

God's Chosen Ones

Sections

Guide us as we work
   and teach us to live
in the Spirit that has made us your
   sons and daughters,
in the love that has made us
   brothers and sisters.
Grant this through Christ our Lord.

DAYTIME PRAYER
THE LITURGY OF THE HOURS

You shall no longer be spoken of as Jacob, but as Israel, because you have contended with divine and human beings and have prevailed.

GENESIS 32:29

Even though you meant harm to me, God meant it for good, to achieve his present end, the survival of many people.

GENESIS 50:20

CHAPTER PREVIEW

Everyone has had feelings of guilt, uncertainty, or fear after wrongdoing. Which experiences of this kind stand out in your memory? How did you come to terms with them? Recall a time when someone rejected or betrayed you. How did you feel? What did you learn from the incident?

Ancient historians often suppressed the faults of their heroes, but the Hebrews were not afraid to tell the truth. They realized that human frailties were no hindrance to God, but only revealed the depth of his mercy and goodness in dealing with his people.

The moral character of Jacob, the younger of Isaac's and Rebekah's twins, left much to be desired. Yet it was to Jacob and not his brother, Esau, that the mystery of God's plan was revealed. Although Jacob's sons betrayed their brother Joseph, God saved Joseph and, through him, all of Israel.

Humanly speaking, Isaac's eldest son, Esau, had the qualities for success in their culture: physical strength, skills of the hunt, and, as the firstborn, upon his father's death the right to a double portion of inheritance and his father's complete authority. Further, the rugged Esau was clearly his father's favorite.

Jacob, on the other hand, was mentally gifted, a quality that hunters could not be expected to value. But Jacob capitalized on his gifts. First he preyed on the weakness of his twin to gain Esau's birthright. Then, encouraged by his mother, who recognized the younger twin's potential, Jacob deceived his father to win Esau's solemn blessing for himself. Even though his actions seem questionable to us, the ancient Hebrews probably delighted in the story of Jacob's cleverness, which also revealed the mystery of God's choices.

Jacob fled from the anger of his brother into the wilderness, where he faced himself and God. In the dream in which he encountered the Lord at Luz (Bethel), God renewed the covenant made to Abraham. In this deeply religious experience, Jacob, like Abraham, was chosen to be the father of the tribes, or nations. From this time on, although he was not yet completely converted, he showed a greater sensitivity to God's presence.

Jacob found shelter with his uncle Laban in Haran. There the cheater was himself cheated when Laban took advantage of Jacob's love for Rachel, a beautiful younger daughter, to extract fourteen years of service from his nephew. Amidst challenging work and constant family haggling, Jacob showed superior farming abilities and learned the important art of reconciliation. Twenty years after his arrival in Haran, Jacob left for Canaan in the south, no longer alone but with a wealth of family, servants, and flocks.

After Jacob had worked seven years, Laban gave him Rachel's less attractive older sister, Leah, heavily veiled. Jacob served seven more years to win Rachel. (See Genesis 29–33 and 35–36.)

Fearing revenge from Esau, he sent ahead gifts, but now he understood that human scheming alone would not bring deliverance. In dependence on God, he prayed, "I am unworthy of all the acts of kindness that you have loyally performed for your servant."

Genesis 32:11

What then took place was so mysterious that it was reported in language using the images of a religious

CALLED BY THE FATHER

dream. In it Jacob received a new name to show the important role he would have on his return to the homeland. Many years later in exile, the Jews derived joy and comfort from this folktale in which God continued to love Jacob even when, as a result of his faults, he was alienated from his own country.

Some historians maintain that the stories of the huntsman Esau and the farmer Jacob explain how Israel abandoned nomadic ways for an agricultural life style. Although the tales were told orally for centuries and were no doubt "touched up" in the retelling, their main purpose was to illustrate the free gift of election and God's faithfulness to his people.

Some of the Jacob stories explain the origin of later practices in Israel. This does not detract from their religious meaning.

■ Have you ever completely succeeded in overcoming a fault? If so, how?

Election refers to God's choice of the Jews to spread the knowledge of himself to the world.

Joseph, Jacob's youngest son, was the fourth and last of the patriarchs of Israel, the link between the wan-

Genesis 46:2 is an exception, in which Jacob receives a direct call to return to Egypt.

dering herdsmen of Canaan and the oppressed people who later made their escape from Egypt under the leadership of Moses. The last quarter of the Book of Genesis portrays Jacob's son in stories that have been loved and repeated for thousands of years. They rank with the world's great literature.

Unlike the earlier patriarchal stories, the Joseph narrative rarely portrays God as appearing supernaturally. There are no mysterious voices, calls, or dramatic appearances in human or angelic form. God's revelation simmers through the ordinary, everyday lives of his people, who are shown as always under the invisible but firm guidance of the divine hand.

God is the Lord of History. Without glossing over even criminal actions, the sacred author showed how God fit both good and evil into his plan of raising up a nation to carry salvation to the world. The message is clearly one of hope: God always wins.

Jacob settled in Canaan with his eleven sons, the youngest of whom, Joseph, was sold into slavery in Egypt by the treachery of his jealous brothers.

When Joseph came to Egypt, the pyramids were already a thousand years old.

Instead of brooding over the injustice done him, Joseph quickly rose to a position of influence in Egypt. Although he was falsely accused of making romantic advances to his master's wife and was imprisoned, he once again made the best of his situation. A kind deed he did led to his appointment as vizier under the pharaoh.

A *vizier* was a high official in the ancient world. History affirms that during the reign of the Hyksos, the foreign invaders who ruled Egypt between 1710 and 1570 B.C., a Semite could very well have gained high office.

When Joseph's brothers were forced by a famine in Canaan to apply to Egypt for grain, Joseph tested the sincerity of their repentance before giving them a choice piece of land on the eastern Nile delta. Thus, by accepting the suffering that had come into his life, he became a savior to his people.

The final stories switch the spotlight back to Jacob's important role in Israel's drama. On his deathbed, Jacob blessed Joseph's younger son in preference to the elder. The scene recalls Isaac's final blessing, except that Jacob was not tricked as his father had been. He died pronouncing oracles about the future status of the twelve

CALLED BY THE FATHER

tribes through whom the knowledge of the true God would be carried to the world.

During the next four hundred years, the seventy descendants of Jacob multiplied in Egypt to become the Lord's Chosen People.

■ Based on what you already know of Joseph, give your impression of him. Of all the road signs you know, like STOP or YIELD, which would be most appropriate for Joseph? Why?

Words to Know

Jacob (**jay**-cub), Esau (**ee**-saw), Edom (**ee**-dehm), birthright, Rachel (**ray**-chehl), Leah (**lee**-eh), Benjamin (**ben**-jeh-mehn), Bethel (**beth**-ehl), Laban (**lay**-behn), Peniel (peh-**nee**-ehl), Joseph, Hyksos (**hick**-sos), Ishmaelites (**ish**-mi-el-lites), Egypt (**ee**-jipt), vizier (**vichz**-i-ehr), Manasseh (meh-**nas**-eh), Ephraim (**ee**-fruhm), Judah (**joo**-dah), Land of Goshen (**goh**-shehn)

JACOB AND ESAU
(Genesis 25:19–34; 27)

Have you ever noticed that fuel and food on a superhighway are usually a little more expensive than on other roads? Why is this so?

■ Would you charge more for something because of someone else's urgent need? Why or why not?

There is always a temptation to capitalize on people's immediate needs. The great patriarch Jacob was not above taking advantage of his twin. To read this famous story with understanding, the following background information will help.

■ *Jacob* means "heel" or "cheater." He was born gripping the heel of his older twin brother, Esau. This symbolized his inclination to take more than his fair share.

Genesis 25:32

- An oracle is a divinely inspired pronouncement. Rebekah, who apparently did not tell anyone what was revealed to her, favored the younger son because of God's choice of him over the older brother.
- Esau instantly accepted the exchange of his birthright for a bowl of lentil stew, saying, "I'm on the point of dying. What good will any birthright do me?" Biblical scholars are puzzled both by the ease with which he gave up his birthright and by his response. Esau was not about to die, and the exchange was grossly uneven. As the leader of his clan, Esau was responsible for preserving the unique faith heritage of Abraham. Esau's carelessness in so important a matter suggests that he lacked a spiritual outlook. Although he was a full-grown man, he refused to deny himself a small pleasure for a long-range good.
- The shrewd Jacob couldn't help recognizing his brother's character weakness, but, as the more thoughtful of the pair, he should have known better than to take advantage of it. Yet God brought good out of the situation.
- With our well-developed consciences, we easily recognize the wrong Rebekah did in helping Jacob trick his father. But perhaps Rebekah was only being true to the oracle, and so to God. Still, Jacob did flee like a guilty man.
- In ancient societies, where hardly anyone was able to write, the oral word was more binding than a legal contract in our day. Once uttered, words could *never* be revoked. This was especially true of curses and blessings.

Read

An *oracle* is a prophecy that is usually given by means of mysterious sign or an allegory and received at a shrine.

Read Genesis 25:19–34 and 27. At the beginning, Isaac did not know about the oracle or about Esau's loss of his birthright. Notice that, in the end, everyone lost—Esau, who was defrauded; Isaac, who was tricked; Rebekah, who would never see her favorite son again; and Jacob, who was forced to flee for his life. Yet God loved his weak and ignorant people. Although they had to

CALLED BY THE FATHER

take the consequences of their actions, God, like a loving and forgiving Father, used their mistakes to further his saving plan for the world.

Recall

1. How old were Isaac and Rebekah when they were married? What is the significance of the twins' names?
2. What oracle was Rebekah given when she consulted the Lord before the boys were born?
3. By what exchange did Esau lose his birthright?
4. How did Jacob deceive Isaac to gain his father's blessing? What did the blessing consist of?
5. What "blessing" remained to Esau?
6. What was Esau's reaction to being replaced? What was Rebekah's advice to Jacob?

Reflect

1. In what way was Jacob like a Christian when he so easily gained Esau's inheritance? What parallel do you see between this scene and your own baptism?
2. Describe how Isaac's senses failed him when he relied on them to discover the truth. What might this symbolize?
3. What can threaten the faith inheritance you received from your parents? How would you keep a 20–20 faith "vision" to safeguard your eternal legacy?

A *legacy* is a legal inheritance.

4. Esau lacked a sense of values. Name one "instant gratification" associated with each of the following that can cut you off from your Father's blessing: a party, shopping at a mall, your job, a date. (For instance, you might trade an hour's sleep for the blessing of God on Sunday morning.)
5. Words are a sacred trust between human beings as well as a way to communicate with God. God communicates with us chiefly by his Word, Jesus, who said "I am the Truth." When do you find yourself most tempted to lie? What are some ways to build up the stability of human words?

John 14:6

JACOB'S DREAM VISIONS
(Genesis 28:10–22, 32:23–33)

On his way to and from Haran, where he fled from Esau, Jacob had two profoundly moving encounters with God in which he grew in self-knowledge and understanding of his and his people's vocation.

Jacob's first dream occurred at Luz, a place in the wilderness that he crossed on his way to Laban's house in Haran. Alone for perhaps the first time, Jacob received a transforming revelation. To emphasize the realness of the experience, the sacred writer repeats the idea that it occurred at a particular "place," "spot," or "shrine." This famous vision is often referred to as Jacob's ladder. The shrine may have been a ziggurat such as Jacob must have passed in the pagan territory. On it, angels—messengers of God—were going up and down to signify a divine revelation. The Lord stood near Jacob and repeated the covenant promise, stressing the idea of the role of Jacob's descendants in blessing the world.

Jacob suddenly saw the purpose of his journey east— to marry and have children, not for himself or because that was what everyone else did, but as a chosen instrument of God's plan. God penetrated his heart with happiness and wonder.

When Jacob awoke, he repeated, as if still in ecstasy, "Truly, the Lord is in this spot, although I did not know it! . . . This is nothing else but an abode of God, and that is the gateway to heaven!" Christians have seen in his words a hint of the Incarnation—God's dwelling with his human creatures on earth. Jacob set up a stone to mark the spot, anointed it, and renamed the place Bethel—House of the Most High God.

The dream left Jacob with a new understanding. His eyes were opened to the mercy of God in choosing him, a sinner, to father God's people. But he was not completely changed; he was still something of an opportunist. He unashamedly bargained with the Lord: *if* God would do thus and so for him, *then* he would worship and give God a cut of his profit. But he was

A *ziggurat* is a temple tower of the ancient Assyrians and Babylonians that has the form of a terraced pyramid with steps leading to the temple on top.

Genesis 28:16–17

Beth–house of; *el*–the most high one

An *opportunist* is someone who takes advantage of circumstances with little regard for principles or consequences.

CALLED BY THE FATHER

no longer 100 percent out for himself. He had made a small step. He was big enough now to direct at least 10 percent of his yearly earnings, produce, or land as a tithe toward something beyond his personal ambition. He worked long years to gain the bride he loved and learned to accept injustice.

Years later, on his way back to Canaan, Jacob received a second dream revelation that affected him deeply. Having developed a life style more suitable to himself than hunting, humbled and more truthful after his experiences in Aram, and wishing to resettle in his own homeland, he feared his brother's power to destroy him and his now-large family. He dispatched servants to meet Esau with gifts, crossed the Jabbok River with his wives and children, and suddenly found himself alone.

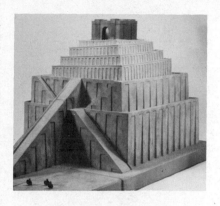

A stranger appeared and wrestled with Jacob all night. At break of day, when the unknown one saw that he had not gotten the better of Jacob, he wrenched Jacob's hip joint, leaving him lame. Jacob struggled on and would not release the dark stranger until he received a blessing. The visitor renamed Jacob "Israel" because, like a strong prince, he had contended with divine beings. Jacob, in turn, named the place of his struggle Peniel—"face of God."

Israel means "you contended with God." This incident explains how Jacob's descendants, the people of Israel, received their name.

Without learning the stranger's name or seeing him in clear daylight, Jacob—and through him, all of Israel—received a blessing. It is a story symbolic of the encounter with God in the darkness of faith, a dangerous meeting that leaves one wounded, but also graced. After this experience, Jacob built his altar, not to the "God of our Fathers" but to the "God of Israel." The man with human failings had become God's chosen patriarch, the father of the tribes.

Genesis 33:20

THE GOD OF THE PATRIARCHS

Just as your knowledge of God has developed, the Israelites grew to know God better through the patriarchs, Moses, and the prophets. Exactly who is this one called Yahweh who breaks into our lives through Jewish history and invites us to be his friends?

Originally the Israelites thought of Yahweh as the God of Abraham's family, the God of their forefathers. Later they came to know him as the highest of many gods, the *supreme* One. No matter how many other "els" there were, there was only one Yahweh, the mysterious "I Am" always present with his people. Then they realized that other gods didn't exist. The Israelites were unique in believing in *one* God, not in a god of good and a god of evil, not in a god for every aspect of nature, not in a god for every nation.

The God of Israel is a *living* God—alert, attentive, responsive. He unendingly gives life. Without beginning or end, he is *eternal*. "From everlasting to everlasting you are God." Israel's God is *spirit*. Invisible, he does not take up space or have weight like man-made gods who "have eyes but see not" and "ears but hear not." No images can be made of the God of the Israelites.

"Though mountains leave their place and the hills be shaken, my love will never leave you," wrote Isaiah. Yahweh's unswerving faithfulness (*emet*) and unfailing tender love (*hesed*) belong to his *immutability*, his unchangeableness. He was unlike the gods of Mesopotamia who inspired fear because no one ever knew when they would become angry and destructive.

Attempting to describe God, the Israelites projected onto him their own ideas of greatness, extending them to the farthest reaches of imagination—to endlessness. Today we use the word *infinite* to describe this divine characteristic. To the Hebrews God was not just powerful, but all-powerful (omnipotent). He was the Creator of heaven and earth. He was not just knowing, but all-knowing (omniscient). "Even before a word is on my

Psalm 47:10

Psalm 90:2

Psalm 115:5–6

Isaiah 54:10

The Hebrew *emet* and *hesed* are key Old Testament words distinguishing God's justice (faithfulness) and mercy.

Psalm 139:4

tongue, . . . you know the whole of it." He did not just exist; he was all-present (omnipresent). "If I settle at the farthest limits of the sea, even there your hand shall guide me." He was all-holy (totally other and different from anything we know), all-good, all-just, and all-wise.

Psalm 139:9–10

The marvel of the God of Abraham was that even though he was so great, he still communicated with his chosen ones. He was more than a force; he was a Person. He was not only approachable, but loving. He revealed himself as friend, helper, and father-protector. Already in his first self-revelation, he showed himself as one who was willing to forgive and save his people.

Christ called God *Abba* (Father), but God had already revealed his personal relationship with us through Moses when he said, "In the desert . . . God carried you, as a man carries his child." Again, in Hosea, God said, "I fostered them like one who raises an infant to his cheeks." The prophets made the great "I Am" the hope of Israel in the near despair of their exile.

Deuteronomy 1:31

Hosea 11:4

This God of the patriarchs is our God. We have additional knowledge of him in that we know Jesus Christ, "the image of the invisible God," who declared "Whoever has seen me has seen the Father." In John, Jesus applied "I Am" to himself. God was no longer a name or simply a word, but a person: Jesus. And Jesus further revealed that the one God is a Trinity. Even for Christians, God remains mystery. Not until the Second Coming of Christ will we "see him as he is," and even then we will never completely comprehend him because of his transcendence.

Colossians 1:15

John 14:9

1 John 3:2

- The worker puts something of himself into his work. What can creation tell us of God?
- Which scenes in the patriarchs reveal what God is like?
- What theme runs through John 17:6, 11, 12, and 26? Find one other example of this theme in John.
- What is the difference between knowing about people and knowing them? How can we know God?

Read and Recall

Read Genesis 28:10–22 and 32:23–32.

1. What was the shrine symbol that Jacob dreamed about?
2. How did God identify with Jacob? What five things were involved in the renewed promise?
3. The Jacob stories are very much concerned with how people and places in Israel received their names. What names and customs are accounted for in these two dream episodes?
4. What was the cost of Jacob's bargain with the Lord after the first dream? How many of his possessions did he promise to return to the Lord?
5. What did the wrestling in the second dream incident symbolize?
6. Why was Jacob renamed Israel?
7. Why do you think Jacob was left with a limp after his encounter with God?

Reflect

1. Describe Jacob's reactions to each of the dreams.
2. Write out a covenant that God might make with you regarding the basic purpose of your existence. Include five things he would give you.
3. Of Rebekah's two sons, Jacob was younger and weaker, but shrewder. Why did God choose him rather than the rugged Esau, who was favored by his father? Why is Jacob's story a source of hope for Israel? For you?
4. God can be found anywhere because his Spirit dwells within, but it seems easier to encounter God at certain places. What made the sacred places of Israel holy? How were they set apart? Name some holy places you are aware of. What connection is there between John 1:51 and the vision at Bethel?
5. Why is truth, especially about ourselves, so hard for us to face?
6. How did Jacob's encounters with God involve both pain and joy? Why were both elements present?

CALLED BY THE FATHER

Why is the Christian life sometimes described as "combat"?

7. How did God use the mistakes of Jacob and others to make them better people? If you have learned something about yourself or God, or other people, by means of a mistake, share it, if you care to.

JOSEPH SOLD INTO EGYPT
(Genesis 37)

William O. Douglas was the only U.S. Supreme Court justice in history to scale the Himalayas alone and to have his picture appear regularly in *Field and Stream* magazine. Even in his seventies he could hike twenty-five miles a day. Who would have dreamed that this child polio victim would become a robust outdoorsman to offset the effects of his disease?

William O. Douglas (1898–1980) was a Supreme Court justice from 1939 to 1975.

- Do you know anyone who developed a strength (it need not be only physical) as a result of a weakness?
- Your weaknesses are often the source of your strengths. Name some of your "potential" strengths.
- What dreams do you have for your future?

Joseph's story inspires courage. As a teenager favored by his father, he was disliked by his older brothers. God's providence turned Joseph's sad circumstances into the means of making the dreams of the pharaoh, of his family, and even of God come true.

As you read the famous story of Joseph's coat (tunic) in Genesis 37, pay attention to the following:

- Joseph's potential. He recognized the wrong his brothers had done. He was obedient to his father. He had an inkling of his future.
- Joseph was favored by his father, and he didn't have to work. Although he was the youngest son, he received from his father a long-sleeved tunic that gave him social status: as the first son of Rachel, Jacob's favorite wife, he was treated as the firstborn.
- Jacob "pondered" Joseph's dream. His action stressed the theological significance of the dream.
- The two versions of how Joseph's life was spared show that the story sprang from two traditions, both so carefully preserved that there was never any thought of dropping either one.
- Although Joseph's story is a sad commentary on Jacob's sons, who caused him heartrending sorrow in his old age, it speaks well of the honesty of Israel's writer in reporting their flaws.

The two versions are in Genesis 37:25–28a and 28b–30. Abandoned wells were frequently used for imprisonment.

Read and Recall

Read Genesis 37.

1. What incidents indicate Joseph's good qualities? Name them.
2. Why did Joseph's brother dislike him?
3. How did the brothers convince Jacob that Joseph was dead?

Reflect

1. Joseph was born to a barren woman only after Jacob's prayers. What is implied by this pattern? Do you know others in the Bible whose birth occurred in similar circumstances? How do these births prepare for the circumstances of Christ's conception?
2. Jacob preferred Joseph, the eleventh child, over Reuben, the eldest son of his first wife, Leah. Later in the story, Jacob preferred Benjamin, Rachel's second

CALLED BY THE FATHER

son, to the others, and then Joseph's younger boy, Ephraim, to Manasseh, the rightful firstborn. For what personal reasons do you think he did this? How do his choices reflect his own background? What theological meaning can it have, considering that God is the great patriarch of all people?

3. What poetic justice do you see in the brothers tricking Jacob by giving him Joseph's bloody tunic?

Poetic justice is the ideal judgment that rewards virtue and punishes vice.

JOSEPH AND HIS BROTHERS IN EGYPT
(Genesis 42–50)

When two people have a falling out, there usually follows a separation—if not physical, then at least mental and emotional. Which of these procedures would you advise for reconciliation?

> The person who started the fight should apologize first.
>
> Both parties should admit their guilt.
>
> The injured party should seek out the aggressor to make up.
>
> Neither party needs to refer to the matter if they begin to interact again.
>
> Both parties should always express their sorrow by words and actions.

The journey of Jacob's sons to Egypt is a story of reconciliation. The jealous brothers were brought to esteem and love their younger brother, who, in becoming a victim, was made their savior. But the account provides good entertainment along with religious instruction. The tricks Joseph pulled on his brothers before revealing his identity could be used in a James Bond film. Spy accusations, the taking of hostages, the planting of stolen goods, attempted kidnapping, demands for ransom, unjust imprisonment, and lawyer-like defenses are all included. The only difference is

Genesis 49:10. David was of the tribe of Judah.

that in the Joseph story, both the "good guys" and the "bad guys" came out on top.

As the curtain falls on the patriarchal drama, the attention returns to Jacob. His deathbed oracles foretold the fate of each of the twelve tribes. Not all were clear, and yet the prophecies about the tribe of Judah placed it in a dominant position in Israel. The "scepter shall never depart from Judah" hints at the messianic prophecy to be made to the House of David.

Joseph lived to what has come down to us in other documents as the ideal age in Egypt—one hundred and ten years. Strangely, this man who kept the faith while holding high office in a pagan culture and who lived to see his dreams come true was not buried with his ancestors near Mamre, but in the alien land of Egypt. This indicates that the story has not ended.

CALLED BY THE FATHER

CREATIVE PARALLELS

Nature contains creative parallels. For instance, butterflies resemble flying flowers, and the development of the human fetus reflects the progress of living things from the cell stage through fish and fowl forms.

■ What other parallels can you think of?

There is a saying that history repeats itself, meaning that patterns are recognizable. Religious history is no exception. When the evangelists reflected on the happenings of the Bible, they recognized parallels between Christian revelation and the people and events of Israel. In John's gospel, for example, Jesus said, "Just as Moses lifted up the serpent in the desert, so must the Son of Man be lifted up."

Evangelists are the Gospel writers.

John 3:14; also see Numbers 21:4–9.

■ Those who looked at the bronze serpent Moses had raised on a pole were healed of poisonous snakebite. What did Jesus mean?
■ What parallels to the fall of manna in the desert did the evangelists see in Jesus's life? To the Passover sacrifice and blood sealing of the Old Covenant?
■ What other parallels do you know? What manna do we have today? What "lifting up"?

The Hebrew writers had not set out to create models for the future; they wrote only what happened. The point of these parallels was to emphasize that God did not change. The Father of Jesus was the same as the God of Israel. He fed his flock and saved his people in every generation.

Typos, the Greek word for "model," provides the word *type*, which we use to characterize the people and events in the Old Testament that seem to parallel or prefigure God's saving action in Christ. As you study the Scriptures, you may want to be open to correspondences between the Old and New Testaments. Learn to

see the Passover and the conquest of the Promised Land as taking place today.

- What parallels with the Christian mystery do you find in these elements of the Isaac story?

  Abraham was promised a son, but waited a long time for him.

  Isaac was Abraham's only and beloved son.

  Abraham was asked to sacrifice Isaac's life on a hill.

  Isaac carried the wood for the sacrifice on his own shoulders.

  Both Isaac and Abraham were willing.

  Isaac was returned to his father alive.

  Isaac was responsible for the life of many, many people.

- How was Joseph like Christ, the Savior of the world? How was he like Saint Joseph?
- Biblical parallels are never perfect. What differences are there between the sacrifice of Abraham and Christ's sacrifice? Is Abraham a type of Christ, or of the Father? What differences do you notice between Joseph and Jesus?
- What parallels can you find between either the Isaac or the Joseph story and your own life, or the life of someone you know?

CALLED BY THE FATHER

Read and Recall

Read Genesis 42–50 and then write a series of headlines that might appear in both the local Canaanite newspaper and the daily bulletin circulated in the pharaoh's court. At least two headlines for each of the eight chapters should tell the story of the famine and migration of Jacob's family to Egypt.

Or, instead, you may prefer to draw the episodes of the brothers in Egypt in a cartoon strip. Identify the characters by particular symbols; for instance, Joseph might always wear a gold chain. Include these main episodes from the given chapters: chapter 42—first journey, encounter with Joseph, return to Canaan; chapter 43—second journey, the goblet: chapter 44—final test; chapter 45—revelation; chapter 46—Joseph meets his father; chapter 47—the pharaoh meets Joseph's family; chapter 48—Jacob blesses his grandsons; chapter 49—Jacob gives his last blessings; chapter 50—the death of Jacob and Joseph.

Reflect

1. Which episodes of this high drama illustrate the following principles of Israelite wisdom?

   a. Hard workers have a good chance of succeeding.
   b. God is not hindered by the actions of human beings, not even by their sins.
   c. Faith can be lived in any culture.
   d. God makes his will known through everyday affairs and ordinary human history.
   e. God's choice of those to carry out his will is absolutely free and unpredictable. He sometimes seems to delight in choosing those who seem to be the least likely persons.
   f. A polygamous society invites certain evils.
   g. God's glory shines through humble people who are open to his will.
   h. Forgiveness takes a great heart, but it also has its own rewards.

Polygamous means having two or more wives or husbands at the same time.

i. Repentance forgives sins.

j. It is God who gives, saves, and improves people's lives, even while he waits for their cooperation.

2. What is the Christian attitude toward work? Toward participation in politics and social welfare? Toward development of personal talent?

3. What New Testament ideals do you find in Joseph's life?

GETTING IT TOGETHER

Jacob is a real, though shadowy, person of the past. At the same time he represents all of Israel itself. Historically, the Jacob stories reflect the tension between the incoming nomads and the settled farmers in Canaan. Esau, who returned to the hunt, lost God's blessings. Jacob, who stayed with the tribe and settled on the land, became prosperous.

Religiously, the stories of Isaac's sons show that God's blessing accompanies those of Abraham's faith. They also make the point that God writes straight with crooked lines. Jacob was not the likeliest candidate for father of the chosen tribes. Because of his conniving, he was rightly forced out of his own household, and by shrewd management he increased his flocks many times over at Laban's expense. It may seem that Esau would have been the better choice.

But the message shines out all the brighter. God's gifts are free. There was no merit on Jacob's part; God chose him out of sheer goodness. Jacob, however, remained open. He showed a faithful love for Rachel, he worked hard for his father-in-law, and he humbled himself and generously shared his possessions with both Laban and Esau. God's gift to him was reconciliation with his brother and repossession of the land.

With their strong details of local color, the Joseph stories, especially, show that the tales of the patriarchs were not invented. The Hebrews were actual inhabitants of Egypt. But what of it? After all, many people have migrated from their native land. Why were these people different?

Local color is the speech, dress, habits, and land conditions peculiar to a certain region at a particular time.

CALLED BY THE FATHER

Despite personal limitations and apparent setbacks, each of the patriarchs accepted Abraham's faith and passed it on to his children. Jacob went on, after squarely facing the conflicts that were part of his intelligent but troubled personality. Joseph did not allow misfortune to keep him from becoming an instrument in God's hand for saving his family from extinction. That family was to pass on the knowledge of the true, living God. So the People of God were born and lived their infancy in these great men and their descendants, who increased to large numbers in the land of Goshen. In the next phase of the story, under Moses, knowledge of the true God knit the tribes into a people and, under David, Israel became a nation that made the God of Israel known beyond Canaan's borders.

The sacred authors did not whitewash the faults of their characters. They showed that God respected his people and left them free. When they failed, he remained constant, continually drawing his children closer as his plan mysteriously unfolded.

The conflicts of Jacob and Joseph were the conflicts of Israel itself, favored with divine election and revelation. Jacob was the people of Israel. During their long history, they struggled with the unknown One who blessed them. Like Jacob and Joseph, they were sent away, acknowledged their failings, and continued to grow. And God led them with a gentle hand ever onward to the Promised Land.

See Genesis 32:29.

Their understanding of God's ways was not yet perfect, as they equated material prosperity with God's favor. And yet the faults and the blessings of Israel were those of every life journey. By hoping in God, the Jacobs of the world became Israel—strong in the Lord. By remaining open to God, as Joseph did, they saved the world.

CALLED BY THE FATHER

REVIEWING THE CHAPTER

Linking Your Ideas

1. Make a list of the good and bad aspects of Jacob's character. Which predominate?
2. The main characters of the Jacob story are obviously flawed, but the minor characters also have weaknesses. Point out the faults of Rebekah, Laban, Rachel, Leah, and Laban's sons. Refresh your memory by a quick reference to Genesis 27–31. What does the sinfulness of these people reveal about God's choice of them as his own?
3. Choose three pivotal events in Joseph's life and create a diary entry he might have written for each one. Focus on thoughts and feelings. One diary page might be about his experience in the well.
4. In the light of what you now know about Joseph, explain the second quotation that appears at the beginning of this chapter.
5. On a map, record the journeys of (a) Jacob, (b) Joseph, and (c) one of his brothers.
6. How is Joseph both like and unlike his father?

Strengthening Your Grasp

1. Defend or disagree with the following statement and supply solid reasons to back your opinion: Jacob's character is unbelievable; without sufficient motivation, he changed radically during his life.
2. Jacob changed from thief to giver of gifts. What gifts did he receive during his life? Which was the greatest?
3. Hold a discussion on the benefits of knowing yourself. Are there disadvantages? How did Jacob get to know himself? How can you?
4. Maturity involves steady growth in insights. From the Joseph stories, tell how Joseph may have learned the following truths: Good often comes out of evil. God is found in unexpected places. Only those converted from the heart can reach out to others.
5. By examples from the Joseph stories, support your agreement or disagreement with the following statement: The good are rewarded and the evil punished.
6. Hold a discussion on the meaning of forgiveness. What is it? How is forgiving different from forgetting? What are its effects on both parties?

Expressing Your Convictions

1. Write a psalm of thanksgiving in which you praise God for the gifts he has given you.
2. In a skit, show how the qualities that generate faults can be directed to positive action.
3. Perform a pantomime to illustrate Joseph's dreams. Select fitting background music. Tell how his dreams came true.
4. Write a TV script for a dream that symbolizes some of your own expectations.
5. Compose a poem or song in which you see yourself as another Jacob.

Extending Your Interests

1. In the Gospel of John, Jesus refers to Jacob's ladder (1:51). Read the entire episode of the call of Nathaniel. Whom did Jesus compare to the ladder? What surprising revelation did he make?
2. Construct a family tree beginning with Abraham, Sarah, and Hagar, and work down to Jacob's twelve sons. Give the names of their mothers as well. (See Genesis 35:23–29.)

CALLED BY THE FATHER

REVIEWING THE UNIT

Patterns

1. How does the unit title "Birth and Infancy" apply to the Chosen People during the patriarchal period?
2. Tell which patriarchs exemplify each of the following: self-knowledge, faith, wisdom. Explain why.
3. On a map, trace the journey of the patriarchs, beginning with Terah's first move.

Focal Points

1. Cite occasions in the stories of the patriarchs when God speaks as a friend and when he seems far above and mysterious to his creatures.
2. The patriarchal narratives show that the great Hebrew ancestors did not believe in doctrinal truths, but in a Person who cared for them. Choose any patriarch to illustrate this statement.
3. Write a poem or composition on what you think it means to be "open" to God's plan. Use any of the patriarchs as illustration.
4. Play music that expresses the personality of any two of the four patriarchs. Tell why you made your choices.

Response

1. Trace your own "patriarchal journey of faith."
2. What view of God did Jesus present—intimate, close, and friendly, or far above, holy, and mysterious? Support your opinion with instances from Christ's life.
3. Find the reference to the patriarchs in Eucharistic Prayer I of the Mass. What connection do the patriarchs have with the Mass?

UNIT 2
Youth and Independence: Moses and Joshua

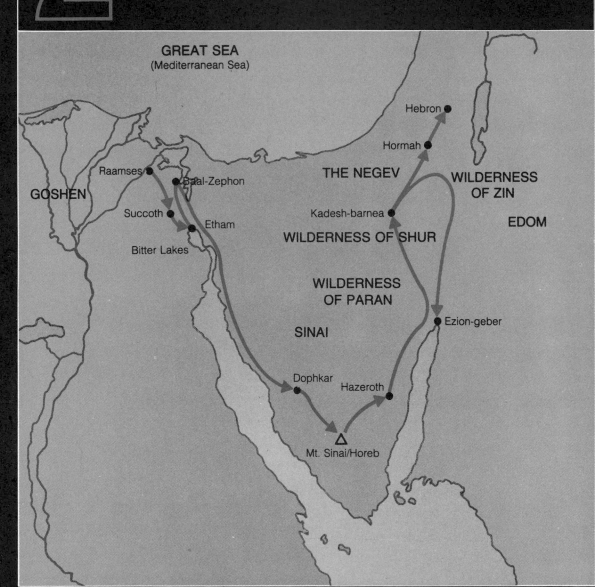

GREAT SEA
(Mediterranean Sea)

Hebron

Hormah

THE NEGEV

WILDERNESS
OF ZIN

GOSHEN

Raamses

Baal-Zephon

Kadesh-barnea

EDOM

Succoth

Etham

WILDERNESS OF SHUR

Bitter Lakes

WILDERNESS
OF PARAN

SINAI

Ezion-geber

Dophkar

Hazeroth

Mt. Sinai/Horeb

Sources

Exodus, Leviticus, Numbers, Deuteronomy, Judges, Judith, Esther, Tobit

■ The Exodus from Egypt to Canaan

■ The Covenant and the Mosaic Law

■ Conquest of the Promised Land

■ Early Government in Canaan

■ Lives of Moses, Joshua, Gideon, Samson, Judith, Esther, Tobit

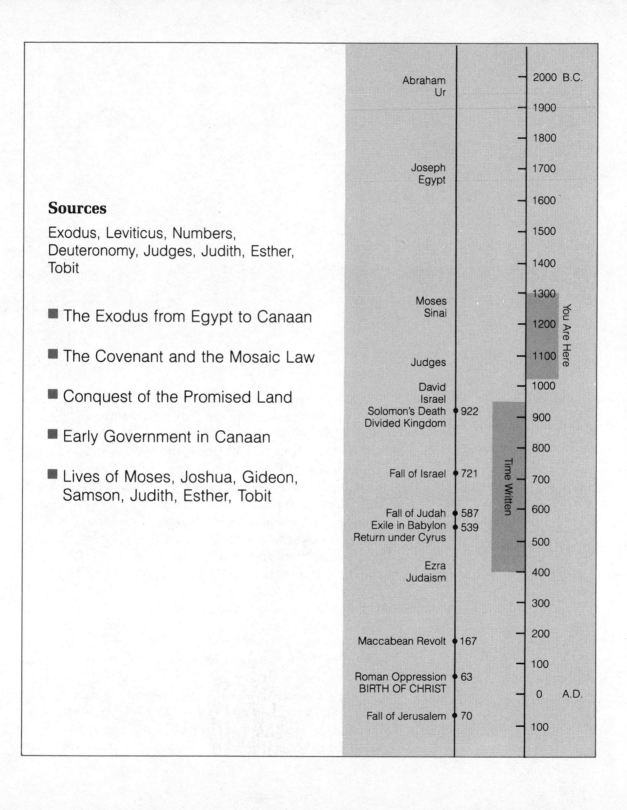

Abraham Ur	2000 B.C.
	1900
	1800
Joseph Egypt	1700
	1600
	1500
	1400
Moses Sinai	1300
	1200
Judges	1100
David Israel	1000
Solomon's Death ● 922 Divided Kingdom	900
	800
Fall of Israel ● 721	700
Fall of Judah ● 587	600
Exile in Babylon ● 539 Return under Cyrus	500
Ezra Judaism	400
	300
Maccabean Revolt ● 167	200
	100
Roman Oppression ● 63 BIRTH OF CHRIST	0 A.D.
Fall of Jerusalem ● 70	100

You Are Here

Time Written

When Israel was a child, I loved him: out of Egypt I called my son.

HOSEA 11:1

UNIT OVERVIEW

Have you ever had a close encounter with death and escaped because someone pulled you out of danger? How did you feel toward the person who saved you?

The Israelites passed from infancy to youth through an experience they never forgot. After Joseph had his relatives migrate to Egypt, they basked in the favor of the pharaohs for many years. Then their friends became their enemies and enslaved them. The Israelites were slaves for over four centuries, until God heard their cry and saved them through Moses.

The deliverance, the Exodus, is the greatest event in Jewish history. It can be compared to Christ's death and resurrection in Christian history. The Exodus remains a liberation event for the Jews, commemorated in the feast of the Passover and weekly in the Sabbath observance. The Exodus remains a liberation event for Christians as well.

God not only saved his people; he fashioned them into a nation. He gave them laws and he gave them Canaan, a land they could call their own. As with Abraham, he entered into a covenant with them, adopting them as his people. After Moses died, God raised up heroes who led the Israelites to military and moral victory. Joshua, the successor to Moses, took them into Canaan. Judges, including Gideon, Deborah, and Samson, directed the people and won important battles for them. Esther and Judith were heroines whose stories have a pattern: God acting to save his faithful people.

Historians believe that the Exodus took place between 1300 and 1200 B.C., probably in the reign of Ramses II. Although the Bible is the sole source of the Exodus story, that an exodus occurred cannot be denied. The Israelites *did* originate in Egypt. They *had* been oppressed. They *did* migrate and settle in a different land. The details are too unusual to be entirely made up. It is unlikely that, in writing an imaginary history for themselves, people would include a period when they held the degrading role of slaves. Furthermore, because Egyptians regularly omitted defeats from their records, they wouldn't have mentioned a small band of slaves escaping the country.

The number of people the Bible states were in the Exodus (600,000 men, not counting women and children) would form a line stretching from Egypt to Canaan and back. This is a symbolic number. Authorities estimate that between two and six thousand would be more accurate. Later on, others merged with these people to form the Israelite community.

Some people explain the Exodus miracles merely as natural phenomena or dismiss them as literary techniques. Certainly God could work miracles if he wanted to. In any case, it is difficult to decide exactly how much of the Exodus account is historical fact. After all, the Exodus events were not written down until about six hundred years after they happened.

A *natural phenomenon* is an unusual but scientifically explainable occurrence.

- Recall one of your childhood experiences. How well do you remember the details? Ask family members who were present to relate what happened. How closely do their stories correspond with your account?

The purpose of the scribes who wrote of the Exodus was to convey a spiritual message through interpreting their history. That message is two-pronged: God offered Israel his love and friendship, and he controlled nature and human destiny. This is the point of the entire Bible. It is the lesson the Israelites learned in their youth, and it was engraved on their memories. The Exodus repeats the story of Abraham: God saves his people.

Reluctant Hero

Sections

My Lord, my Creator, you always know what is best.
Open my mind to your plans for me.
   Enlighten me so that I may know
   What you want me to do and how to do it.

Open my heart to respond with love.
Give me the courage to say Yes to you
   in all my life decisions.
I rely on you for whatever I need to see them through.

No prophet has arisen in Israel like Moses, whom the Lord knew face to face. He had no equal in all the signs and wonders the Lord sent him to perform.

DEUTERONOMY 34:10–11

CHAPTER PREVIEW

What person is most written about in the Bible? The perhaps surprising answer is that there is more about Moses in the Bible than any other person, including Jesus. Like a giant, he towers over the whole Old Testament and ranks as the greatest Jewish hero. The authorship of the first five books of the Bible is attributed to Moses. With Elijah he appears with Jesus in the Transfiguration. And he is the subject of one of the world's most striking and memorable sculptures, Michelangelo's *Moses*.

Moses holds many titles: prophet, savior, lawgiver, judge, mediator, leader. Even so, little is known about him for certain. The Israelites who repeated his life story and the scribes who wrote it down gave him the marks of a national epic hero, out of pride and as a way of emphasizing certain truths.

In any case, Moses played the leading role in the most stupendous event of Jewish history: the Israelites'

An *epic* is a grand story celebrating episodes of a people's heroic tradition and recounting the deeds of a national hero.

deliverance from the land of slavery to the land of promise. Like other biblical characters, he was portrayed alternately as a superman and as a flawed human being.

While Moses was hiding in the desert because of a murder in defense of a Hebrew laborer, God commissioned him to lead the Israelites out of Egypt. Although reluctant, Moses obeyed and managed to saved his people.

In the desert, Moses acted as mediator between God and the Chosen People. When they complained, he supplied food and drink for them. He received and proclaimed the law of God and he negotiated a covenant between the Israelites and their God. Throughout the ordeal in the desert, Moses bore the burden of leadership. More than once he wished that he did not have to do the job God had called him to do, but, supported by his faith and sustained by an intimacy with God, Moses overcame his fears and doubts and persevered.

Moses was an important link in the chain of faithful people that connected Ur with Bethlehem. More than any other biblical personage, he pointed to Christ as prophet, savior, and lawgiver.

God is calling you to some role: student, daughter, son, brother, sister, babysitter, club officer, Christian witness. Perhaps he is hinting about a call he has in store for you. At the end of life you will be judged on your response to God's calls. How are you cooperating with your present vocation? Because it's no simple matter to accept God's invitation wholeheartedly, it's a good idea to ask his help in prayer as Moses did. Focus on an important life decision you are facing. Pray the prayer on the chapter-opening page with that decision in mind.

Words to Know

pharaoh (**fehr**-oh), Passover, Moses (**moh**-ziz), Mount Sinai (**sigh**-nigh), prophet, Jethro (**jeth**-roh), Yahweh (**yah**-weh), Aaron (**ehr**-on), plague (playg), Reed Sea, Exodus, manna, bronze serpent

THE NAME OF ISRAEL'S GOD

The early peoples had numerous gods. There was Chemosh (**kehm**-osh) of the Moabites, Amon-Re (**ah**-mohn-ray) of the Egyptians, Baal (**bay**-ehl) of the Canaanites. Little wonder, then, that when God spoke to Moses, Moses asked what his name was. The Lord responded, "I am who am . . . the Lord, the God of your fathers, the God of Abraham, the God of Isaac, the God of Jacob."

Exodus 3:14–15

Prior to this revelation, the patriarchs referred to God by the word *El* or by the majestic plural form *Elohim*, which indicates that he possessed all the divine attributes.

High officials sometimes use the plural in speaking of themselves. A king might say, "We think our crown is too heavy."

Once the God of the patriarchs called himself "I Am" or "Yahweh," the Israelites knew his personal name. "Yahweh" is related to the verb "to be," but this Hebrew verb means more than "exist"; it means to be actively present. A common interpretation of the name Yahweh, then, is that it reflected the Israelites' belief that God was with them to help them.

Some translations read "I shall be who I shall be."

The Jews have so much reverence for the holy name of God that they do not even pronounce the word "Yahweh." They use the substitute "Adonai." Since Hebrew words are written only in consonants, "Yahweh" in English is JHWH. When vowels were inserted into the Hebrew text, the vowels of "Adonai" were written under "Yahweh" as a reminder that the reader must say "Adonai" instead of "Yahweh." By mistake, Christian translators put these vowels into the JHWH, resulting in the word "Jehovah," which doesn't exist in the Hebrew but has come down as the name of God.

■ How do Christians today show respect for the name of God? What are the Divine Praises?

MOSES AS PROPHET: THE CALL
(Exodus 1–3, 4:1–17)

Were you ever in the uncomfortable position of being asked to do something you didn't feel qualified for? How did you respond?

Moses found himself in a similar predicament. Through a spiritual experience symbolized by a burning bush, God made known to Moses that Moses was to be his prophet. Using Moses, God would conduct the Israelites out of slavery and deliver them to a land that would be theirs. Asking the pharaoh to let the Israelites go was as ridiculous as asking the Soviet Union to free Poland completely.

Moses reasoned with God, pleaded with God; he even used his speech defect as an excuse. But God was unyielding. Moses, with his brother Aaron as spokesman, was to approach the pharaoh.

Although Moses lacked self-confidence, he was the man for the job. Raised in the pharaoh's courts, he knew Egyptian ways but was not afraid to identify with his own people. Hadn't he killed an Egyptian for striking a Hebrew? He also had the makings of a hero, demonstrated once by his defense of seven girls against a band of shepherds.

The call of Moses on the mountain of God was the beginning of a personal relationship between God and Moses that led to a personal relationship between God and Moses's people. As usual, God made the offer. He revealed his name.

■ Why do people in love write the name of the one they love all over their notebooks or carve it into wood? Why are you offended if people ridicule your name or mispronounce it?

There is a close bond between you and your name because it represents you. Telling your name to people is a sign of trust, a first step toward friendship; in a sense it is putting yourself under their power. In the story of Adam and Eve, Adam named the animals as

Prophets are instruments of God through whom God speaks and acts.

According to the Bible, during the persecution of the Jews the daughter of the pharaoh found Moses hidden in the Nile, and she raised him as her son.

Mount Horeb and Mount Sinai are used interchangeably in the Bible for a mountain of God. The location of either mountain is uncertain.

Throughout the Bible, God's name is identified with God himself, as in Psalm 7:18: "Sing praise to the name of the Lord Most High." Also see Psalm 8:2, Psalm 34:3, and 2 Chronicles 20:9. Christians pray in the Our Father, "Hallowed be thy name."

CALLED BY THE FATHER

a sign that he was master over them. To the Jews, a person's name was a reflection of his or her personality. Jacob, whose name meant "he is cunning," was in fact a deceiver. Thus, to reveal your name to someone was to reveal the secret of your being.

When God told Moses his personal name—I Am, or Yahweh—he not only struck up a friendship but disclosed the kind of god he is: the God who is. This can mean "I am there," emphasizing his presence for Israel; "I call into being," referring to his role as creator; and "I am always the same."

Encountering God that day motivated Moses to accomplish a feat he himself considered impossible: to mold a group of escaped slaves into a community with God as its king, freedom as its hallmark, and God's law as its constitution. He learned that with God all things are possible.

Read

Read Exodus 1–4:17. As you come across the numbered events that follow, match them with the truths they demonstrate from among statements "A" through "F" below.

1. Being drawn out of the water and adopted by the pharaoh's daughter
2. The killing of the Egyptian
3. Singlehanded defense of the seven girls from the shepherds
4. The burning bush
5. Removing sandals, hiding face
6. The snake staff, leprous hand, and bloody river

A. God is all-holy and almighty.
B. Fire, so mysterious, is a sign of God's presence. Moses had a mystical experience one day.
C. Ancient legends described how the hero escaped death early in life in order to fulfill a high destiny.
D. Moses was sympathetic toward his own people although he lived as a royal Egyptian.

E. God was with Moses to help him carry out his mission.

F. Moses was courageous.

Recall

1. What features of Moses's early life marked him as the Exodus hero?
2. How was Moses like the ordinary man on the street?
3. What two things did God reveal to Moses at their first encounter?

Reflect

1. How was Moses a prophet? How does a person become a prophet?
2. In what situations may God ask you to do something that you are not too eager to do? Describe some ways to handle such situations when you feel like echoing Moses's words and feelings: "If you please, Lord, send someone else."
3. The Israelites never spoke the name of God, but used a substitute. Why? Why do we say "God" so casually in the course of conversation?
4. Moses could have led a life of comfort in the pharaoh's palace, or at least a life of peace tending flocks. Instead, he endangered his life by casting his lot with the people of God. Who are some other people who have sacrificed a secure life because they would not compromise their convictions?

MOSES AS SAVIOR: THE EXODUS
(Exodus 5:1–9, 7:8–12:39, 14:5–15:21)

Some heroes enter history's Hall of Fame because of a skill, a talent, or an outstanding achievement. But the heroes who most inspire admiration are those who risk or give their lives for others.

■ Name some heroes that fit into this last category. Can you think of any "unsung heroes"?

CALLED BY THE FATHER

One night Will McLaughin and his uncle, a minister, were discussing the passage "For this cause came I into this world." Will offered to take his uncle's materials for the next day's sermon to the large new Iroquois Theater of Northwestern University. When he arrived, the building was on fire, and he rushed to the balcony where screaming people were trapped. The fire escapes had not yet been completed, so Will laid a plank from a balcony window to a window of the building next door, enabling many people to escape. By the time Will stepped onto the plank, the fire had weakened it and he crashed to the concrete below. Before he died he said to his uncle, "Maybe your text fits me: 'For this cause came I into the world.'" The university inscribed the passage and Will's name on that plank and it is cherished as a memento.

Even though he was not cooperative at first, Moses eventually submitted to God's call and became a charismatic leader who saved his people. This was the cause for which he had come into the world.

Charismatic means being endowed with special gifts for the good of others.

Originally Joseph's descendants were welcomed into Egypt by the Semitic Hyksos, a foreign invader in control of the country. When the Hyksos were expelled, about 1500 B.C., the native Egyptians probably turned against the Hebrews too, who were related to the Hyksos. Enslaved, the Israelites were forced to construct the cities of Pithom and Raamses in the eastern part of the Nile Delta. To control their number, all Hebrew male infants were killed.

Egyptian bricks were made from wet clay mixed with straw. Wooden molds with handles were used to shape the clay into bricks, which were dried in the sun.

Imagine Moses's frustration when his first trip to the pharaoh backfired. Instead of freeing the Israelites to celebrate a three-day feast as Moses had requested, the pharaoh complicated their lives. He stopped supplying straw for brickmaking but demanded that they continue to produce the same quota of bricks.

God's renewal of his promises encouraged Moses to return to face the pharaoh again. What followed was a contest, with God and Moses on one side and the pharaoh and his magicians on the other. Ten times God sent plagues to Egypt. These plagues were all natural phenomena. For instance, the Nile will turn red when

A *plague* is a terrible calamity.

An explanation of the final plague is that the decayed matter from the previous plagues caused the spread of a deadly epidemic.

certain algae are present. The miracle was in timing and the source of the plagues: God intervened to save his people.

The first plague—the water turning to blood—had no effect. The court magicians also did this, possibly with Satan's help. With the second plague, the last one the magicians could imitate, the pharaoh agreed to let the people go. But he took back his promise each time Moses removed the plague.

The tenth plague was the climax. Every firstborn Egyptian died at midnight. The Israelites were spared, however, when they sprinkled their doorways with lamb's blood. This time the pharaoh, grieving for his son, begged Moses to leave with the Israelites.

Without even taking time to put yeast in their bread, the Israelites departed. (*Exodus* means "departure.") But the pharaoh had second thoughts, and sent troops after the slaves. The people, seeing the approaching horses and chariots, were terrified. But God, their champion, came to their aid by causing a strong wind to dry up the Reed Sea so that they were able to cross. However, the chariot wheels of the Egyptian warriors got stuck in the mud, and the waters, perhaps tidal, returned to drown them. The Israelites celebrated with a victory song, and the women danced.

The name of the Reed Sea was translated as "Red Sea" in the Greek version of the Bible. Tides are caused chiefly by the gravitational pull of the moon. In some estuaries, bodies of water with a wall-like front, known as tidal bores, surge beyond the estuary.

The Jews have never stopped celebrating the Exodus. Moses commanded them to hold a Passover feast every year to recall the night the Angel of Death passed over the Israelites as they passed over into freedom. During the meal of roasted lamb, unleavened bread, and bitter herbs, the story is recounted.

Unleavened bread is bread made without yeast.

This feast combines two rituals of primitive nomads in the region. In the spring, at the full moon, they sacrificed an animal and marked the entrances to their tents with its blood to ward off evil spirits. Pastoral nomads celebrated the first harvest for seven days by eating only unleavened bread made from the grain of the new harvest. The Israelites adapted these rituals to signify God's saving action. Later, Christ transformed the meaning of Passover by using it as the setting for his saving sacrifice, his passing over to the Father, and his communion with his people in the Eucharist.

Pastoral means rural or related to the shepherd's life.

The Exodus event was a preparation for the greatest saving act of all, the redemption of the human race from the slavery of sin by the Son of God, the new Moses.

Read and Recall

Read Exodus 5:1–9, 7:8–12:39, and 14:5–15:21. As you read of the struggle between the Chosen People and the Egyptians, keep a scorecard for the Israelites with two columns, one for wins and the other for losses. Enter each event in one column.

Reflect

1. Have you ever undergone a period when things got worse instead of better before God answered your

prayers? Why do you suppose God allows such things to happen?

2. Looking back at your life, can you see God's providence at work?
3. Must God work miracles in order to have people believe he exists? Explain your answer.
4. What elements in the Exodus narrative reflect the Israelites' belief that God was the direct agent of everything that happened?

MOSES AS LAWGIVER: THE DESERT EXPERIENCE

(Exodus 15–34; Numbers 11–12; Deuteronomy 34:1–12)

Some experiences either make or break you. What are some crisis points a person your age might meet?

Because of divinely directed detours, it took forty years for the Israelites to reach Canaan, the so-called land of milk and honey. Circling south, they fought the Amalekites, they were forbidden to pass through Edom, and they did battle with Og, King of Bashan, and Sihon, King of the Amorites.

Just as a loving father disciplines his son and allows him to face trying situations in order to toughen him and make him a man, so God treated his maturing people. The mob of refugees had to undergo an inner transformation. Through the desert, God whipped this stiffnecked people into shape. Repeatedly in their trials God aided this grumbling ragtag crowd. He entered into an alliance with them, offering them his love and his Law to make them a unified people. As the Song of Moses put it, "He found them in a wilderness, a wasteland of howling desert. He shielded them and cared for them, guarding them as the apple of his eye."

Moses intervened on behalf of the people, and God used him to answer their pleas. He gathered the group into a community that had God as its king. Through Moses, God showed himself God of Israel, establishing the Convenant and giving the Law on Mount Sinai.

Forty is a symbolic number in the Bible. It means a holy period of time, a time of preparation.

Deuteronomy 32:10

CALLED BY THE FATHER

But even the great Moses had to be purified. Because he did not trust God enough to follow directions exactly in getting water from a rock, God forbade him to enter the Promised Land. When finally in sight of Canaan, the Promised Land, Moses went to the mountain for the last time to meet his Lord.

Read

Read the following imaginary log of the journey to Canaan. For more details about the incidents, you can refer to the passages noted in the margin.

Sunday: We hadn't seen water for three days, until today. As luck would have it, the water here at Marah was too bitter to drink. The Lord answered Moses's prayer, though, and showed him what tree would sweeten the water. What a relief!

Exodus 15:22–27

Monday: It's been a month since we left Egypt. Now that we're in the desert, it's difficult to get food. All of us complained to Moses and Aaron that we wished we had died in the plague in Egypt where there was food, instead of coming out here to die of starvation. The Lord told Moses we would have meat tonight and bread tomorrow. True to his word, a flock of quail provided us with meat this evening, but how we'll ever get enough bread out here in the wilderness to feed everyone remains a mystery.

Exodus 16

Tuesday: This morning when we awoke, strange white flakes covered the ground. Moses told us this was the promised bread and had us gather enough for our families for one day. He explained that only on the day before Sabbath are we to collect a double portion because we are to rest on the Sabbath.

Saturday: Even though it was the Sabbath, out of curiosity I went out to get the bread we call manna, but there was none on the ground. I felt as foolish as my neighbor did when he tried to save two portions Wednesday and it rotted.

Exodus 17:1–7

Wednesday: Today we're encamped at Rephidim, a place where there is no water. We grumbled to Moses and were on the verge of stoning him, until he called out to the Lord. At the Lord's direction, Moses struck a rock with his staff and drinking water flowed out. Who can deny that our God is with us?

Finish this imaginary log of the journey to Canaan by supplying entries for the events in these passages: Exodus 17:8–15, 18; 19:1–15, 16, 20–26; 32:21–29, 32, 34; Numbers 11, 12.

Recall

1. Name instances when God came to the aid of his people on their journey to the Promised Land.
2. How did Moses stand out as a strong leader during the wandering in the desert?

CALLED BY THE FATHER

3. What indications are there that Moses had a close relationship with God?
4. What were the main events in the formal establishment of the covenant?

Reflect

1. The labor gang of Israelites was the raw material out of which God, the master architect, formed a nation. What tools did he use? What does he use today to transform individuals?
2. What occurrences in the desert foreshadowed Baptism and Eucharist? How?
3. The food miracles during the forty-year sojourn had natural explanations: *manna* is a type of pellet formed from the droplets of the tamarisk tree; *quail*, migrating from Europe, fell exhausted to the desert floor; *water* deposits lay trapped within limestone rock until they were tapped; leaves and bark of certain trees can *sweeten water*. Why then do we say that God worked miracles for his people?
4. Show that God has never spared his friends from suffering. Why shouldn't you reject God when he lets you suffer?
5. In the spiritual life there are "mountain experiences" and "desert experiences." Having read Exodus, what would you say is characteristic of each type of experience? What life events would you put in each category?

GETTING IT TOGETHER

God stepped into history and, through his servant Moses, worked the great saving act that is the core of the Jewish faith. When the Israelites were in bondage, God raised up a hero to lead them to a promised land of freedom. After Moses heard the Lord's call on Mount Sinai, he forced the pharaoh to release the Israelites by a series of plagues. On the last night, the sign of the lamb's blood saved the Israelites from the death that struck down the firstborn of the Egyptians. The Chosen

People still eat a special Passover meal to commemorate their escape.

The climax of the liberation occurred when the Israelites passed safely through the Reed Sea, while the Egyptians pursuing them were drowned.

Because the Israelites had to be formed as the People of God, they journeyed for forty years, suffering discomfort and trials. Eventually their confidence in God began to grow.

Again, on a mountain, God communicated with his people. He set forth his law and promised to be their God if they would follow his will. Yahweh wasn't a god who merely demanded sacrifice of animals on certain days; he wanted to be worshipped through the use of free will. He asked love—to be chosen through trust and fidelity—throughout one's life. The people entered into this solemn covenant with their God and sealed it with a blood-sprinkling ceremony.

Still imperfect even after agreeing to do all that the Lord commanded, the Chosen People broke the first commandment by making an image of God. They found it difficult not to see and yet believe. God forgave them and continued his purifying process. At last they reached the Promised Land, and Moses died on Mount Nebo. No doubt God greeted him with "Well done, good and faithful servant."

REVIEWING THE CHAPTER

Linking Your Ideas

1. Create an edition of *The Desert Herald* with typical newspaper features.
2. Construct a collage or mural incorporating key images from Exodus.
3. Prepare a script for a TV tribute to Moses. Why was Moses so great?
4. Why were the Israelites called the Chosen People? What were they chosen to do? How were they privileged?

Strengthening Your Grasp

1. The New Testament is rich in references to the Hebrew Scriptures. Skim the Gospel of John or the Letter to the Hebrews to find mention of the Moses events. Write a paragraph detailing your findings.
2. Talk to a Jewish person about the celebration of Passover today and report to the class.
3. Your passage through life is itself an exodus. As a Church member, you belong to a pilgrim people, the new Chosen People. Set up a chart comparing these events to parallels in your life: slavery, Reed Sea, covenant, law, manna, water, battles, Canaan.
4. Compare the birth of the Israelite nation to the birth of the United States. Point out similarities and differences.

Expressing Your Convictions

1. Psalms 105, 135, and 136 celebrate the Exodus. Recite them aloud, alternating verses with someone.
2. Write an essay entitled "Be Not Afraid." Refer to the experiences of the Israelites to show that anyone who believes in Yahweh has no cause to fear.
3. In your notebook or journal, write a list of experiences in your life that parallel the following experiences of the Israelites: burning bush, Exodus, Reed Sea, golden calf, desert, manna, the Law, bronze serpent, enemy tribes. For example, the "burning bush" in your life might be the way God speaks to you through the Bible, insights, other people, homilies, and so on.

Extending Your Interest

Research the customs of the Egyptians or peoples of other ancient cultures. How did they rest and relax? How did they spend their holidays?

FOUR YAHWEH
Faithful Friend

Sections

*O Jesus, through the Immaculate Heart of Mary, I
offer you all my prayers, works, joys, and
sufferings of this day, for all the intentions of Your
Sacred Heart, in union with the Holy Sacrifice of
the Mass throughout the world, in reparation for
my sins, and for the intentions of all Christians
and our Holy Father.*

If you hearken to my voice and keep my covenant, you shall be my special possession, dearer to me than all other people.

CHAPTER PREVIEW

Were you ever hurt when a friend told your secrets to others, wouldn't help you, or stopped being your friend for no apparent reason?

Because human beings aren't perfect, relationships aren't perfect. Whenever you open yourself to friendship, you risk being hurt. Likewise, you may sometimes hurt your friends. Only God is the truly perfect friend.

The history of the Israelites is the story of God's efforts to be friends with human beings. The gap between God and people could not be wider. God is "a merciful and gracious God, slow to anger and rich in kindness and fidelity." On the other hand, human beings are weak, fickle, and unreliable. As the psalmist said, "What is man that you should be mindful of him?" Yet not only does God think of human beings, but he never ceases appealing to their hearts. A mystery of the universe is that God accepts people as they are and loves them.

Exodus 34:6

Psalm 8:5

Blood is a symbol of life; sprinkling it on the altar (God) and on the people symbolizes their union. The pillars stand for the commitment of the twelve tribes.

Cherubim are probably winged-lion creatures with human heads. They guarded Mesopotamian palaces and temples.

After Yahweh demonstrated to the Israelites by his act of salvation that he cared for them, he invited them to unite with him in a covenant, which is like an engagement in that two parties pledge themselves to each other in love, trust, and fidelity. God promised to be the God of the Israelites, to bless them, and to give them land. The Israelites promised to be God's people, to do all that he commanded. The Covenant was sealed when Moses sprinkled blood on the altar and on the people. They then shared a sacrificial meal and erected twelve pillars, one for each tribe.

God fulfilled his part of the Covenant by his abiding presence. He visibly guided his people as a pillar of cloud by day and as a pillar of fire by night. He was with them in a dwelling, a meeting tent that housed the ark of the covenant. This ark was a chest containing manna and the tablets of the Law. On the gold-plated top between two winged cherubim was the throne of God. Here God met his people: Moses presented their petitions and God spoke to him. God was also close to

CALLED BY THE FATHER

the Israelites in countless saving acts in the desert. The writer of the Book of Deuteronomy exclaimed, "What great nation is there that has gods so close to it as the Lord, our God, is to us whenever we call upon him?"

Deuteronomy 4:7

The Israelites fulfilled their part of the Covenant by obeying. They promised that "all that the Lord has said, we will heed and do." Yahweh set forth his Law as a way of life for his people. He called them to be holy as he was holy, to love what he loved and hate what he hated. The crowning command of the Covenant was the Shema, the Jewish confession (statement of belief): "The Lord is our God, the Lord alone. Therefore, you shall love the Lord, your God, with all your heart, and with all your soul, and with all your strength." The Law expressed in the commandments and in their prescriptions was a gift from God. It organized the Israelites into a community that would become a mighty nation. It kept them from falling back into slavery to false gods and to their own drives and desires, and it led them to true happiness.

Exodus 24:7

Jews pray the Shema twice daily. Some men wear on their left arm and forehead small leather boxes (tefillin or phylacteries) containing scrolls of the Shema and other passages. A similar box (mezuzah) is hung on the doorposts and touched devoutly.

Subsequent events proved that Yahweh got the worst end of the bargain. Even though he constantly manifested his loving-kindness to the Israelites, they broke the Covenant. Then God showed himself to be a truly great friend: he forgave them.

God continued to extend his love to all people. Some rejected him; others were friends for a time, but then forsook him; still others were off-and-on friends. But he was always there waiting.

■ To see where you stand with the Lord, think over yesterday, or the past week. In your journal, jot down evidence that you are keeping the covenant you made at baptism.

Words to Know

ark of the covenant, meeting tent, tabernacle, dwelling, Decalogue (**dek**-ah-log), Pentateuch (**pen**-teh-took), Torah (**tohr**-ah), Shema (sheh-**ma**), theocracy (the-**ock**-reh-ce)

THE GOD WHO LOVES: THE COVENANT
(Deuteronomy 5:1–10, 28:1–19, 31:14–32:1)

In what ways is an adopted child like a natural child? Adopted children are proud that their parents wanted them and chose them. God chose to adopt the Israelite slaves. He had Moses tell the pharaoh, "Israel is my son, my firstborn." God's human children could even share in his divine life; they were to be holy through the Covenant of Sinai.

To be holy is to be like God, who is all good, all merciful, all loving.

Through this covenant, God again offered the joys of the lost paradise to the human race. This generous gesture was not due to any merit on the part of Israel. Also, God bore the greater responsibility and was the chief giver.

Other peoples became nations because of geographic boundaries, war, or a common form of government. When the Israelites ratified the Covenant, they became a community formed by their relationship to their God. The Israelites were bound together not by a natural tie but by a supernatural one: belief in Yahweh.

To *ratify* means to confirm formally.

Read

Read Deuteronomy 5:10–21, 28:1–19, and 31:24–30. The Mosaic covenant conformed to the structure of the Hittite treaties. Hittite kings and vassals (lesser leaders) made pacts by which the vassals accepted certain obligations in return for the assurance of protection. Skim through the readings on the establishment of the Covenant between Israel and its God and identify these characteristics:

Hittites were an ancient people whose empire in northern Syria collapsed around 1300 B.C.

Opening with the name of the great king
Description of the benefits the king has bestowed on his vassal
Detailed obligations of the vassal and demand for exclusive loyalty
Depositing of text in a sanctuary and periodic rereading
List of witnesses to the treaty (gods of nature)
Blessings and curses

CALLED BY THE FATHER

Recall

1. What were the obligations of both parties bound by the Mosaic covenant?
2. How was the Covenant a tremendous gift of God to his people?
3. How was God like a king to the Israelites? Like a father?

Reflect

1. What does Christ's New Covenant, which ended the Mosaic covenant, involve? How are the two covenants the same? Different?
2. Saint Thomas More was executed when he refused to break his covenant with God to please the King of England. In the play *A Man for All Seasons*, dramatist Robert Bolt has More say, "When a man takes an oath, Meg, he's holding his own self in his own hands. Like water. And if he opens his fingers, then—he needn't hope to find himself again." What did he mean? What evidence is there that some people take their promises lightly today?
3. Why did God call himself a jealous god?
4. What is God's response when someone falls out of love with him and breaks the Covenant? How do you renew the Covenant?
5. There is a saying "To have a friend, be a friend." How can you "be a friend" to God?
6. How did the Covenant of Moses prepare for the covenant you made at baptism? What do these two covenants have in common?
7. What does it take for a teenager to be holy today?

THE GOD WHO IS PRESENT: THE ARK OF THE COVENANT

(Exodus 25–40)

Why do Catholics "make a visit" to churches and chapels when there are no services?

We believe that God is with us in a real, physical way in our churches. The Israelites believed that on

their journey God was with them, localized in a sacred place called the tabernacle.

From the beginning they experienced his presence through his actions on their behalf: the plagues, the passages through the Reed Sea, the food and water in the wilderness. They saw his guidance visibly as a pillar of cloud during the day and as a pillar of fire at night.

But after the Sinai Covenant, God promised that he would actually dwell in their midst. He gave instructions for constructing a portable sanctuary, called a dwelling, meeting tent, or tabernacle, that would house the ark of the covenant, his throne. This dwelling was the source of strength for the Israelites, for because of it they were able to meet and consult with God. In the meeting tent Moses spoke to the Lord face to face and presented the people's petitions. This place where God

The ark was a gold-plated wooden box about four feet long, two and a half feet wide, and two and a half feet high. On top was the throne flanked by gold cherubim, who covered it with their wings.

CALLED BY THE FATHER

"pitched his tent" with his people became the center of their political and religious life.

The ark of the covenant within the dwelling contained manna and the tablet of the commandments. They served as a reminder and pledge of the Covenant in which God had promised, "I will work such marvels as have never been wrought in any nation anywhere on earth, so that this people among whom you live may see how awe-inspiring are the deeds which I, the Lord, will do at your side."

The ark remained with the people about six hundred years, until it was lost in the destruction of Jerusalem in 586 B.C.

Exodus 34:10

Read

In reading about the dwelling, be alert to the features it has in common with churches today.

These passages are about the physical makeup of the dwelling:

You will encounter these new words in your reading: *showbread* refers to the twelve sacred cakes that are renewed every Sabbath and eaten only by the priest; a *propitiatory* is thought to be the cover of the ark; a *laver* is a basin for washing.

| Exodus 25–28:5 | gold, tabernacle, altar, utensils, bread, lamps, priests, vestments |
| Exodus 30:1–38 | contributions, water, oil, incense |

These passages reveal the uses of the dwelling:

Exodus 33:7–11	for consultation
Exodus 40:34–38	for guidance on the journey
Numbers 7:89	for communication
Leviticus 1:1–9	for worship

Recall

1. What was the purpose of the dwelling? Of the ark of the covenant?
2. In what ways was the dwelling like a modern-day church?

Reflect

1. Explain how, even in the time before Christ, God had showed himself as Emmanuel, which means "God with us."

2. What are some signs that God is with you?
3. Johnny was afraid to sleep in the dark. His mother reminded him that God was with him. "I know," said Johnny, "but I want someone with a face." Moses's encounter with God was described as face to face. Who else is said to have seen God? How do you explain these so-called visions? How will you see God in heaven?
4. A disturbing quotation is: "God often visits us, but most of the time we are not at home." How can you be "at home" when God wants to step into your life? How can you be prepared to welcome him?
5. People use various techniques to recall God's presence. One man trained himself to think of God whenever he went into a different room. Churches used to ring the angelus bells three times a day. Are such crutches valuable? Necessary? What does Saint Paul mean when he says, "Pray always"?
6. Why do you make a sign of the cross with holy water when you enter a Catholic church?
7. Where do you most sense the presence of God? Why?

THE GOD WHO GUIDES: THE LAW

(Exodus 20–23; Leviticus; Numbers 35, 36; Deuteronomy 6, 11–25)

Take a minute to jot down words that pop into your mind when you hear the word "law."

If you were an Israelite, your list would be composed of positive words like "happiness," "security," "peace," "guidance," "love," "strength," and "freedom." Although the Israelites were bound to the Law as their covenant obligation, they saw it as a gift from God. The Law was not just a legal code; it was a way of life. It was not confining, but liberating. It allowed them to follow what God had marked out as the path to happiness. Therefore, the Jewish people loved the Law.

The Ten Commandments, called the Decalogue (ten words), are the ground rules of human existence. Found in the Pentateuch, they reach back to Moses himself. Since these early rules are very broad, other codes explained them in detail. Moses probably worked out the specifics of the Law as he settled cases at the meeting tent, and these decisions were then handed down through generations. This is what occurs when the Supreme Court decides on issues that are not spelled out in the U.S. Constitution: decisions on any new cases set the precedent for similar cases. As new economic and social circumstances arose, new laws (based on the spirit of the old code) were added to the Mosaic law. Moses was the author of the entire Law because all rules can be traced back to him.

Archaeological research reveals that ancient codes very similar to the Mosaic law were in existence even before the time of Moses. This indicates that the Israelites borrowed from the tribes with whom they came in contact. The major difference in the Hebrew laws is reflected in the first commandment: "I, the Lord, am

The Pentateuch consists of the first five books of the Bible—Genesis, Exodus, Leviticus, Numbers, and Deuteronomy. "Pentateuch" refers to the five jars or cases the scrolls were kept in. Jews call these books the Torah, which means "instruction."

The earliest known code dates from about 2050 B.C. The most famous is the code of Hammurabi from Babylon, dated about 1750 B.C.

Deuteronomy 5:6–8

The Jews were forbidden to make and worship statues (idols) as other people did. To do so would have been to commit the sin of idolatry.

A *theocracy* is a state or nation governed directly by God and not by any human individual or group.

When the hungry disciples picked grain on the Sabbath and the Pharisees rebuked them, Jesus quoted the text "It is mercy I desire and not sacrifice" (Matthew 12:7).

your God, who brought you out of the land of Egypt, that place of slavery. You shall not have other gods besides me. You shall not carve idols for yourselves." Other nations wrote laws just to keep order in society. Israel's purpose is clear in the Shema, the very greatest commandment and the heart of the Law. The Shema demands an exclusive and complete loyalty and love of God. It is the connection of the Mosaic law with the worship of God that sets it above all others. The Israelites accepted God as their only ruler and became a theocracy. This was the beginning of God's kingdom on earth.

Ideally, God's people were governed, then, by faith and observance of the Law. As time passed, the Israelites, like ourselves, found it difficult to keep their sight fixed on true, interior worship. They forgot that the measure of their life was God himself and not the Law as a list of prescriptions. In the time of Jesus, some of the Jewish leaders exaggerated the importance of external actions to such a degree that they evoked his criticism. Jesus emphasized worship from the heart. In line with the progressive Pharisaic movement of his day, he redirected attention to the *spirit* of the law of Moses.

Read and Recall

Read completely the account of the bestowal of the Ten Commandments and the Shema: Exodus 20:1–17 and Deuteronomy 6:4–9.

Skim through these sections, reading only the headings within each chapter to see what was included under the Law: Exodus 21–23; Leviticus; Numbers 35, 36; Deuteronomy 11–25. Read these interesting passages to get the flavor of the Law: Exodus 21:12–23 and 33–35; Leviticus 11:1–8 and 16:20–22.

1. What relationship did the Law have to the Covenant?
2. What did the Law mean to the Israelites?
3. What aspects of life did the Mosaic law regulate?
4. What law is at the heart of the Mosaic law?

94

THE DEAD SEA SCROLLS: TREASURE IN A CAVE

In 1947 on the northwest side of the Dead Sea, a shepherd boy searching for his lost goat in the desert of Judea tossed a stone into a cave and discovered an archaeological treasure. Excavations made from 1949 to 1956 revealed that the cave was one of eleven in which were housed what appeared to be the library of an ancient religious community.

Altogether this find yielded about six hundred precious manuscripts or portions of manuscripts, including every book of the Bible except Esther. The scrolls had been wrapped in linen and preserved in jars. Until the Dead Sea discovery, the oldest copies of Scripture were from the ninth century A.D. The Dead Sea Scrolls originated a thousand years earlier, in about 100 B.C.

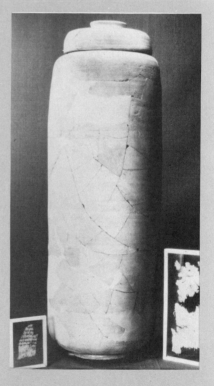

Scholars believe that the monks who owned the scrolls were the Essenes, who were opposed to the Jewish Pharisees and Sadducees. They formed a community and moved to the desert to prepare in their own way for the Kingdom of God. (John the Baptist may have been acquainted with them.) The Essenes were organized under a leader known as the Teacher of Righteousness. A Manual of Discipline for the Essenes was among the scrolls in the caves. The scrolls were probably hidden in the caves to keep them out of the hands of the invading Romans, who eventually did destroy the community in A.D. 68.

Since the Dead Sea Scrolls are near ruins called Khuibet-Qumran, they are also referred to as the Qumran Scrolls.

■ How do people nowadays, both Christian and Jews, show their reverence for the Bible?

Reflect

1. In making decisions, is it better to ask yourself "What must I do to be saved?" or "What can I do to please the Lord?" Why?

2. An actress once remarked, "Some people regard discipline as a chore. For me it is a kind of order that sets me free to fly." What is discipline? How can discipline set you free?

3. Why could Jesus say that if you are to be perfect, follow the commandments and the Shema?

4. The commandments are in the form of Thou shalt . . . or Thou shalt not . . . , which gives them a negative tone. What is the virtue demanded by each commandment?

5. A privilege usually implies responsibility. Why wouldn't you be fulfilling your Christian obligations if you merely lived up to the standards of the Ten Commandments?

6. The invention of the car required a multitude of new laws and regulations. What other inventions or changes in society have made new laws necessary? On what are these laws based?

CALLED BY THE FATHER

GETTING IT TOGETHER

If you look at the biblical history of the Israelites as an epic, the real hero is Yahweh. It was Yahweh who reached out to rescue the captured, who performed miraculous feats, and who fought off Israel's foes. If was Yahweh who formed his people into a strong nation.

To the Israelites, every happening stemmed from the loving-kindness of Yahweh, their faithful friend. The relationship between the Israelites and their God was expressed formally in a covenant, which can be represented by a hand. A hand has two sides: turned up, it receives; turned down, it gives. In the Covenant, the Israelites received God's commitment; in return, they gave themselves to him by following the Law. But the Law was not a burden, for if two people love each other with a total love, no sacrifice is too great on behalf of the other. Moreover, the Law was a blessing because it guided the Israelites to a good life. They prayed in Psalm 119:105, "A lamp to my feet is your word, a light to my path."

Through the covenant relationship, Yahweh became the sole ruler of Israel. As a theocracy, Israel had no

central government or machinery of state. A loosely gathered people of mixed origins, without even a land of their own, the Israelites maintained an identity as a people for about two hundred years. God elected them and prepared them for a special destiny. Their life anticipated the time when the Word of God would become the Word made flesh.

When God appeared in person, he established a new, eternal Covenant with all people. As Moses sealed the Covenant with the blood of animals, Christ sealed the New Covenant with his own blood. God fulfilled the Covenant by saving the new Chosen People from sin and death. He asked that they obey his new commandment to love one another as he loved them.

Christ did not destroy the Law of Moses, but fulfilled it. When a man asked him how to be perfect, Christ first referred him to the commandments and the Shema. The law of Moses was to be brought to fuller development by the law of Christ. Human beings are a continuing work of God. The Mosaic law, with its 612 regulations, was designed for the Israelites, a particular nation. Christ's law is for all people, the universal church. The Israelite society ruled by God's will was the seed of the kingdom. The New Moses would bring it to full flower, but Jesus, like Yahweh, declared, "Anyone who loves me will be true to my word."

God continues to be Emmanuel in the Church of Jesus Christ. The new People of God can repeat the Jewish prayer, "You, O Lord, are near, and all your commands are permanent."

John 14:23

Psalm 119:151

REVIEWING THE CHAPTER

Linking Your Ideas

1. Construct a replica of the ark of the covenant.
2. Read Psalm 19:8–11 and Psalm 119 on the Law. List passages that reflect the Israelites' attitude toward God's law.
3. What was the Covenant between God and Israel? How did each party carry it out?
4. How does someone who loves God regard his law?
5. What distinguished Israel from other nations?

Strengthening Your Grasp

1. Through the ages architects have tried to design suitable places for people to meet God. The meeting tent—constructed according to elaborate directions—was such a place. Describe or draw what you would consider to be the ideal church.
2. Make a collection of songs that reflect on God's presence.

Expressing Your Convictions

1. Your baptismal certificate is the document of your personal covenant with God. However, it is not very detailed. Draw up a document expressing your personal relationship with God. Use the six characteristics of the treaty explained on page 88. Just as the Jews reread the terms of their covenant every seven years at Shechem to renew their dedication, you might want to save your covenant paper and read it at times like your birthday or retreat days.
2. Write a story or a poem recalling a time when you were very aware of God's presence in your life.
3. In speaking of Yahweh, the Israelites used specific images that symbolized what he meant to them. These symbols are not only valid today but have even deeper meaning because Christ has come. Decide why God can be compared to each thing because of his action in the Church and in your personal life; then choose one and compose a prayer that addresses God by that name.

Extending Your Interest

Read the birth announcement of Jesus in Luke 1:26–38. What imagery is drawn from the experience of the Israelites in the desert?

FIVE

JOSHUA AND OTHER GIANTS

Conquerors of the Promised Land

Sections

Joshua: Man with a Mission
Joshua 1–24

The Judges: God's Generals
Judges 1–21

Judith and Esther: Women Liberators
Judith 1–16; Esther 1–10

I will give thanks to the Lord with all my heart
in the company and assembly of the just.
Great are the works of the Lord,
exquisite in all their delights.
Majesty and glory are his work,
and his justice endures forever.
He has won renown for his wondrous deeds;
gracious and merciful is the Lord.
He has given food to those who fear him;
he will forever be mindful of his covenant.

PSALM 111:1–5

How fortunate you are, O Israel! . . . The Lord is your saving shield, and his sword is your glory.

DEUTERONOMY 33:29

CHAPTER PREVIEW

Do you know what it's like to be on a winning team? To hold a coveted trophy or medal in your hands? To hear the wild cheering of the crowd? If so, did you acknowledge that thanks were due not only to the team members and the coach but to God?

As the Israelites overtook Canaan, they knew that it was God who was giving them the victory. The scribes who compiled their history arranged and enriched the facts to stress the fact that loyalty to God puts God on your side.

According to Jewish divisions of Scripture, the books of Joshua and Judges are prophetic, not historical—that is, they provide religious instructions and encouragement rather than an accurate record of the past. Their overriding truth is that those who love and trust God are rewarded.

Joshua assumed the leadership of the Israelites when Moses died. He had demonstrated his faith when the Israelites first learned that the land of milk and honey

Archaeologists have found that the cities of Jericho and Ai mentioned in the Bible were already ruins when the Israelites came to Canaan. The battles described there probably took place at another city, such as Bethel.

Holocaust is a sacrifice to God in which the offering is completely destroyed so that no man can claim it.

Fourteen judges are named in the Bible. (See the list headed "Judges in the Book of Judges," p. 107.)

was also the land of fierce warriors. He and Caleb were the only two who relied enough on Yahweh to move into Canaan immediately. God made good his promise to Abraham when, under Joshua, the Israelite tribes fought their way into Canaan and divided the land. Excavations in Western Palestine confirm that several important cities (Bethel, Lachish, Debir, Hazor) were destroyed in the latter half of the thirteenth century B.C., the proposed date of the Israelite invasion.

For two hundred years, the Israelites engaged in battles to hold their land. They fought the original peoples of Canaan as well as such invaders as the seacoast Philistines and the camel-riding Midianites. During this time Palestine was never totally under Israelite control.

The Chosen People believed in holy war—that is, a war that is justified because of religious reasons. If they were obedient to Yahweh, he would choose a leader to take them to victory. The Israelites also practiced *herem*, or "the ban," which meant that they totally destroyed enemy cities as a holocaust. Only the land was theirs; the booty and captives belonged to Yahweh.

God frequently provided for the Israelites a military leader known as a judge to lead them to peace. You are probably familiar with the judges Deborah, Gideon, and Samson. Some of the judges ruled over certain tribes at the same time that other judges ruled over other tribes. The judges were by no means of sterling character, but God used them because of their faith. That imperfect men and women could become heroes and heroines offers hope for sin-scarred people.

The stories of Judith and Esther echo the theme of Joshua and Judges. Many scholars agree that these two books are mostly fiction and are meant to illustrate that when the Jews were faithful to the Covenant, God rescued them from their foes.

■ Can you foresee any challenging situations or problems in your future? Compose a prayer of trust in God to bolster your confidence and help you cope with any conflict. In your prayer, refer to God's love for you and to the evidence of his past help. Ask him for his strategy in conquering the problem.

Words to Know

Joshua (**josh**-uh-eh), Caleb (**kay**-lehb), Philistines (**fil**-is-tinz), Midianites (**mid**-ee-eh-nightz), holocaust, ban, Jericho (**jer**-eh-koh), judge, Rahab (**ray**-hab), Shechem (**shek**-ehm), Shiloh (**shigh**-loh), Gideon (**gid**-i-ehn), Samson (**sam**-sehn), Jephthah (**jef**-theh), Deborah, Barak (**bayr**-ehk), Sisera (**sis**-eh-ruh), Jael (**jay**-ehl), Judith, Nebuchadnezzar (neb-eh-kehd-**nez**-ehr), Holofernes (hoe-leh-**fair**-nees), Esther, Mordecai (**mohr**-deh-kigh), Haman (**hay**-mehn), Uzziah (eh-**zigh**-eh)

JOSHUA: MAN WITH A MISSION
(Joshua 1–24)

Have you ever had the uncomfortable experience of standing alone or nearly alone when a majority of people held a different opinion from you? How did you feel, then, when you were proved right?

Joshua, Moses's successor, was one of the two men who wanted to seize Canaan as soon as the Israelites arrived, even though scouts on reconnaissance had reported that the Canaanites were giants, adding, "We felt

Numbers 13:33

like mere grasshoppers." No one over twenty survived to enter the Promised Land except Joshua and Caleb, the two who had trusted in Yahweh. The people were sentenced to forty years of wandering in the desert before winning Canaan.

Joshua was marked as a hero. His name "Yeshua," like "Jesus," meant "Yahweh saves." Summoned to the meeting tent with Moses, Joshua had been divinely commissioned to lead the people into the Promised Land, and he distinguished himself as a commander in desert skirmishes.

In all likelihood, the tribes of Israelites infiltrated Canaan gradually and more or less peacefully, settling it over a period of three hundred years. But the sacred writer painted the conquest of Canaan in glorious colors and as if all of Israel had participated in a grand military onslaught under Joshua's leadership. This served to reaffirm that Yahweh had given the land to these people.

That the Israelites' success is the Lord's doing is evident in the Bible. When the Chosen People entered Canaan, the Jordan River stopped and allowed them to cross, just as the Reed Sea had parted for them at the beginning of their trek. They overtook their first city, Jericho, because of the kindness of Rahab, who believed in their God, and because the city walls miraculously collapsed. They won a battle against five Amorite kings in a surprise attack and with the help of a hailstorm that killed the enemy. In this same battle, the sun stood still for Joshua.

In all favorable circumstances, the Israelites interpreted events as God's intervention on their behalf.

You may think it unjust for God to have fought other peoples so that his people could have land. Wars, like any evil, are the result of sin. God only takes human agents and conditions as they are and accomplishes his own purposes. The Israelites felt it was good to conquer Canaan because the Canaanites were a wicked, immoral people. Besides, they reasoned, hadn't God promised their fathers that they would own Canaan? From a wider perspective, God was leading humankind to a greater destiny than the Israelites understood.

The banks of the Jordan last collapsed and dammed the river in 1927.

Rahab was rewarded in that she became an ancestor of David, the forefather of Christ.

Scholars today interpret the miracle of the sun as part of a victory poem: the words mean that the hailstorm caused darkness. Another theory is that Joshua exclaimed, "O sun, stand still," wishing for time to win, and when the Hebrews won, they used the image of the sun standing still.

CALLED BY THE FATHER

The Promised Land was divided among the twelve tribes by lots, an Israelite means of discerning God's will. Each tribe received a section except for the priestly tribe of Levi. Because of the Lord's commands, the Levites were given cities in every tribe's portion.

Before Joshua died, he had the tribes renew their covenant at Shechem. Because many people had joined the Israelites since the original covenant, the renewal made it possible for them to unite with the first-covenanted people in their solemn promise. Thus the weakest of peoples was on its way to becoming the greatest of nations. But everything depended on their continuing fidelity to Yahweh.

Lots, called *urim* and *thummin*, were probably two stones or sticks marked "yes" and "no."

Shechem is believed to be the first shrine city. After the conquest, the ark was moved to Shiloh, which became the tribal center.

Read and Recall

Read Joshua 2–6. After reading these chapters about the entrance into Cannan, you should be able to answer these questions:

1. What sign protected Rahab's house?
2. What led the line of march into the Jordan?
3. What was the perpetual memorial recalling the Jordan River miracle?
4. Which Israelite practice was renewed on reaching Canaan?
5. What was discontinued once the Israelites were in Canaan, the land of milk and honey?
6. What did the Israelites do at Jericho when the signal horn sounded?

SOME HEBREW NUMBER FACTS

If you had to choose between plane seats seven and thirteen, you would probably select seat seven. For us, seven is a lucky number, and thirteen is unlucky. Some hotels skip the thirteenth floor because people are reluctant to stay on an unlucky floor. To the Eskimos, five is special. The Israelites shared our preference for seven, believing that it was the perfect number.

Three was also significant for the Israelites; it stood for deliverance and victory. In Scripture, Yahweh appeared to the Israelites on Mount Sinai, Esther saved her people, and Jonah was delivered from the whale.

Forty stands for one generation or an extended but uncertain period of time. It usually signifies purification and preparation—a holy time—as in the rainstorm of Noah and the wandering of the Hebrews.

The desert experience of Christ lasted forty days.

A *discrepancy* is a disagreement or inconsistency.

The discrepancies in Hebrew numbers in Scripture have some interesting explanations. You may have heard the expression "as old as Methusaleh." The Bible says that Methusaleh lived to be nine hundred and sixty-nine years old, and his grandson Noah fathered three sons when he was only five hundred years old. These long life spans are symbolic: high numbers signify power, importance, and faithfulness to God. This explains the census of the Israelites in Numbers.

Other factors also make interpretation difficult. Hebrew numbers are the same as the letters of the Hebrew alphabet, and the word for "thousand" can also mean "family," "clan," or "soldier." These confusing similarities and the fact that, in Hebrew, words are written without vowels or separating spaces, gave rise to errors of interpretation. Also, scribes who copied the texts could easily have omitted or added a digit by mistake. Archaeological findings and biblical research continue to solve the problem of numbers in the Bible.

CALLED BY THE FATHER

Reflect

1. It is amazing how one person's life can influence thousands. Who are some individuals who have changed the world for the better? How? What role did faith play in their lives?
2. Sometimes fear keeps people from achieving their potential. What is at the root of this fear? What advice would you give fearful people?
3. You get nothing for nothing. The Israelites had to earn their land. What is required of someone who strives for a high goal?
4. What would Jesus say about the practice of the ban? What makes you think so?

THE JUDGES: GOD'S GENERALS
(Judges 1–21)

What lessons have you learned in the school of life?

The Israelites had been told: "If you . . . serve other gods and worship them, the anger of the Lord will flare up against you and you will quickly perish from the good land which he has given you." However, they had to find out for themselves that Yahweh did not tolerate unfaithfulness.

Joshua 23:16

Not only did the Israelites compromise by allowing idol-worshipping Canaanites to exist, but they themselves worshipped idols. As a result, God allowed them to be attacked. The Israelites were attracted to idols because neighboring tribes worshipped them. The Israelites found it just as difficult to be different as people today find it hard to be "odd" or "not with it." Moreover, because human beings are so dependent on their senses, praying to a visible god is more satisfying than praying to an invisible one.

The Israelites were slow learners. No sooner had they become contrite to Yahweh and in return received his forgiveness and help than they abandoned him again for false gods. This four-phase cycle—(1) sin/idolatry, (2) punishment/attack, (3) repentance/prayer, and (4) deliverance/a leader brings victory—was the life style of Israel throughout the period of judges (1200–1120

Judges 21:25

B.C.). This time is referred to as the dark ages of Jewish history because of its conflict, lack of culture, and low moral standards. Judges states, "Everyone did what he thought best."

In war the tribe or tribes involved were led to victory by a leader who then became a local hero. This person, guided by God's spirit, was called a judge. The Book of Judges names twelve judges. The six judges described in detail in the Bible are called major judges (they are starred in the following list); the other six are called minor judges.

Judges in the Book of Judges

*Othniel of Judah	Tola of Issachar
*Ehud of Benjamin	Jair of Gilead
Shamgar	*Jephthah of Gilead
*Deborah of Ephraim	Ibzan of Bethlehem
and Barak of	Elon of Zebulun
Naphtali	Abdon of Ephraim
*Gideon of Manasseh	*Samson of Dan

An Israelite judge was not a judge in the legal sense, although some of the judges served as tribe consultants. Nor was a judge a king. The only judges who led all of Israel were Eli and Samuel, who appear in the Book of Samuel.

Furthermore, the judges were not necessarily models of virtue. They were people of their time, often crude, even savage. For instance, the judge Jephthah made a vow that if he conquered the Ammonites he would sacrifice to God the first person who came from his house to meet him. When he returned home in triumph and his young daughter came out dancing to welcome him, he kept his vow and killed her. The judge Samson was a colorful character whose deeds were spectacular but who spent much of his life indulging his own passions and desires.

One judge, Deborah, was a woman, and in her story it was also a woman who delivered the Israelites. The people were once again guilty of idolatry. God let them suffer at the hands of the Canaanites, with their nine

Human sacrifice was a practice common among pagans.

Probably the exploits of Samson were performed by several men, but as the legends were passed down all the feats were attributed to Samson. No doubt they also grew more impressive with each retelling.

CALLED BY THE FATHER

hundred iron chariots under the command of Sisera. Deborah told Barak that God wanted him to gather the nearby tribes and attack Sisera's army. Barak agreed to go, on the condition that Deborah went too. The "Canticle of Deborah" reveals that heavy rains flooded the battlefield, rendering the enemy chariots useless. Every Canaanite was killed except Sisera, who took shelter in the tent of the woman Jael. When Sisera fell asleep, Jael drove a tent peg through his head, thus breaking the revered rule of hospitality but obtaining victory for the Israelites.

The "Canticle of Deborah" celebrating the Jewish victory over Sisera is one of the most ancient pieces of Hebrew poetry in existence (Judges 5).

Two of the major judges were Gideon and Samson. Before their appearance, the Israelites had broken the Covenant and were being harassed by other people. God let the Midianites plague the Israelites in Gideon's time. In Samson's time, the Philistines were a long-standing foe. This sea people, who had settled on the coastal plain, engaged in guerrilla wars with the Israelites of the highlands for possession of the desirable hill country that lay between them. Through Gideon and Samson, God brought his people back to him and destroyed their enemies.

Samson was a Nazarite, which means he had taken vows never to drink wine or cut his hair.

The predominant lesson of the Book of Judges is that obedience to God's law brings prosperity and security, while disobedience invites disaster.

Read

Read the following outline of Gideon's life as described in Judges 6–8. Make a similar outline for Samson after you have read his story in Judges 13–16.

I. The call comes to Gideon
   A. Gideon is an "insignificant" man trying to save his father's wheat before the Midianites destroy it when an angel commands him to save Israel.
   B. Because Gideon asks for a sign, fire consumes his sacrifice.
   C. At the Lord's bidding, Gideon destroys his father's altar to the god Baal and builds one to Yahweh.
   D. Gideon summons the tribes against the Midianites.

After he destroyed the altar and challenged Baal, Gideon was called Jerubbaal ("let Baal take action"). Baal (lord) was the chief Canaanite god. These gods were creators and destroyers linked to the forces of nature.

E. Twice, Gideon asks God for a sign that he will save them.
  1. Fleece becomes wet with dew while the ground remains dry.
  2. Then the fleece remains dry while dew covers the ground.
II. Gideon achieves victory
  A. God reduces Gideon's army from thirty-three thousand to three hundred.
    1. Those who are afraid are allowed to go home, leaving ten thousand.
    2. At a stream, the three hundred men who drink water that is raised to their mouths with their hands (rather than kneeling and drinking from the stream like dogs) are chosen to fight.
  B. Gideon hears a man telling about his dream predicting victory for Gideon.
  C. There is a surprise attack at night with torches, horns, and the breaking of empty jars.
  D. People at Succoth who refuse bread to the army are killed on the return march.
  E. Gideon refuses to become king because Yahweh rules.

Major headings for the Samson outline might be: I. Samson is consecrated; II. Samson and the Philistines contend; III. Samson's weakness leads to his downfall.

Recall

1. What role did the judges play in Jewish history?
2. Describe the cyclic pattern of the Israelites' lives throughout the period of the judges.
3. How did Gideon live up to the title "judge"?
4. What exploits gave Samson a reputation for strength?

Reflect

1. "It's not the size of the dog in the fight; it's the size of the fight in the dog that counts." What was God demonstrating by making Gideon's army smaller? What other Old Testament encounters can you think

CALLED BY THE FATHER

of where the size of the army or of an individual did not determine the outcome? What did?

2. In Catholic tradition, Gideon's fleece stands as a symbol for Mary. Why?

3. How can someone your age be imitating the sin/punishment/repentance/deliverance pattern of the Israelites?

4. In the time of the judges, how was God like the father of the New Testament prodigal son? How was he different?

5. The cutting of Samson's hair was the direct cause of his blindness and bondage, but what fault was at the root of his downfall? What are some nagging habits or negative attitudes that may lead you to your destruction?

6. "All that is necessary for evil to prosper is for good men and women to do nothing." Newspapers and television provide evidence that life is filled with brutality and sin today, just as it was three thousand years ago. What can you do about it?

7. Throughout history, people have come to the fore in crises just as the judges of old did. Joan of Arc, who led the French in defending Orleans from the British, is one of them. Who are others?

JUDITH AND ESTHER: WOMEN LIBERATORS
(Judith 1–16; Esther 1–10)

Michelle's mother and father didn't set down rules for her behavior or issue warnings about what would happen if she misbehaved. Instead, they told Michelle stories that had a point.

■ What are some stories that teach a lesson?

Many nations have a store of folktales and favorite stories that illustrate truths. You are probably familiar with Greek and Roman myths, Aesop's fables, and Hans Christian Andersen's stories. The Jews are among the best storytellers. In teaching through parables, Jesus was following a well-established Jewish practice.

It is no surprise, then, to find that the Bible contains several books that are exciting and absorbing short stories. Two of these, the books of Judith and Esther, share the same lesson: God saves his faithful people. Both books reflect the Exodus event. In Judith, God uses the hand of a woman to keep his people from total destruction by foreign invaders. In Esther, God uses the bravery and loyalty of a woman to spare his people in Persia from the sentence of death.

The Book of Judith was written late, probably in the second century B.C. The chief foe, Nebuchadnezzar, who was really king of the Chaldeans, is called an Assyrian king. It is difficult to identify the conflict and the people described with any known historical event. Scholars propose that these glaring errors are the author's way of informing people that the story is not to be taken literally but, rather, symbolically. Nebuchadnezzar stands for all people who make themselves gods. Judith, whose name means "Jewess," stands for the nation as it should be: devout, careful in observing the Law, and trusting in Yahweh.

The Book of Esther was most likely written at the close of the fourth century B.C. Again, neither the people

Since the Book of Judith was written when legal observance was emphasized, the heroine's lie and murder were not considered sinful, yet her eating of unlawful food would be.

CALLED BY THE FATHER

nor the events can be traced. The story explains the origin of the Jewish feast of Purim that is celebrated on the fourteenth and fifteenth of Adar (February and March). The author must have lived in Persia to have been able to relate this story set in that country. Because the book did not directly deal with God, although his saving presence is assumed, writers added parts like Esther's prayer to make it more acceptable as religious literature. Protestant and Jewish people do not believe the additions to the Book of Esther are inspired, but the Catholic Church holds that the book, with its additions, is the Word of God.

The Book of Esther is the only Old Testament book not found among the Dead Sea Scrolls of Qumran.

Judith and Esther both served to bolster Jewish national pride. The purpose of the Israelites' delight in revenge was to demonstrate that evil against God's faithful people returned on the heads of the plotters.

Even though the authenticity of these two accounts as history cannot be proved, the message of both is certainly true: those who make God the foundation of their lives, conform to his wishes, and never doubt his love, not even in the worst situations, are invincible.

Invincible means not able to be conquered.

Read

For the story of Judith, read the key sections from your Bible and the following summaries, which link them together.

King Nebuchadnezzar was determined to destroy the whole world because the neighboring countries refused to be his allies. He wanted all people to worship him as a god. As a result, Holofernes, his general, led the Assyrian army on a rampage of destruction.

When the Israelites heard of the approach of Holofernes, they prayed, fasted, and did penance. In the meantime Holofernes asked Achior, the leader of the Ammonites, about the background of the Israelites. Achior warned him that the Israelites' God shielded them when they were faithful to him. This angered Holofernes, who saw Nebuchadnezzar as the only god. He threatened to annihilate the Israelites, and sent Achior to them to be killed with them.

The strategy the Assyrians used in besieging the Israelite city of Bethulia was to capture their water sources and guard the mountains so that no one could escape. By the thirty-fourth day, the Israelites were begging Uzziah and the other city rulers to surrender. Uzziah asked them to hold out for five more days.

Once Upon a Time—read 8:1–12, 28–36.
The Heroine's Prayer—read 9:1, 12–14.
Enter the Villain—read chapter 10.
The Heroine's Plan—Judith flatters Holofernes. Then she tells him that she fled from her people because they had broken God's law and thus would be destroyed by the Assyrians. She says she will pray every night, and God will let her know when Israel has sinned. Then she will tell Holofernes the ideal time to attack and lead him into the city. Holofernes trusts her.
The Plot Thickens—read chapter 12.
The Climax—read 13:1–10.
Good Triumphs—Judith is received in the town with great rejoicing. She directs the Israelite warriors for the next siege of battle and then relates

The words the Israelites used to praise Judith (15:9) are applied by the Church to Mary in the liturgy.

CALLED BY THE FATHER

her adventures to the people. Achior becomes a
Jew. Read 4:11–15:14.
Happily Ever After–read 16:18–25.

Regarding the Book of Esther, as part of the two-day
celebration of Purim the Jews act out the story of Esther.
Sometimes the audience participates by applauding the
hero and heroine (Esther and Mordecai) and by either
booing the villain (Haman) or using noisemakers to
show their dislike. After you read the Book of Esther,
you may want to act out the important scenes.

The feast of Purim commemorates the rescue of the Jews from Haman's plotting. The word *purim* (*pur* means "lot") indicates that Haman cast lots to determine the day the Jews would be destroyed.

Recall

1. Why is it fitting that the books of Judith and Esther
   are included in a unit on the Exodus?
2. What is the purpose of each book?
3. How were Judith and Esther alike?
4. Why did Yahweh save the Israelites from the Assyrians? From the Persians?

Reflect

1. Judith and Esther are types of Mary. What parallels
   can be found in their lives and hers?
2. What do the Judith and Esther stories reveal about
   the Israelites' attitude toward women?
3. Stories in which the enemies receive their just punishment are satisfying. Why doesn't just punishment
   always happen in real life?
4. How can people today be Nebuchadnezzars? Ju-
   diths?
5. How do Judith and Esther exhibit courage? What is
   the source of their courage?

GETTING IT TOGETHER

Sometimes a piece of music is a series of variations on
a theme, with the melody repeated in different ways:
lower or higher, faster or slower, with a new rhythm
or another combination of instruments. But no matter

what the disguise, the basic melody line is always recognizable.

This is true of the literature in the Bible. There is one message flowing throughout the Old Testament: the loving God of Israel saves his faithful people. The vehicle for this message varies. Looking backward at their history, the Jews interpreted favorable happenings as God's saving action. After the Exodus, Yahweh continued to save his people. Through the faithful Joshua, he led them into Canaan and aided them in conquering the inhabitants. As long as the Israelites followed him, he provided judges who gave them victory in war.

This theme of God's intervention in the lives of those who trust him and worship him alone recurs in new forms in books like Judith and Esther. In these books God uses women of faith to destroy the enemy.

Later, the books of the New Testament tell about another saving act of God, the sending of an even greater Yeshua, his Son.

CALLED BY THE FATHER

REVIEWING THE CHAPTER

Linking Your Ideas

1. Create a pictorial Hebrew Hall of Fame. Draw symbols for the Jewish heroes and heroines and write explanations of why they are worthy to be included.
2. What do all the stories in this chapter have in common?
3. How did the Sinai covenant affect the course of the Israelites' lives once they were in the Promised Land?

Strengthening Your Grasp

1. Construct a relief map of Canaan. Mark off and label the tribal divisions of the land.
2. Research the excavations that have been made in Jericho and other ancient cities of the Holy Land.
3. Adapt the story of Judith or Esther to modern-day times. Keep the theme the same, but update the situations.
4. Judith, Esther, and their fellow Israelites put on sackcloth and ashes and fasted to obtain God's favor. Investigate the Church's teaching on penance and fasting. When, why, and how do Catholics do penance nowadays?

Expressing Your Convictions

1. Adapt the stories of Gideon, Samson, Judith, Esther, or Tobit to comic-book form, or present one of them as a puppet show.
2. Make a photographic essay on sin/punishment/repentance/deliverance today.
3. God is still the Lord of History, working out the pattern of events for the good of those who love him with their whole heart. Compile a list of the times in this chapter when God assisted the Israelites. Next to it, list major or minor events in your life during which you can see God saving you, too.

Extending Your Interest

In the book of Tobit an angel and a fish bring healing. Like the books of Judith and Esther, the Book of Tobit conveys a message through the medium of a religious novel. The story of Tobit, probably written in the second century B.C., could possibly have its roots in a historical event. As it stands, it is a delightful combination of Jewish tradition and Oriental folklore. It is a classic tale illustrating that goodness is rewarded. Luther wrote about the Book of Tobit, "Is it fiction? Then it is a truly beautiful, wholesome, and profitable fiction, the performance of a gifted poet."

The framework of the story provided the author with opportunities to incorporate prayers and psalms along with Jewish wisdom themes. For this reason, Tobit is considered just as much a wisdom book as a historical book, but it is usually classified as a historical book.

Read the Book of Tobit in its entirety. Watch for the Jewish themes woven throughout the story: respect for law, burial of the dead, God's intervention, and the reward of the faithful.

Your class would probably enjoy acting out its colorful story.

REVIEWING THE UNIT

Patterns

1. How did Yahweh show himself a true Father to the children of Israel?
2. What response did God desire from his people? How did he react when they failed to respond according to his desires?
3. Describe the qualities that make these people heroes or heroines: Moses, Joshua, Gideon, Esther, Judith, Tobit.

Focal Points

Which of the following concepts would be objectionable to the authors of the Hebrew Scriptures?

1. Yahweh is worshipped best when you can see an image of him.
2. God's name is I Am.
3. The plagues were coincidences that led to the freeing of the Hebrews.
4. Yahweh chose Israel because of its potential to become a great nation.
5. When you trust in God, you can do impossible things.
6. God always calls outstanding and talented people to do his work.
7. Wickedness is punished in the next world, not in this life.
8. Those who are faithful to Yahweh will always be victorious.

Response

1. Skim through the Catholic Easter Vigil service and note the references to ideas that were covered in this unit.
2. Write a comparative character study of Christ and Moses or Christ and Joshua, or of Mary and Esther or Mary and Judith.
3. Write a ballad or original verse about Moses, Joshua, Gideon, Judith, or Esther.
4. If Moses were to come back today, what message would he have for our Church? Write a homily that he might give at your parish.

Adulthood and Maturity: The Monarchy

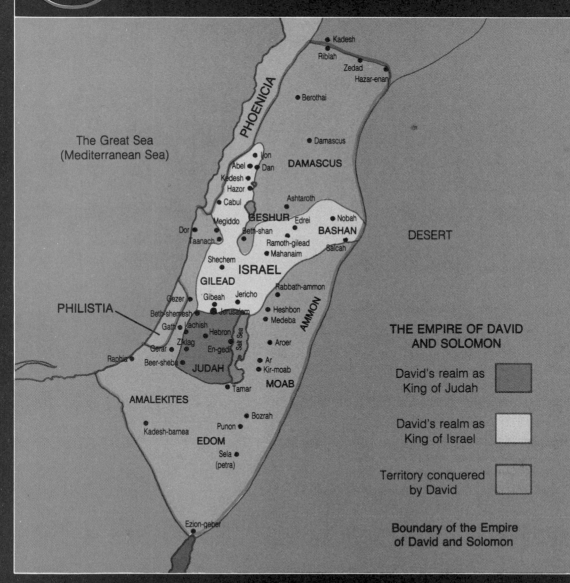

Kadesh
Riblah
Zedad
Hazar-enan

Berothai

PHOENICIA

The Great Sea
(Mediterranean Sea)

Damascus

Iyon
Abel • Dan
Kedesh
Hazor

DAMASCUS

Cabul

Ashtaroth

GESHUR

Megiddo
Dor
Taanach

Beth-shan

Edrei

Nobah

BASHAN

Ramoth-gilead
Mahanaim

Salcah

DESERT

Shechem

ISRAEL

GILEAD

Gezer
Gibeah
Jericho

Rabbath-ammon

PHILISTIA

Beth-shemesh
Gath • Lachish
Ziklag
Gerar

Jerusalem

Hebron

En-gedi

Heshbon
Medeba

AMMON

Aroer

Raphia
Beer-sheba

Salt Sea

JUDAH

Ar
Kir-moab

MOAB

Tamar

AMALEKITES

Bozrah

Kadesh-barnea

Punon

EDOM

Sela
(petra)

Ezion-geber

THE EMPIRE OF DAVID AND SOLOMON

David's realm as
King of Judah

David's realm as
King of Israel

Territory conquered
by David

Boundary of the Empire
of David and Solomon

Sources

1 and 2 Samuel, 1 Kings 1–11

■ Founding of the Israelite Monarchy, 1000? B.C.–922 B.C.

■ Careers of Samuel, Saul, David, and Solomon

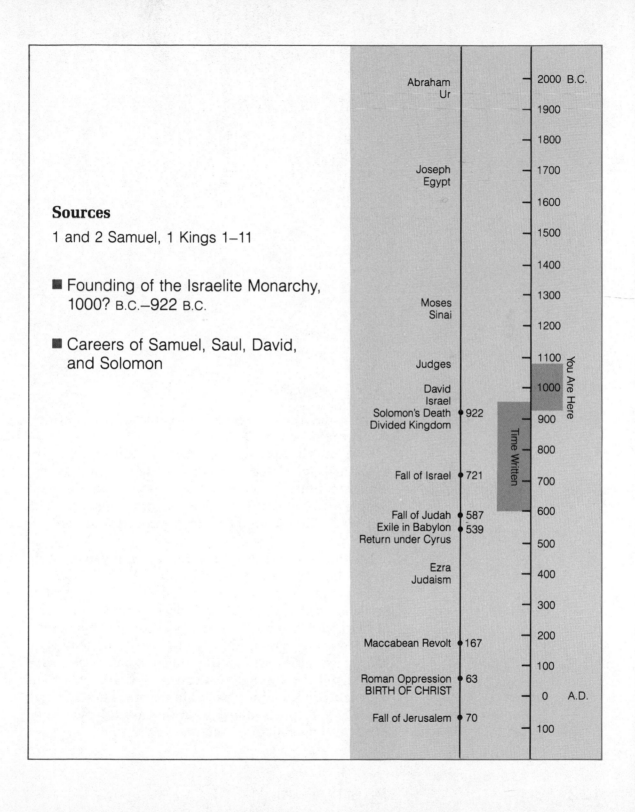

Abraham Ur	2000 B.C.
	1900
	1800
Joseph Egypt	1700
	1600
	1500
	1400
	1300
Moses Sinai	1200
	1100
Judges	1100
David Israel	1000
Solomon's Death	922
Divided Kingdom	900
	800
Fall of Israel	721 · 700
Fall of Judah	587 · 600
Exile in Babylon	539
Return under Cyrus	500
Ezra Judaism	400
	300
	200
Maccabean Revolt	167 ·
	100
Roman Oppression	63 ·
BIRTH OF CHRIST	0 A.D.
Fall of Jerusalem	70 ·
	100

You Are Here

Time Written

Speak, Lord, for your servant is listening.

1 SAMUEL 3:9

UNIT OVERVIEW

If everyone in school agreed to wear jeans every Friday, what would you wear? Why?

Israel was becoming self-conscious. She was growing to maturity now that she had been settled on the land for some time. "There must be a king over us," the people said. "We too must be like other nations, with a king to rule us and to lead us in warfare and fight our battles."

1 Samuel 8:19–20

For the two previous centuries, when loyalty to Yahweh—the one thing that had united them in the first place—had grown cold, the tribal leaders had tended to bicker among themselves and place their individual needs above the good of all. Declining morals and a divided army made it difficult to ward off enemies invading from the east and the south. In each crisis, God had raised up a judge to save the day. But when the determined Philistines gained in numbers and strength and began to push inland from the coast, Israel found itself on the brink of extinction.

CALLED BY THE FATHER

Onto the stage stepped the holy and deeply respected Samuel. His influence on the history of the Chosen People was great enough to merit having one entire scroll, later divided into two books, named after him. He led them from near disaster into the most glorious period of their history—the monarchy. It was to be a shining hour of independence. In her maturity, Israel would produce a king who could serve as a model for every Israelite and who would foreshadow the King of Kings, Christ himself.

But Israel's golden hour was all too brief. Although the monarchy lasted almost five hundred years, its only greats were the first three kings to sit on the throne, and even these great men were flawed. The warrior king, Saul, kept the enemy from devouring the tribes, but he went mad out of jealousy. The great-hearted David unified the nation in the worship of the living God, but he sinned grievously by stealing another man's wife. The wise King Solomon introduced culture into Israel and built a magnificent empire. In the end, however, he also strayed by allowing the worship of foreign gods, which led to the division that ultimately destroyed Israel.

Of the three, it was David whom the people would look back to as their ideal king. After hard fighting, he had brought them a period of peace. He was their messiah. But more—by repenting of his sins, he showed Israel the true source of their strength: love of God. One of the world's most famous monarchs, David was to be the ideal of every future king of Israel. The people would come to expect that their final savior would come from among his descendants.

Later, when the monarchy crumbled and disappeared, some prophets saw that the king they awaited—the true Messiah—would be like King David and yet, somehow, he would be different from, and greater than, the best king Israel had ever had.

When the Hebrew scrolls were translated into Greek, the Greek alphabet took one-third more space than the Hebrew alphabet, which was then composed only of consonants. The scroll had to be divided for ease in handling.

SIX

SAMUEL AND SAUL

Victory and Defeat

Sections

The Birth and Vocation of Samuel
   1 Samuel 1–3, 8–10

Victory, Rejection, and Election of David
   1 Samuel 11:1–11, 13; 15:1–16:13

Mood Music for a Tortured King
   1 Samuel 16:14–23

Saul's Jealousy, Despair, and Suicide
   1 Samuel 18:1–19:7, 21, 22, 24, 31

Sing to the Lord a new song;
   sing to the Lord, all you lands.
Sing to the Lord, bless his name;
   announce his salvation, day after day.
Tell his glory among the nations;
   among all peoples, his wondrous deeds.
For great is the Lord and highly to be praised;
   awesome is he, beyond all gods.

PSALM 96:1–4

If you wish with your whole heart to return to the Lord, . . . worship him alone. Then he will deliver you from the power of the Philistines.

1 SAMUEL 7:3

Obedience is better than sacrifice.

1 SAMUEL 15:22

CHAPTER PREVIEW

When someone gives you directions, what is the greatest challenge you face?

God had shown himself Israel's faithful friend, freely speaking his Word to them. As in our own time, the biggest challenge Israel faced was carrying out God's plan.

In the struggle to possess the land, the Israelites gradually adopted the customs of their neighbors and drifted away from the Lord. Their worship continued at Shiloh, a central shrine where the ark was housed, but the priests who performed the ceremonies were corrupt, taking the offerings for themselves and leading the people into false worship. Once again, God raised up a savior for Israel.

The priests in the Samuel narrative are represented by the sons of the chief priest, Eli.

As was true of other important persons of the Bible, Samuel's birth and call are played up in stories that highlight God's special assistance. He is shown as coming to the most helpless.

A poor, childless woman, Hannah, prayed fervently for a son. When her prayer was answered, she returned the boy, Samuel, to the Lord at the shrine. There he was trained to priestly service under Eli, who taught him to respond to God's call, which came to him unexpectedly during his teenage years.

Samuel responded to his call with generosity and courage, and became Israel's first prophet after Moses, as well as its last judge.

A prophet does not necessarily foretell the future.

As a prophet (an official spokesman for God), he reawakened the Israelites' conscience by turning them from idol worship. As a judge, he summoned military forces sufficiently powerful to contain the invading Amonites, Amalekites, Moabites, and Edomites. Samuel led his men to victory over the fierce Philistines, the sea people who had successfully captured the ark and threatened Israel's very existence, and restored the ark. For twenty years the people remained faithful to Yahweh, and for twenty years there was peace.

The Philistines were called the sea people because they lived on the coast of the Great Sea, the ancient name of the Mediterranean Sea.

But as the Philistines planned another attack, the tribes, like the American colonies, saw the need for more than military unity. They recognized the godless sons of the aging Samuel as unfit to lead. Envying the strength of other nations, they asked Samuel to appoint a king. Samuel was divinely directed to grant their wishes, despite Israel's tradition of tribal independence and direct obedience to God. Warning them of the abuses of human kings, Samuel named Saul as Israel's first king. When Saul later usurped Samuel's role and proved unfaithful to Israel's Law, Samuel rejected him and anointed David at Bethlehem. Then Samuel retired from the limelight and died, mourned by all as a man who had remained true to the Lord.

The tribe of Benjamin was the least important in Israel.

The Benjaminite Saul reigned for twenty years, more a warrior hero than a king. An unusually tall and strong man, Saul was far from a giant in social status, disposition, or character. He had begun his career with many advantages: he had been anointed by God, counseled by the holy Samuel, and accepted by the elders. He was deeply religious and something of a military genius.

CALLED BY THE FATHER

Yet he lacked self-confidence, and his sense of inferiority led him to desperate acts.

Although Saul successfully rallied the tribes to a unified military effort against the Philistines, who continued to invade the borders, two fatal mistakes marred his record and provoked the anger of Samuel and God. First, fearful that without offering a sacrifice he would lose a battle, Saul took over the priest's role and offered the sacrifice when Samuel was delayed. Rightly angered, Samuel prophesied that, because of Saul's superstition and pride, Saul's descendants would never rule in Israel.

Second, Saul disobeyed Samuel's command to put the Amalekites under "the ban" (discussed in the preceding chapter). Saul made a show of conformity by ordering all the people killed, but he saved the king, whom he greatly admired. To win favor with his men, he allowed them to keep the best animals, offering the lame excuse that he had intended the men to sacrifice the animals when they reached home. Samuel prophesied that God would reject Saul, and then parted company with the king. Relieved to be free of Samuel, who was like his conscience, Saul nevertheless understood the evil he had done and was torn by a guilt that eventually led him to near insanity.

The Amalekites had forced Moses and the Israelites to detour unnecessarily through the desert by forbidding passage through their land.

Saul's natural impulse to like David, the talented musician and warrior he had appointed to his court, was overshadowed by an uncontrollable jealousy as David's charm and military success made him a popular hero. After almost killing him, Saul forced David to flee the country and live for years among the Philistines. Depressed and suspicious in his last days, Saul consulted a witch to learn of his future—a thing absolutely forbidden by Israel's faith.

In the belief that God alone knows the future, the Israelites regarded consulting spirits as going against the first commandment (Leviticus 19:31).

But Saul was unable to muster enough strength from among the tribes to permanently defeat the Philistines. Wounded in the fateful battle of Gilboa, he committed suicide after learning of the death of his sons, among them Jonathan, whom he himself once almost killed because of Jonathan's friendship with David.

Saul became the victim of an overheated imagination, fear, and lack of self-control. He is an example of a person of great promise brought to disaster because of flaws that he allowed to master him.

- Someone has said that waiting is the hardest part of trust. Do you agree? Why or why not?
- What personal faults do you recognize in Saul?

Words to Know

Elkanah (ehl-**kay**-nuh), Hannah (**han**-eh), Peninnah (pin-**een**-uh), Eli (**ee**-ligh), Samuel, Shiloh (**shigh**-loh), Philistia (fi-**lis**-tih-uh), Ashdod (**ash**-dod), Kiriath-jearim (**keer**-ee-aht yeh-har-**eem**), Dagon (**day**-gon), shrine/sanctuary, Hophni (**hohf**-nee), Phinehas (**phin**-ee-uhs), Kish (kihsh), Saul, Ammonites (**am**-uh-nights), Jonathan, Amalekites (eh-**mal**-eh-kights), Agag (eh-**gog**), Jesse (**jes**-ee), David, Gibeah (**gib**-i-eh), Jabesh-gilead (**jay**-behsh **gil**-ee-ehd), Michmash Pass (**mick**-mash), Bethlehem, Judah (**joo**-dah)

THE BIRTH AND VOCATION OF SAMUEL
(1 Samuel 1–3, 8–10)

Two men were walking along a crowded city sidewalk. Suddenly one of them remarked, "Listen to the lovely sound of that cricket." His friend protested that nobody could be expected to detect the sound of a cricket amid the roar of traffic and the noise of the crowds. The first man, a zoologist, didn't explain. He simply dropped a half dollar onto the sidewalk. At once a dozen people began to look about them. "We hear what we listen for," he said.

- Do you agree that we hear what we listen for? Give examples to back up your answer.
- When and how do you listen to God?

Disgraced by her barrenness, Hannah cried to the Lord for a son. When Samuel was born, she dedicated him to God's service at the central shrine of Shiloh,

Barrenness, or childlessness, was considered a curse in Israel, because having children was God's will.

CALLED BY THE FATHER

where, under the chief priest Eli, he learned God's service. In the Shiloh Temple, Samuel heard the difficult call of God to admonish Eli, whose sons he had allowed to offer pagan sacrifices and take the sacrificial meat before it was offered. Samuel revealed God's curse on Eli's corrupt priestly family, whom Israel would reject in favor of Samuel, the bridge between the old tribal league and the monarchy. Samuel was both a judge and a prophet in Israel.

When the elders of Israel approached their prophet with the request for "a king over us, as other nations have, to judge us," Samuel at first refused, seeing only trouble ahead if Israel tried to copy the government of their Canaanite neighbors, whose kings were like gods, with absolute power. In Israel's tribal confederation, God had been the sole source of the law. The request for a monarchy was directly contrary to the faith of the Chosen People.

1 Samuel 8:5

1 Samuel 11:6

These books are 1 and 2 Samuel; 1 and 2 Kings; 1 and 2 Chronicles.

The sacred author gives the historical reasons for Israel's desire for a change in government: the pounding of the Philistines at the back door, the weakening of the priesthood, the aging of Samuel, and the corruption of his sons. Yet the author also shows that none of these would have been of any importance if God had not somehow indicated the change. God did approve, giving a revelation to Samuel in prayer and pouring out his spirit upon Saul, whom he urged to save his people, who were under attack from the Ammonites. Saul came into office, then, by appointment of the established authority in Israel—Samuel—but he was also chosen because he was personally qualified for his role.

Samuel listened to God and left the people free to bind themselves to a human king. He anointed Saul, but only after warning the nation of the abuses that could creep in when human beings rose to power. In fact, the theme that runs through all the books on the history of the monarchy confirms Israel's original belief: everyone—even the king—is subject to God's law.

Read and Recall

Read 1 Samuel 1–3 and 8–10.

1. In your own words, tell the story of the "marvelous conception" of Samuel (chapters 1 and 2) and the sad condition of the priesthood in Israel. Include these words: Elkanah, Hannah, Peninnah, Shiloh, Eli, double portions, Hannah's song, three-pronged pitchfork, a little garment, Hophni, Phinehas.
2. Dramatize the call of Samuel (chapter 3) using these characters: narrator, Eli, Samuel, the Lord. Discuss the source of the communication and what it says about Israel's God, Samuel's character, and Eli's response.
3. Write or act out the drama between Samuel and the elders of Israel as they asked for a king (chapters 8–10). Bring out Saul's timidity as well as the reasons for and against initiating a monarchy, and the rights of kings as Samuel lists them.

CALLED BY THE FATHER

Reflect

1. Obstetricians say that the chemical effects of a mother's sadness, anger, and discontent affect the development of a fetus. A child can know whether he or she is loved or not wanted even before birth. What natural effect would prayer for God's blessing have on an unborn child? What other effects might it have? How can the father have a positive effect on a child before it is born?

2. What would Hannah have said to a modern woman who was thinking of having an abortion? (See 1 Samuel 1:4–8.)

3. How can modern parents return their children to the Lord as Hannah did? (Don't say by giving them to "religious life.")

4. Samuel obeyed Eli, even though Eli was not a good priest. Who communicates God's will to you? Why can't obedience be based on the commands of perfect people? What does the statement "Praying is listening" mean? How can you discern God's will?

5. Why do you think the elder Eli so willingly received Samuel's criticism? In what circumstances might a teenager today be required to show courage in standing up for the Word of the Lord?

6. Which other people in the Old or New Testament are noted for their openness to God? How did their faithfulness affect the world?

7. The elders would not have accepted a king without Samuel's approval. How important is it to have the Church's blessing on the important events of your life? Would you marry outside the Church? Why or why not?

8. Is leadership in the Church based on the approval of the Church community?

9. Saul apparently met Samuel by chance. Does anything happen by chance? Why did God choose a farm boy from the smallest tribe for Israel's first king?

An *obstetrician* is a physician specializing in the care of women during pregnancy. A *fetus* is the baby in the mother's womb.

SUPERSTITION VERSUS TRUE FAITH

What do superstitious people believe about a rabbit's foot or the number seven?

The now elderly Eli was upset. Frightened after losing a key battle with the Philistines, the men of Israel had carried the ark with them to war. Eli knew that they were substituting for repentance a belief that the ark would work like a lucky charm to defeat the sea people, who, with their iron weapons and chariots, were ahead in the arms race.

But not even the holy ark could replace genuine worship. As Eli sat at the city gate pondering these things, a messenger came running to announce that the ark had been captured and thirty thousand Israelites slain, Eli's sons among them. Stunned, Eli "fell backward from his chair [and] died of a broken neck."

Just as walking under a ladder makes us expect bad luck, the sea people saw the ark as an omen of evil. They were suspicious of its power. Triumphant at having captured the shrine city of Shiloh, they placed the ark before their god Dagon in their own city of Ashdod. But strange things happened whenever the ark was moved. Even the gods fell off their pedestals! Finally, remembering the stories of the Egyptian plagues, the Philistines returned the ark to the borders of Israel and sent atonement offerings of gold images.

Samuel then led a revival in Israel in which the people renounced the rites they had performed to the Canaanite Baal and Ashtaroth, gods they superstitiously had believed would repay them with good crops. They enshrined the ark and offered sacrifices of repentance for forgetting God's faithful care.

At the next Philistine battle at Mizpah, with the help of a minor earthquake, the Israelites won a decisive victory and enjoyed peace. For twenty years, Samuel visited the cities of Israel regularly to stir up faith and unite the people.

At this time the people of Israel had strayed far from God (see 1 Samuel 4:18).

1 Samuel 4:18. Eli's death at the news symbolizes that the power of the established priesthood in Israel was at an end. From then on, Israel would follow prophets and kings.

To demonstrate that the possession of the land was God's gift, Israel traditionally accompanied its military victories with signs of God's intervention: earthquakes, crumbling walls, angels of death.

132

The sacred author attributes Israel's success in holding back the Philistines to the return of Yahweh under Samuel's leadership.

■ Read 1 Samuel 4–7 and trace on a map the movements of the ark from its capture to its return.

■ What events in the story of the ark's capture show Israel learning these lessons?

> God demands fidelity to himself alone.
>
> Unlike other nations, Israel is God's no matter how advanced other nations seem.
>
> The special places of God's presence demand reverence.
>
> Self-reliance is doomed to failure.
>
> God speaks through his representatives.
>
> We should pray at all times, not only in crises.
>
> When things go wrong, it isn't God's fault so much as the result of human foolishness.
>
> Religious objects can't be made into lucky charms.
>
> Faith should inspire our actions.

■ Discuss the difference between faith and superstition as illustrated in the episodes of the capture and return of the ark.

VICTORY, REJECTION, AND ELECTION OF DAVID
(1 Samuel 11:1–11, 13; 15:1–16:13)

The passages listed above vividly recount Saul's first military success, his boldness in taking Samuel's place, Samuel's anger, the unholy "holy war," and God's choice of David to replace the rejected king.

Read and Recall

Read 1 Samuel 11:1–11, 13, and 15:1–16:13. To save time, consult the references given for each of the questions below as you answer them.

1. Explain how the incident surrounding Jabesh-gilead established Saul as military leader in Israel. (1 Samuel 11:1–11)
2. Why was Israel forced to use wooden weapons while the Philistines used iron? (1 Samuel 13:19–22)
3. Before the battle of Michmash Pass, why did Saul offer sacrifice in place of Samuel? How did Samuel react? What prophetic pronouncement did he make? (1 Samuel 13:5–14)
4. Draw soldiers to represent the position of the Israelite and Philistine contingents before the Philistine invasion. (1 Samuel 13:15–18) What other wars did Saul fight? (1 Samuel 14:47, 52)
5. How did Saul again incur Samuel's anger? How did it affect Saul's relationship with Samuel? With God? What happened to Agag? (1 Samuel 15)
6. Where did the Lord send Samuel after Samuel left Saul? (1 Samuel 16:1–3)

Reflect

1 Samuel 15:22

1. Samuel said, "Obedience is better than sacrifice," referring to Saul's failure to observe the ban on the Amalekites. How might a person offer a sacrifice but not follow the law?

1 Corinthians 3:18

2. What are some things Christ might have done rather than submit to death in obedience? Saint Paul said that the Christian vocation is to become a fool for

134

Christ's sake—that is, to do what God commands, no matter what. Describe a situation in your life that might demand taking a little ridicule for following God's will.

3. Samuel looked over all the sons of Jesse and chose the youngest and most unlikely. What unlikely people do you know who have been chosen for important missions in life? What unlikely thing might you be called to for God's kingdom?

MOOD MUSIC FOR A TORTURED KING
(1 Samuel 16:14–23)

Music has a mysterious power. It can be creative, hypnotic, or destructive. Children who have been sung to during their mother's pregnancy seem happier. Experiments show that plants exposed to pleasant melodies flourish, while jarring sounds cause them to wilt and even die. Music is used for propaganda, to increase work output, to heighten morale, and to soothe.

■ What does music do for you?

ISRAEL'S MUSIC

Name someone you think is the greatest musician alive. What effect does he or she have on people?

David was Israel's most inspired musician. He soothed Saul in his dark moods. He chanted an elegy over the graves of Saul and Jonathan, and as king he had such a heart for the music of worship that he commanded competent Levite chanters and accompanists to march with the ark as it was carried in solemn ceremony to Jerusalem. He established a special group to sing and accompany the psalms of Israel at their religious festivals. He himself composed psalms—the songs of praise to be accompanied on the harp.

His son Solomon followed his lead, setting aside rare cabinet wood imported from Ophir for harps and lyres. Cantors led the people, singing the more difficult parts of the psalms and often improvising their own melodies. Since Israel's system of musical notation was limited, cantors or lead singers had to memorize hundreds of melodies. The cantors were regarded as so important in Israel that they were paid as professionals in money and produce.

The singing in Israel was joyful and enthusiastic, loud and full of the praise of God. This was because the cantors were expected to understand their music and their religious tradition, be skilled in singing, have a flair for leading the people, and be sensitive to whatever would help the people pray better.

The tradition of good leadership in congregational worship continued in Israel for hundreds of years. New psalms were added to the nation's repertoire until 300 B.C., when the Psalter—the songbook of Israel—was completed. The early Christian Church, composed mainly of Jews, followed Jewish musical tradition for three hundred and fifty years. Then in A.D. 367, a council of bishops decreed that only appointed cantors could sing in church.

An *elegy* is a poem of grief for the dead.

Levites were members of the priestly tribe of Levi.

1 Chronicles 15:16–22, 27–28

Ophir, thought to be located in southwest Arabia, was rich in gold and fine woods.

A *repertoire* is a list of pieces that a group is prepared to present.

The school of cantors was known as Schola Cantorum in the Middle Ages, when Latin was used universally in the Church. Latin is still the Church's "official" language.

136

Fourteen centuries passed in which Christian worship was a matter of congregational watching and listening. Today the right to full participation in the liturgy has been restored to all the people. The *Constitution on the Sacred Liturgy* of Vatican II devotes an entire chapter to sacred music. The document invites the hundreds of millions of Catholics who make up the Church to lend their musical talents to the worship of the Lord.

The modern Church encourages people who play a musical instrument, as well as those gifted with good voices or ability in musical direction, to lend their talents to worship. If congregational singing is to accomplish its purpose, every voice is needed. Saint Augustine said that when you sing, you pray twice. You too can be a David. All it takes is good will and love of God.

1. How did David promote liturgical music? How did the tradition of liturgical singing develop? What was expected of cantors? Briefly trace the history of Christian liturgical participation.

2. What talents can you contribute to make the liturgies you celebrate more meaningful?

3. Joan Baez writes in her autobiography, *Daybreak*: "To sing is to love and affirm . . . to coast into the hearts of people who listen to tell them that life is to live, that love is there. . . . To sing is to praise God and the daffodils." What does she mean? How does what she says apply to church music? Listen to one of her recordings or to another album, keeping her words in mind.

4. Research the life of a great church musician such as Giovanni Palestrina or Alexander Peloquin. Present your findings to the class. Or find out who is responsible for the music in your parish and ask what the problems and satisfactions are. Are the ministers of music paid as professionals? Make a report.

Read and Recall

Read 1 Samuel 16:14–23.

1. The Bible says that the Spirit of the Lord left Saul and he was depressed. What bothered him?
2. Where might David have gotten the inspiration for the songs he sang at court?

Reflect

1. Why is music good for tortured minds? Does it soothe from without or within?
2. The Bible says that the evil spirit that tormented Saul was "sent by the Lord." Why would his depression be sent by God?

SAUL'S JEALOUSY, DESPAIR, AND SUICIDE
(1 Samuel 18:1–19:7, 21, 22, 24, 31)

Two-year-old Teddy's world has been changed by the arrival of his baby sister. Now Mom as well as other people pay more attention to her than to him. Whereas before he used to fight to be free, now Teddy goes to people and says, "Hold me!"

CALLED BY THE FATHER

Of the emotions that enrich our lives, most come in pairs. You can name the opposites of joy, despair, and fear. Your capacity for a positive emotion also includes your capacity for the negative. People who can love deeply can also hate fiercely.

■ One of the most destructive emotions is jealousy. How do you know when someone is jealous? Whom and what does jealous destroy? What emotion is its opposite?

In Saul, the Hebrew Scriptures present a classic jealous personality. As you read of his exploits in the following selected episodes, determine how, in trying to destroy others, Saul actually destroyed himself.

Classic means serving as a standard.

Read

Read the introductory material to each passage before you turn to the biblical account itself.

The victory march home. It was a great day in Israel when Saul's armies marched home, victorious over the dreaded Philistines. Everyone ran out to meet them. The girls danced and sang in the streets. There was one young warrior in particular whom the Israelite maidens had their eye on: "Saul has slain his thousands," they sang, "and David his ten thousands."

1 Samuel 18:7

■ Put yourself in Saul's army boots as he trudged back from the war. How would you feel?
■ If you were Saul's son, the same age as David, how would you feel about the popularity of someone who could take your rightful place as the next king?

The characters in the Bible are by no means stereotypes. They are unique, real, flesh-and-blood people. Did Saul burst with pride over the success of his rookies as you might expect a general to do?

Stereotype means cast into a set mold; lacking uniqueness.

■ Read 1 Samuel 18:6–9 for the account of the victory march home.

Saul attacks. All night Saul must have tossed and turned, tormented with the thought of David's growing popularity. The next morning he was overcome by a deep depression. Raving like a madman in a fit of passionate jealousy, he paced back and forth before his royal seat, carrying his spear as if ready to spring on some invisible enemy. On the floor in a corner, David gently strummed his harp.

■ Read of one of the most famous "misses" in the Bible in 1 Samuel 18:10–16.

A famous friendship. Jonathan's friendship with David is not easy to explain, considering that Jonathan was the rightful heir to the throne. But David's complete trust—even to putting his life into Jonathan's hands— is just as inexplicable. After all, Jonathan had good reasons to do away with his political rival.

Inexplicable means unable to be explained.

■ Read about one of the most beautiful friendships in the world and of the way that friendship successfully foiled a great warrior's tyranny in 1 Samuel 18:1–5 and 19:1–7.

The fugitive and the slaughter. After the second attempt on his life, David fled the country, taking refuge with the hated Philistines. Saul deliberately hunted him down in order to kill him. Ask yourself how the people must have felt when their chosen king, who had given the priests shelter at Nob, probably the home of the ark, suddenly and senselessly massacred them on the excuse that they had aided David in his flight from his court. It was Saul's final rejection of all that Israel stood for. He might as well have been a worshipper of the foreign gods. He was no worshipper of Yahweh.

Nob was the place where the priests lived under their leader Ahimelech.

■ Read the frightful account, including the "intelligence report" delivered by Doeg, in 1 Samuel 21:2–22:23. Notice the two items David asked for and who escaped the massacre.

David spares Saul's life. Try to get some sense of David's superb generosity in more than once sparing his persecutor's life when he had him right in his hands. Notice his freedom and independence in not fearing that his own men might think him weak. Far from let-

CALLED BY THE FATHER

ting them rule him, David taught them reverence for kingship. The result of his lessons would come back to him someday: he would always have the loyalty of his followers. Saul's littleness seems all the uglier next to David's unselfishness and strength of character. In his clear moments Saul recognized David's greatness and was even attracted to him, but then, in his insecurity, he lashed out at him. All this seemed only to tear him apart even more.

■ Read the episodes in 1 Samuel 24:1–16, 26.

The death of Saul and Jonathan. As you read of the final hours of Saul's life, try to capture the agony that caused him to turn his violent emotions onto himself when he learned that the Philistines had not only won the battle but killed the son he had hoped would succeed him.

■ Read the sad end of Saul in 1 Samuel 31.

Recall

By means of pictures or stick figures, depict the emotions of the people in these situations in 1 Samuel:

1. *The march home*: Saul, David, the village girls—read 18:6–9.
2. *Playing for the king*: David the King—read 18:10–16.
3. *In the cave*: David, Saul, David's men—read 24:1–16.
4. *David after leaving Saul's camp*: David, Abner, Saul—read chapter 26.
5. *David at the graveside of Saul and Jonathan*—read chapter 31.

Reflect

1. The sacred author paints Saul in a disagreeable light. What were his faults? Did he have any redeeming qualities?
2. What actions show that Saul suffered feelings of inferiority? What events encouraged his feelings? How would David have handled the same events? Why?

3. Jealousy eventually caused Saul to lose his reason. Do you think Saul was responsible for this? Why or why not? What other passions, when left uncontrolled, are dehumanizing? What help might Saul have received today to control excessive jealousy?

4. Suspicion often begins with fear. What is the role of imagination in fear? In self-control? What are some of the fears of young people your age? How can they be eased?

A foil serves as a contrast to another person.

5. As the king was being rejected, the author introduced David in a kind light. Saul was a foil for the future king. What personality traits in David contrast with Saul's?

6. David's reverence for authority shines through in these episodes. Where? Since Saul was not a good king, why was David so respectful of him? Is respect for authority an old-fashioned quality, or is there still a place for it in today's world? Why or why not? Name some people to whom you owe obedience. Who will owe you obedience in your life?

7. In sparing Saul's life in the cave and camp, David showed that he had learned to handle the honors that came to him so early in life. Why do tragedies very often mark the careers of people who achieve early fame? What was David's secret of survival? Name someone who, even after success, continued to grow as a person.

GETTING IT TOGETHER

Samuel is one of the few biblical characters whom we know from infancy to death. In that entire span he is presented as a man of God, a man of prayer. A child of his mother's prayer, a boy who knew how to listen and to do courageous things for the Lord, Samuel became a leader. He consistently brought victory and peace to his people by leading them to God. As an elderly prophet he consulted the Lord when the nation wanted a king. As Samuel had rebuked Eli, so he was to judge

CALLED BY THE FATHER

Saul. Saul's mistake was to reject Samuel, who stood for the true religion of Israel and God's plan.

Once Samuel's work was finished, he gracefully stepped back and let others take over, as only a man of prayer would do. He died quietly in his own hometown, mourned by all. His public role in Israel was an extension of his own deep convictions—that true religion, happiness, and order are not to be found in external things like hereditary priesthood or a particular form of government but only in keeping God at the center of life. In the darkness of faith, the beacon that kept his ship on its steady course was his constant communication with God.

Israel's first king, on the other hand, possessed a giant body but a dwarfed heart. Unlike Samuel, Saul was a military leader whose personal life was not rooted in prayer. He couldn't believe that God had chosen him just as he was, or that God wanted to use him. Lacking faith, Saul depended superstitiously on sacrifice, instead of offering the sacrifice God asked—patience. His god was as small-minded as he.

Saul couldn't believe that others might like him for himself. Even after winning important wars and being accepted by his countrymen, he was fearful of losing the loyalty of his soldiers. Instead of considering David's talents as a gift to enhance his own reign, he regarded David as a threat.

A religious man to start with, Saul gradually forgot his true center, forgot who walked beside him in supreme command of the world. As a result, he felt his weakness keenly, and eventually steered himself and his nation off course. Instead of leading Israel to peace as Samuel had done, he introduced violence into his court and country. Finally he turned that violence onto himself. In the end, the sacred author says, Saul's life showed that it is lack of faith that destroys—distrust of God, yourself, and others.

REVIEWING THE CHAPTER

Linking Your Ideas

1. How is the story of Samuel's birth similar to that of John the Baptizer as given in Luke 1:5–25, 67–80? What do both marvelous birth stories point out about these children?
2. Why was Samuel called both a judge and a prophet?
3. Write a letter of outrage to Eli complaining about his sons' activities at the shrine. Speaking as a deeply concerned Israelite, tell why you are so anxious about the nation.
4. The Israelites had followed their religious leaders for hundreds of years. How did Saul break that tradition? What was the result?
5. Why wasn't the monarchy of Israel hereditary?
6. What contributed to Saul's madness?
7. The sacred author slowly built up to the idea that Saul was not a king according to God's and Israel's hearts. Make a list that tracks the condemning evidence. What faults led to Saul's behavior?

Strengthening Your Grasp

1. Reread Hannah's hymn of gratitude in 1 Samuel 2:1–10. Which lines say the following? (a) God helps the weak and suffering. (b) God casts down the mighty and raises the lowly. (c) God is the only source of true strength.
2. Compare Hannah's hymn with Mary's song to Elizabeth in Luke 1:46–55. How are they alike? Write a hymn of gratitude for some gift you have received, using modern English.
3. What things did Jonathan do for David? Why?
4. What do you think is the real reason that Saul massacred the priests? Did he achieve his purpose?
5. What political reasons might David have had for not killing Saul and for praising him at his graveside? Do these things detract from any religious motive, or is politics a form of religion? Explain.

Expressing Your Convictions

1. Write or act out a skit showing a situation in which a young person would need courage to stand up for something asked by God.
2. Write a letter to a modern Eli whose children are corrupting the morals of your younger brother or sister. Be sure to give reasons for your concern.

3. Investigate how one of the following discovered his or her vocation from God: Saint Francis of Assisi, Saint Joan of Arc, Mother Teresa of Calcutta.

4. Make an entry in your journal telling what has led you to earnest prayer in your life so far. What things might lead you to pray in early, middle, and late adulthood? In old age?

5. Imagine that David and Saul were to be represented by animals. Decide which of the following would best symbolize each man: serpent, panther, fish, dog, lion, horse, bear, chameleon. Explain your choices.

6. Associate David and Saul with particular colors. Which would you choose for each? Why?

Extending Your Interest

Israel's religion was very physical. Samuel didn't merely announce that God had chosen Saul and David to be kings, but that he anointed them. Like other cultures in the area, the Israelites used the oil of pressed olives for anointing. Christianity follows Israel's lead in using real objects and actions to symbolize God's comings. In which sacraments were you anointed? What was the meaning of each anointing? Create a slide presentation featuring all the functions of the oil used in anointing, with a script that reflects the spiritual blessings shown by the natural powers of this kind of oil.

SEVEN DAVID
Man After God's Own Heart

Sections

Turn away your face from my sins,
   and blot out all my guilt.
A clean heart create for me, O God,
   and a steadfast spirit renew within me.
Cast me not out from your presence,
   and your holy spirit take not from me.
Give me back the joy of your salvation,
   and a willing spirit sustain in me. . . .
My sacrifice, O God, is a contrite spirit;
   a heart contrite and humbled, O God, you
      will not spurn.

PSALM 51:11–14,19

Your house and your kingdom shall endure forever.

2 SAMUEL 7:16

CHAPTER PREVIEW

When you leave your family home to begin a life of your own, what new freedoms will you enjoy? What problems will you face?

The hour of glory was at hand: Israel was about to become independent! The charismatic (spirit-filled) King David would bring to fulfillment the promise the Lord had made to Abraham centuries earlier: "I will give you this land as a possession." Under David's dazzling leadership, Israel's borders would be extended from Mesopotamia to Egypt. They were never to reach farther.

Genesis 15:7

With the judges, and even under Saul, Israel had been only a loose federation of tribes who barely succeeded in beating back their enemies. When public sentiment swung against Saul, some of the men deserted to David's side and the Philistines won a decisive victory at Mount Gilboa. With Saul's beheaded body impaled on the walls of the Philistine fortress, the Israelite army, now leaderless, scattered into the hills for cover, leaving the sea people in complete control of the valley route from the Great Sea to the Jordan valley. Conquest of the surrounding Israelite territory seemed only a matter of time.

David, who no doubt had learned war strategies during his association in exile with the fierce Philistines, returned to Hebron in Judah to be crowned by the southern tribes. With amazing swiftness, he reorganized the army and dealt a fatal blow to the Philistine power. His next task was to win over the ten northern tribes ruled by Saul's son, Ishbaal. Instead of forcing himself upon the North, David shrewdly waited. His instinct proved correct. Weakened by intrigue and corruption, the House of Saul came begging his protection.

Within seven short years, David had unified the nation both militarily and politically. He moved his capital from tiny Hebron to the more central and strategic Jerusalem. To cement national unity, David revived devotion to Yahweh by establishing the ark in the midst of the people. He dreamed of building a temple to house it, but this task was to remain to his son. Through the prophet Nathan, however, God promised David a house—a kingdom that would last forever.

Under David's reign, Israel abandoned its nomadic existence entirely. The nation's control of the great east-west trade routes enabled agriculture and commerce to flourish. Links with important seagoing nations of the Mediterranean were established, and literature and architecture made their appearance. Israel experienced its finest hour.

Then, at the peak of his career, David succumbed to human weakness and committed adultery and murder. Unlike Saul, he did not despair, but through sincere repentance became one of the Bible's most attractive characters. His dynasty was to last for more than four hundred years.

David's career displays some surprising parallels to Israel's history, falling into three divisions: the rise to power, the building of a mighty nation, and a time of human mistakes that teach wisdom. Two strengths—friendship and administrative ability—helped David

The fact that Saul's son was named after the Canaanite Baal may have been a sign of Saul's idolatry.

A *dynasty* is a succession of rulers of the same line of descent who maintain power for several generations.

CALLED BY THE FATHER

achieve his dreams and gain an outstanding place in history. They were also responsible for his problems. But it was David's greatest gift—a deeply personal love of God—that saw him through. Until his death he remained a man according to God's heart.

- As an Israelite, what fears and dreams would you have had at the election of a new king?

Words to Know

Goliath (geh-**ligh**-ehth), Michal (**migh**-kehl), Abner, Achish (eh-**keesh**), Joab (**joh**-ab), Ishbaal (ish-**bay**-el), Jebusites (**jeb**-yeh-sights), Zion (**zigh**-ehn), Absalom (**ab**-seh-lehm), Nathan, Bathsheba (bath-**shee**-beh), Uriah the Hittite (you-**rye**-eh), Gath (gah-t), Ziklag (**zik**-lag), Jerusalem, ephod (**ef**-od)

DAVID AND HIS FRIENDS
(1 Samuel 18:20–29, 19:11–17, 20:1–4, 20:25–34)

As conceited and arrogant as Napoleon was, he was a general for whom his men were glad to die. As chief commanding officer, he did not hesitate to take the night watch for a private who was exhausted or ill.

- What qualities does it take to inspire loyalty in friends? What do you do for them? How do friends improve your life?

David was more than a flashing-eyed redhead. He also had a flashing personality, and with it a talent for friendship. All who knew him not only loved him but were willing to risk their lives for him. In his rise to power, David could honestly have said, "I got through with the help of my friends." David's friends helped him unfold God's plan. Probably during his years as a shepherd, while he pondered the stars, David had first realized his need for God and for other people. All his life he remained humble before his Lord and respectful toward others. His forgiving and generous heart endeared him to all, even to God.

The friendship of David with Saul's son Jonathan is renowned. Loyalty to David caused Jonathan to renounce his own right to the throne. He informed David of plots against him at court, and several times he laid his life on the line by taking David's part against Saul, who was insanely jealous. Jonathan devised a clever scheme to warn his friend of danger, and rather than see David hurt, he chose never to see him again.

Saul's daughter Michal was one of many women who loved David, who easily fulfilled the condition Saul set before he would permit David to marry her. On their wedding night, Michal saved David by tricking the officers sent by the king to kill him.

After a last painful farewell to Jonathan, David fled to Nob for overnight shelter. Saul subsequently murdered the priests there for sheltering his young rival. This caused the people to turn against Saul for good.

2 Samuel 23:15–17

David inspired loyalty in his family and Judean friends. A man's man, he was able to persuade some four hundred who owed him favors or who disapproved of Saul to fight as guerrillas with him in the hills. During the skirmishes, the men repeatedly risked their lives to fulfill David's slightest wishes, even to bring him a drink of water.

When in danger, some people expect God to save them by a miracle. David relied entirely on God, but he also took the necessary measures to preserve his life against Saul. In fact, the story of David in exile is very exciting. Surmising that Saul would not follow him there, David shrewdly decided to hide on the borders of Judah, the country of the Philistines. But this placed

You may want to read about David among the Philistines in 1 Samuel 29–30.

David in a dilemma. He had to convince Achish, the Philistine leader who knew of his victories over the Philistines, that he was an outcast in his own land and would not betray them to the neighboring Judeans. On the other hand, neither in conscience nor before his men could he take the side of the Philistines against his own people. Only a person with David's charm, ingenuity, and faith in God could have come through with integrity. While seeming to do battle for the foreign king, he plundered the Philistine towns and split the

Integrity means honesty.

CALLED BY THE FATHER

booty with Achish and his countrymen in Judah, making himself popular with both.

Acting as a successful double agent, David won the confidence of Achish, and his winning ways drew many Philistines to join his unit. But other Philistine generals were not so trustful. When the sea people rallied their forces for a united attack against Israel, David, to his great relief, was found suspect and commanded to return home. Both Saul and Jonathan were killed in this attack.

At Saul's death, David returned to Hebron, the center of the southern tribes. There, after mourning Saul and Jonathan, he was crowned King of Judah. During his seven-year reign in the South he was not bothered by the Philistines, but his armies skirmished constantly with the House of Saul, where Ishbaal held power backed by Abner, Saul's general. Gradually the northern armies lost vigor and, as a result of in-fighting, both Ishbaal and Abner were killed. At thirty-eight, David became the unchallenged ruler of all Israel, in about 1000 B.C. He ruled for thirty-three more years, launching a welcome time of peace in the land.

Read and Recall

After reading the sections given below, answer the questions following each.

> 1 Samuel 20:1–4, 25–34—*David consults with Jonathan*. Why did David doubt that Saul would discuss his plans for David with Jonathan? Why was Saul upset with David and Jonathan?
>
> 1 Samuel 19:11–17—*David in love* and *Michal's strategy*. Saul offered David his daughter Michal if he would kill a hundred Philistines. David killed two hundred. How did Michal trick the officers who came to kill David?

Reflect

1. David's friendships had all the qualities that bring out the best in people. Point out examples of the following: (a) a friend thinks of the other's good; (b) a friend helps the other to grow; (c) a friend is a support in hardship; (d) a friend is loyal.

2. What does it mean to say that some people never really say hello to anyone because they don't want to say goodbye? What do you learn about true friendship from the fact that Jonathan sent David away? What other risks does friendship involve? Do you agree with the poet Alfred Tennyson, who wrote, "Better to have loved and lost than never to have loved at all"?

3. In a poem, song, story, or composition, fantasize about what good things might have happened to Saul if he had kept David at his side. Think of the good things that might occur if you were to become friends with someone you don't get along with.

4. Subjects owe obedience to their king. Were Jonathan and Michal right in defending David against their father, the king? Why or why not? Describe their love of David.

5. Listen to a contemporary song of friendship. Discuss: (a) what the song says about friendship; (b) in what ways these elements are evident in David's life;

CALLED BY THE FATHER

(c) which qualities in David's character contributed to his friendship.

6. Tell which of the following positions describe David's friendship with God: (a) total trust in God; (b) total confidence in himself; (c) half and half; (d) both.

7. What kinds of moral dilemmas do young people often face? Is it possible to get through without God's friendship? Be honest.

DAVID AS BRILLIANT LEADER
(2 Samuel 5:6–25, 6, 8:15–18)

In a few years you will be eligible to vote. Decide which of these qualities you would consider helpful in a political leader: intelligence, courage, administrative ability, friendliness, military genius, a sense of humor, personal charm, diplomatic ability, character, speaking ability, artistic interest, understanding of people. Which *one* quality would be most vital?

David was graced with all the gifts of an outstanding leader. He believed God needed him, and he made the most of his talents, yet he knew how to wait.

A *chancellor* is a chief officer of state.

Anointed as a young man, David did not claim the throne until God's will was clear, although he twice had the chance to kill Saul himself. He had to learn the ways of kingship—not in the court, as might be expected, but as a fugitive, getting to know the people and learning the battle tactics of the enemy he was to defeat. Even after Saul's death, he didn't push his destiny but waited until the elders elected him King of Judah. Then, for seven years, he learned to govern in the smaller state before accepting the responsibility of national leadership.

Finally, after receiving the Lord's signal, David strove for all he was worth and ascended the throne of Israel fully prepared. His royal achievements included the creation of a central government, expansion of power, cultural progress, religious unity, and the establishment of a shrine for the Lord.

To weaken tribal leadership, David concentrated political power in himself. In a brilliant move, he captured the old Canaanite fortress of Zion, held for centuries by the fierce Jebusites, and made it his capital city, Jerusalem. The new "City of David" was less vulnerable, and its central location made it acceptable to both the North and the South. From there he governed wisely and launched Israel's golden age.

David was a keen judge and administrator. He knew how to delegate authority and had a sharp eye for talent and character. By personally choosing his chancellor, cabinet, armed forces commander, and other officers, he surrounded himself with men he could trust. He was careful to place honest people in charge of public welfare and distant posts.

As a military leader, David was inspired. He replaced untrained military volunteers with a standing army of professional soldiers headed by his own generals. By this action he accomplished two things: he eliminated the power of the tribal chieftains and he insured military strength for expansion. He conquered some neighboring lands completely and set up occupation forces in others.

CALLED BY THE FATHER

Unlike Saul, who had been content with a rustic fort for his headquarters, David dreamed of a better life for himself and his people. With the treasures of conquest pouring in, David could afford to hire expert carpenters and stonemasons from the coastal city of Tyre to build a magnificent House of Cedar. Taking his cue from other kings, he increased the number of his concubines and he ordered scribes to keep the historical records that developed into the two books of Samuel, Israel's first work of literature.

By taking foreign concubines, David gained the favor of other nations.

David saw Israel as a melting pot of twelve tribes held together only by a common faith. To reinforce Israel's sacred heritage, David rescued the ark from its forgotten residence in a private home and brought it to Jerusalem with pomp and ceremony. Thus the City of David became Zion, the City of God, for the Lord was present once again in the midst of his people.

Unified in military strength, government, and religion, Israel became the most powerful small nation in the Near East. David's forces delivered two last solid thrashings to the Philistines, breaking their power once and for all.

In yearly campaigns, David gradually subdued all his foes. Before his death, David saw Israel increase to sixty thousand square miles—ten times the territory he had inherited.

Some people may believe that all a leader needs is a forceful personality, but when the top aides to several U.S. presidents were asked recently what quality was most needed for the presidency, their unanimous response was "character." By this they implied that high office requires high moral principles. David was successful, the sacred writer says, because "the Lord went with him." Put in today's language, David possessed a strong moral character and never outgrew his humble obedience to God. He sought God's guidance in every decision, and then, with faith in God's help, he insisted on honesty in his administration. He was willing to risk being ridiculed when he forgave his enemies and showed his love of God publicly.

DAVID: SAVIOR OF ISRAEL

A teenager wrote this poem about David's famous encounter with the Philistine giant, Goliath. What does the last line mean?

> David
> Against Goliath
>   of Gath
> from the stream
>   of eternity
> Five smooth stones
>   have I
> Which will nearly be
>   the death of me.*

You may wish to read the account of the Goliath story in 1 Samuel 17:1–11, 26–54. While it is probably a legend representing Israel's victory over the Philistines, it also portrays human character realistically. In one verse, David's reasons for slaying the giant are purely religious—to keep Israel, God's country, from insult. But in another, David asks what he will get out of it if he wins.

■ If David represents Israel, what symbolism do you see in the following: David's youth and Goliath's size; the staff, five pebbles, and a slingshot; the combat itself; the heavy armor Saul puts on David; the victory of David and the defeat of Goliath; the army of Israel.

■ In what ways does David foreshadow Christ? How is he a figure of yourself?

*Adapted from Gretchen Meyer, "God Gives His Word," in *Roots of Faith* (New York: Harcourt, Brace, Jovanovich, 1966), p. 75.

Read

Before consulting the following recommended Bible passages, read the notes preceding them.

1. *A new capital.* Because the city had no natural water supply, the Jebusites had cut a deep shaft through the rock on which the fortress was built in order to reach a spring just outside the city walls. In certain seasons the water level of the tunnel dropped. Read 2 Samuel 5:6–10.
2. *Government organization.* The specific details of this section imply authentic history. Read 2 Samuel 8:15–18.
3. *Progress of culture.* David's interest in beauty, music, and literature showed him to be a gifted person. He used all three to further religion and culture in Israel. Read 2 Samuel 5:11–16.
4. *Transfer of the ark to Jerusalem.* During Saul's rule, so much effort had been spent on military defense that religion took a back seat in the lives of the Israelites. Futhermore, Saul had caused confusion by killing the priests to whom the people looked for leadership. Although he was not of a priestly family, David was a priest-king like Melchizedek, a much earlier king of (Jeru) Salem (Genesis 14:18). Read 2 Samuel 6.
5. *Military achievements.* David understood the psychology of victory: the side with faith and confidence is the likeliest to win. Read 2 Samuel 5:17–25, 8.

Recall

After doing all the readings, choose only one of the following activities.

1. Using stick figures, show the strategy Joab and David might have used to conquer the fortress.
2. Make a chart of the chief officeholders in David's administration. Label the last one "Head of the Guard." Don't forget to include David.

3. List five new things you might have noticed at court as a result of David's desire "to be like other nations."

4. Assume you are a scribe describing the transfer. Incorporate these terms into your account (they need not be in this order): thirty thousand, Abinadab, a new cart, Uzzah, tambourines, Nodan, Obededom, three months of blessings, City of David, sacrifice, dancing, meat and raisin cakes, Michal, David's reply, childlessness.

5. In the way you would diagram a football play, show the method by which Israel routed the Philistines. Name some countries or rulers David's armies defeated or occupied.

Reflect

1. What does it mean to be a leader? Someone has said that necessity is the creator of leadership. Can anyone—should everyone—be a leader? Why or why not? Who are your leaders? To whom are you now a leader in some way? What aspects of leadership did David demonstrate?

2. What qualities in David's character are brought out by his transfer of the ark to Jerusalem? How can a student council officer "transfer the ark" in a school community?

3. What was Michal's problem? What does the incident reveal about David? Who are the modern Michals? Who are the modern ridiculed Davids?

4. What "arks" do Christians have in their midst? What leaders does the Church pray for at the Eucharist? Why is the Mass an appropriate time both to learn and to pray for good leadership?

5. Jesus is addressed as Son of David in the Gospels. How is David like Christ?

6. Catholics honor Mary as the Daughter of Zion, the old name of the Jebusite fortress city that David renamed Jerusalem. How does the name apply to her?

7. How is the government of David's Israel like the government of this country?

GOD'S PROMISE TO DAVID
(2 Samuel 7)

If you have ever worked hard to achieve some goal, how did you feel when the job was done?

Loaded with success in every undertaking, David remained restless. He felt guilty living in a palace of imported, fragrant wood while the Lord dwelt in a crude ark. He dreamed of building a magnificent temple. God solved his problem with an unexpected and mysterious pronouncement made through the prophet Nathan: "I will build a house for you. . . . Your kingdom shall endure forever." From this time on, Israel looked to David's descendants for its final deliverance.

2 Samuel 7:27, 16

The amazing thing is that this prophecy has as much meaning for Christians today as it had in David's time. While the Temple built by David's son, Solomon, was destroyed, David's rule lasted even beyond the end of time in Jesus, as the Lord had promised.

Read and Recall

Read 2 Samuel 7. Try to put yourself in David's place when his dream was frustrated and God made him a momentous promise.

1. What was David's concern?
2. What answer did the Lord give?

Reflect

1. The promise made to David is one of the most important of the Old Testament. How is it connected with the covenant made with Abraham and Moses?
2. In his prayer, David recalled Israel's privileged place among nations. Since the coming of Christ, it is clear that God loves all people. What was God's purpose in entrusting Israel with his self-revelation? Christians have the fullness of God's word in Christ. What is our role in the world? (See Luke 24:47–49 and Acts 1:8)
3. David was astonished at God's promise. What greater and even more astonishing gifts has God given his people since then?
4. God cannot go back on his promises, and yet David's "house" no longer exists (see Romans 11:29). Can you explain this?

DAVID AS REPENTANT SINNER
(2 Samuel 11:1–12:25, 18:1–19:1)

Everyone makes mistakes. Think of a time when you did something you regretted. Did you give up, or did you get up and start all over? Why? How did others react to what you did?

CALLED BY THE FATHER

With Israel at peace, there was leisure to learn to read and write. A gifted writer, today known as the court historian, rose up to write some of the most colorful stories of the Hebrew Scriptures. Even though the author portrayed the conflict surrounding the choice of David's successor in these stories, he emphasized the person of David, and the result is that suddenly a flesh-and-blood hero springs out of the Bible's pages. David's fine qualities shine out, but his faults are not covered over.

David had reached the peak of his career. He was well into middle age and a little bored. His court, with its fine cedar walls and ornate stone pillars, its large harem and quarters for many officers of state, began to resemble the luxurious courts of the great Oriental rulers. David started to use his kingly office for his own purposes rather than for God and God's people. His strong point—love for people—grew into lust as he stooped to the sins of the powerful and wealthy. It all began with a little thing—idleness. For the first time, he did not accompany his men into battle, and then curiosity led him into temptation and sin. But even in his moral failures, David continued to develop as a person. He humbly repented and willingly accepted the misfortunes that flowed from his sins.

His gift for organization was also turned to disadvantage. He took a census to be sure that everyone paid taxes. When the people grumbled, God sent a plague. Once again, David's mistake was turned to advantage when, through prayer, he was directed to buy the land on which the first temple of Israel would stand.

Despite many troubles, David died as one of Israel's most loving and beloved figures. Something of the flavor of his great-hearted spirit has been captured in the psalms, Israel's ancient religious songs, many of which are attributed to him.

Saul was a man's king; David was God's—a man after his own heart, as God had revealed to Samuel. Faithful friend, brilliant leader, religious model, humble penitent, and loving father, David has captured the imagination of people in every generation.

The story of David begins at the end of 1 Samuel, is treated almost biographically in 2 Samuel, and continues into 1 Kings 1–2.

A *harem* consists of the wives and concubines, with their servants, who form part of a king's household.

1 Samuel 13:14

THE WORLD'S MOST POPULAR SONGS

What songs are popular today? Most song hits have a short life. The top ten are different from week to week. You may know only a few of the "golden oldies" that your grandparents sang. Some songs, like "Greensleeves" and "Amazing Grace," are unusual for having survived for several hundred years. Songs that might last a thousand years would have to be very special.

The psalms, Israel's religious songs, are special. They've lasted three thousand years and are still going strong wherever Christians and Jews gather to pray.

You will find the psalms in the Book of Psalms or Psalter of the Bible. Although all hundred and fifty are attributed to David, a talented harpist, no one knows who really wrote them because they were composed over a period of six hundred years and contain references to all stages of Israel's history. Like riverboat songs or the spirituals of the South, the psalms were learned in childhood. They molded the traditions and faith of the people more than the Torah itself. For this reason, the psalms are considered the heart of the Jewish Scriptures. Significantly, they fall at just about the center of the Bible.

Psalm means "song with stringed-music accompaniment." The psalms mirror David's great worshipful heart, which delighted in the glory of God, their main theme.

The Psalms as Prayers

Jesus grew up on the psalms, which formed part of all Jewish celebrations. In the Temple, they were performed in high style. Whereas it may take you half a minute to read a psalm, at the coronation of a king one psalm might have taken up to two hours to perform. The setting included a colorfully dressed leader, a chorus, dancers, and a group of musicians playing instruments like those suggested in Psalm 150. Stage directions are built into some psalms.

The psalms originated between 1000 and 600 B.C.

Someone divided the Book of Psalms into five books to make it resemble the Pentateuch, but this division is strictly artificial.

Psalm 72 is an example of a group called the "royal psalms."

See Psalm 81:3–4

CALLED BY THE FATHER

In the home, the psalms were the people's way of speaking with God. As you easily pick up the words of popular songs, the Jews knew many psalms by heart. Jesus quotes them in the gospels. The apostles and the early Church used them as prayers and hymns. Later, Christians ended each psalm with the Glory Be to the Father to honor the trinity whom Jesus had revealed. The psalms remain part of our heritage.

Today, the Jewish people use the psalms in their prayers, and Christians pray and sing them in their liturgies and in the daily Liturgy of the Hours.

Long ago, when people became less literate and could not read all the psalms in Latin, Hail Marys were substituted for the psalms. This practice developed into the rosary, which has a hundred and fifty beads and fifteen mysteries, one for each decade.

The Psalms as Lyric Hymns

The lyrics of the psalms possess a mysterious power to touch the heart. They comfort us with God's greatness and nearness. They show that he protects those in danger and is concerned with all who call on him. They inspire hope as they proclaim God's mercy and forgiveness. In the psalms, all creation sings of God's love.

■ Look up these psalm verses—69:2–3, 47:2–3, 35:1–5, 13:2–3—and match them with the following emotions: anger, sadness, fear, happiness.

The psalms take on a deeper meaning for Christians. Those that particularly refer to Jesus are called messianic, because they were prophetic of the Messiah. What fuller meaning do you see in the following verses?

As far as the east is from the west,
    so far has he put our transgressions from us.

Psalm 103:12

Yours is princely power
    in the day of your birth, in holy splendor;
    before the daystar, like the dew, I have begotten
        you.

Psalm 110:3

All you who see scoff at me;
    they mock me with parted lips, they wag their
        heads.

Psalms: 22:8

The Psalms as Poetry

The psalms are among the finest examples of Hebrew poetry. Although they make abundant use of images, their main poetic technique is balanced phrasing, called parallelism. The Hebrews often restated *similar* ideas in different words as a way of stimulating contemplation:

Psalm 9:16

> The nations are sunk in the pit they have made;
> in the snares they set, their foot is caught.

Two lines placed together may express the same thought from *opposite* points of view, then be repeated:

Psalm 27:1

Statement (1)	The Lord is my light and my salvation;
Contrast (2)	whom should I fear?
Repetition of (1)	The Lord is my life's refuge;
Repetition of (2)	of whom should I be afraid?

Entire stanzas repeat preceding stanzas from an opposing point of view. The following verses stand in opposition to the stanza just above:

A *verse* is a single line of poetry.

Psalm 27:2

> When evildoers come at me to devour my flesh,
> My foes and my enemies themselves stumble and
> fall.

What theme runs through the verses in both stanzas?

Because of this structure, there are three styles of recitation: *whole group*—everyone recites the entire psalm (example: Psalm 23); *antiphonal*—the community is divided into two choirs that alternate verses (example: Psalm 115); *responsorial*—a leader reads the main verses and the congregation responds by repeating the same verse (refrain) after each verse the leader reads (example: Psalm 136).

In this psalm, Sihon rhymes with "high on"; Bashan, with "nation."

Using Psalm 136, divide your group into two choirs that will read alternate lines. Begin the introduction in an everyday voice, clear and definite. Recite lines 1–9 quietly, almost whispering. In lines 10–22, work up to a loud, joyous shout by the last verses. Read the concluding lines (23–26) strongly and slowly, as if closing a musical composition. Let a "choir director" guide the tempo and volume.

CALLED BY THE FATHER

Read and Recall

Read 2 Samuel 11:1–12:25 for the account of David's fall, Nathan's warning, and David's punishment and repentance. Read 2 Samuel 18:1–19:1 for the tragic end of Absalom, the favored son who rebelled against his father.

Draw a stick-figure cartoon strip to tell the story of David's fall, or answer these questions.

1. Why was David at home in the spring, the time of war campaigns?
2. What predicament did he get into?
3. How did he first plan to cover up his sin? Why didn't his plan work?
4. How did he use his power to arrange a cover-up?
5. What does Nathan's parable mean? Why did he use a parable to correct David?
6. What was David's reaction? His punishment? His response to it?
7. How did Absalom die? What was David's reaction?

In order to obtain God's favor for their battles, soldiers abstained from having sexual relations while on campaign.

Reflect

Think about the meaning of David's life as you read this commentary, and then answer the questions that follow.

It may be surprising that the sacred author included in his account David's sins—his selfishness in taking Bathsheba from Uriah, one of his own loyal soldiers, and the cold-blooded plans for Uriah's murder. But if the great King David fell into sin, his sincere repentance revealed him at his best. He did not try to continue the cover-up by getting rid of Nathan, who wakened the king's conscience by means of a story. Nathan only spoke the truth that David recognized in his own heart: the God of Israel held authority even over the king.

With courage, David faced his sin, did not try to excuse himself, and accepted the consequences. He regretted the injustice done to Uriah, the child, and Bathsheba. But his overriding concern was his offense against his Lord who had so favored him. "I have sinned against the Lord," he said simply.

2 Samuel 12:13

2 Samuel 12:10

After this, things were all downhill for David, in his private as well as his public life. Nathan's prophecy did indeed come to pass: "The sword shall never depart from your house." In every generation, David's family would know violent death. The death of his child, crime among his children, the rebellion of his own son, and plague throughout the land led to a trail of suffering that was to extend beyond his lifetime to that of his descendants. But for all his misfortunes, David's character only grew brighter.

1. What might Saul have done if he had fallen into David's sin? Why do you think so? Make a list of all the bad things that happened to David. What quality did David possess to enable him to make the best of every situation?
2. We all have within us a bit of the pessimist Saul and a bit of the optimist David. Which do you think is more important to cultivate? Why? How can admitting your sins be an act of optimism? Why is it an important habit to acquire?
3. What good has come out of apparently bad things in your life or in the lives of other people?

GETTING IT TOGETHER

David's life, like everyone's, was filled with both joy and misfortune. The secret of his success was tied to a kingdom, but not the kingdom of Israel. The independent empire he worked so hard to build has gone the way of all the other ancient Asian empires. Only fragments of glory remain, now painfully pieced together in archaeological digs, which proclaim how quickly glory fades. David's fame, however, endures. His name is more famous than those of the pharaohs or caesars, and today he is loved by both Christians and Jews. Why?

Many figures of history have been loyal friends, brilliant leaders, loving fathers, and even repentant sinners. But to have been all these as the humble servant of a greater king—this is David's glory.

It was David's faith in an invisible kingdom—the kingdom of the Lord—that marks him a giant. Although saints are often presented as strictly "good guys," David's halo is all the brighter because of his mistakes. He knew how to bring that invisible kingdom to birth through whatever he did, whether shepherding, living as a fugitive, working with his family and friends, governing his people—even through his sins. His life shows what it means for God to reign.

The gifted warrior, Saul, was a loser because his pride and rebellion turned him into a guilt-ridden, suspicious, and bitter man. With all his faults, David became a winner by continuing to trust in spite of everything.

He bowed his head in humble acceptance when the child of his love was born dead. He forgave his political enemies. His rebel son Absalom taught him yet a deeper forgiveness. Even as he was forced to send troops to quell Absalom's uprising, David instructed his generals, "Be gentle with young Absalom for my sake." The success of his men in subduing the rebels became meaningless in the face of his son's death.

2 Samuel 18:5

David was first a human being, then a king. Although his heart was broken, he remained ready to love without limit. He sought no revenge because he had learned to forgive himself the sins God had forgiven him. He saw that he must extend that same forgiveness to others.

REVIEWING THE CHAPTER

Linking Your Ideas

1. Draw an upside-down pyramid entitled "David's Growing Role in God's Plan." Place David as shepherd at the lowest point to represent his starting role, and rearrange his other achievements (listed below) so that they move up the pyramid to King of Israel at the top.

Shepherd	Victory Over Goliath
Victory Over All Enemies	First Victory Over Philistines
Successful Getaway	Transfer of the Ark
Dream of a Temple and God's Promise	Repentance and Glory
	Final Victory Over Philistines
Unembittered Exile	Reorganization of Government
King of Hebron	Transfer of the Capital
Service at Court	King of Israel
Sin and Shame	

2. List the occasions on which David showed generosity to someone. Who was loyal to him?
3. How is the covenant God made with David connected with the coming of Christ? With you?
4. Why did the Israelites preserve the events of David's reign in great detail?

Strengthening Your Grasp

1. What characteristics of leadership did David have? Cite an example of each. What other qualities did he possess?
2. Tell how the following things from David's early career figured in his reign: shepherd's staff, sheep, bears and lions, harp playing, outlaws, the open fields.
3. Americans love to make up titles: Jolly Green Giant, Mr. Hero, Father of Our Country, The Lone Eagle, Mr. Entertainer. What titles would you give King David? Be ready to explain each. Your first might be Forgiving Father. The titles need not all be complimentary.
4. Humor trickles through the David stories. Tell where you see humor in these accounts: (a) David presenting himself to Saul and Goliath as Israel's champion; (b) David's being sent home by Achish, king of the Philistines; (c) the Lord's response to David's dream of building

a fitting house for his Lord; (d) the taunts of the Jebusites from the wall of their "impregnable" fortress.

5. Why is it hard to forgive yourself? Why is it impossible to believe in God's forgiveness if you can't forgive yourself?

6. What does the saying "Life can make you bitter or better" mean? What effect did the suffering in David's life have on him?

7. What were some situations in which David, unlike Saul, waited patiently for God's will to be fully revealed? (a) In becoming king of the South? (b) In becoming king of all Israel? (c) In regard to the punishment of his sin with Bathsheba?

Expressing Your Convictions

1. Sculptors have depicted David as a dynamic and passionate leader (Bernini), as a strong-bodied man (Donatello), and as a brave youth with the head of Goliath at his feet (Michelangelo). In Michelangelo's version, with its emphasis on great strength and deep goodness, David symbolizes the best in youth. Express what David means to you in an essay, a poem, a slide presentation, a song, or a comparison with some contemporary person or historic figure. If you are artistic, use your talents with paint or pencil.

2. The modern novelist Erich Segal has one of his characters in *Love Story* say, "Love means never having to say you're sorry." Would David agree or not? Why?

3. Read David's last instructions to his son Solomon (1 Kings 1–4). Write an essay on what it means to be a man or a woman according to the ideal presented by the sacred author in the story of David.

4. Choose a symbol, a color, a word, or a season that you think best expresses David's character. Put them together in a collage to represent your idea of the king.

Extending Your Interest

A second version of the David story appears in 1 Chronicles 10–29, written six centuries after David lived. The later scribe erased David's faults and painted his character in glowing colors. Which version do you think you would prefer? Why? You may enjoy reading the later account and noting the differences.

EIGHT SOLOMON
Magnificent Failure

Advance, O Lord, to your resting place
  you and the ark of your majesty.
May your priests be clothed with justice;
  let your faithful ones shout merrily for joy.
For the sake of David your servant,
  reject not the plea of your anointed.

PSALM 132:8–10

Judah and Israel lived in security, every man under his vine or under his fig tree from Dan to Beer-sheba, as long as Solomon lived.

1 KINGS 5:5

CHAPTER PREVIEW

The humorist Sam Levinson once quipped that we should not allow prayer to be taken out of school because "that's the way most of us got through."

■ When you get a good grade on an exam, to what or to whom do you attribute it? Study? Luck? God? Explain.

When Jesus said "The man who holds out to the end . . . is the one who will see salvation," he was teaching a lesson that had a long history in Israel. The need for perseverance is the moral of Solomon's story.

Matthew 24:13

Solomon, the son and successor of the great King David, brought the golden age of Israel to its zenith. Before his death, David kept his promise to Bathsheba and saw that Solomon was made king, although Solomon's older half-brother had already claimed the throne for himself. Unlike his father, who had begun as a humble shepherd, Solomon was born to the purple—a king, conscious of his role from the time of his ascent to the throne in 961 B.C. to his death forty years later. He

Zenith means high point.

started out as the model of wisdom—that quality in Israel uniting know-how in practical things with the knowledge that all success comes from God. The result of his later fall into idolatry became another reminder to Israel of its call to remain faithful to Yahweh.

Despite his advantages, Solomon began his reign humbly, asking the Lord for wisdom and an "understanding heart" in order to deliver just laws to his people. His vast knowledge made him the patron of the Wisdom Movement in Israel and gained him credit for the Bible's wisdom literature.

After eliminating his enemies, Solomon turned to the tasks proper to kingship. On the home front, he rezoned Palestine for fairer taxation and launched an extensive building program that included a magnificent temple and two palaces of cedar. He fortified the walls of strategic cities thoughout the land, establishing them as "chariot centers" for defense. He charged tolls on all the trade routes through Palestine, and, to build up the economy, hauled imports from distant ports in Ophir and Arabia in fleets he had built with the help of the King of Tyre. He also mined and refined copper in the southern deserts of the land. His dedication to the God of his father led him to secure the best materials for the temple and to perform his religious duties faithfully.

But gradually Solomon deserted Israel's ideal of wisdom by relying too heavily on human means of success. To gain favorable diplomatic relations with foreign nations, he brought into his harem many wives and concubines from other countries. The most famous of Solomon's wives was the Egyptian pharaoh's daughter. By building her a separate palace, he demonstrated not only his need to stay on friendly terms with powerful Egypt but also the extent of Israel's international influence.

Puffed up by prosperity and power, Solomon yielded to the temptation of the newly rich. While claiming only to be open-minded to other ways of life, in actuality he was too eager to please Israel's neighbors. By building shrines to the gods of his foreign wives and

Wisdom literature is the collections of wise sayings that teach how to succeed in life.

Excavations at Hazor, Meggido, and Gezer have uncovered city walls of the tenth century B.C., all of the same pattern, thus confirming the authenticity of the biblical texts describing Solomon's building program.

1 Kings 9:16. Traditionally, princesses of Egypt did not leave the country to marry. In the tenth century B.C., under weak dynasties, this rule was broken, enabling Solomon to receive his bride.

CALLED BY THE FATHER

participating in idol worship himself, he compromised his faith. He lost wisdom, the quality for which he had been most praised, and he forgot Israel's one law: to please God first.

Beneath Israel's blossoming landscape there smoldered the restlessness of the people. Excessive taxation, forced labor, and the cost of luxurious court life were like volcanic pressures waiting to erupt into another civil war.

Solomon learned that Jeroboam, the foreman of forced-labor teams in the North, was planning to lead the ten northern tribes in rebellion, and he ordered Jeroboam killed. But Jeroboam escaped to Egypt, to emerge after Solomon's death as a leader. The volcano would then spew forth the dark lava of intrigue and crime that would layer Israel's fortunes for centuries to come. The sacred writers realized it was the corruption of Israel's religious tradition that eventually brought about Israel's burial.

Recall that David's rebel son, Absalom, led an uprising in the North against his father.

- Solomon is known throughout the world for his wisdom. What is your idea of wisdom? If you know someone you consider wise, describe that person.

Words to Know

Solomon, Hiram (**high**-rehm), Queen of Sheba, Phoenicia (fi-**nee**-sheh), Port Ezion-geber (hesh-yon-**geh**-ber), Gulf of Aqaba (**ahk**-eh-bah), wisdom, proverb, vestibule, nave, Holy of Holies

THE WISDOM OF SOLOMON
(1 Kings 3, 5:9–14)

If you were given one wish—anything you wanted (except more wishes)—what would you ask for?

In the beginning of his reign, Solomon was as humble and devoted to the Lord as his father had been. One night, God told Solomon in a dream to ask for whatever he wanted, and Solomon's request so pleased the Lord

1 Kings 3:13–14

In ancient times, the king was also the chief justice in the land.

that he promised even more than Solomon had asked for. God then made a request of the king.

When he awoke, Solomon realized that God had come very close to him during the night. To celebrate God's goodness to him, he gave a banquet for all his courtiers in Jerusalem. As the royal judge of Israel, he sought to be as good to his people as God was to him. His wisdom in dealing with human nature is shown in the familiar story of the two mothers who claimed the same baby.

Read and Recall

Read 1 Kings 3:2–15 for Solomon's coronation prayer and 1 Kings 3:16–28 for the story of the wise judgment. Then go on to 1 Kings 5:1–14 for examples of Solomon's practical wisdom.

1. What did Solomon ask for? What did God promise and ask of him?
2. Draw a cartoon strip depicting the story of the squabbling women, or write it in verse.

ISRAEL'S WISDOM

Which of these proverbs can you complete? A stitch in time . . . , Birds of a feather . . . , Necessity is the mother of . . . , A bird in the hand . . . . How many more do you know? Why are such sayings popular?

Short sayings that capture the wisdom of the people are part of every culture. Those given above are from Benjamin Franklin's *Almanac*. He gathered and published these bits of wisdom that were part of American life. Israel, too, had its folk wisdom, which it recorded centuries before Columbus.

Benjamin Franklin (1706–1790) was an American statesman, printer, scientist, and writer. His *Almanac* was a calendar that included many bits of wisdom and useful information.

What has been called the Wisdom Movement of the Old Testament had its beginnings under Solomon, the sage or wise one of Israel and its promoter of the arts. In his court, three thousand proverbs were preserved by the scribes. Because authorship was attributed to the patron of a work, other books of sayings and wisdom stories, added later, were also attributed to Solomon.

Many of these are now in the Bible.

A *patron* is a wealthy person who sponsors a project.

The Book of Proverbs is the first of the biblical books known as the wisdom writings. It was probably not completed until five hundred years after Solomon, in the early fifth century B.C. Other wisdom books include Job, Psalms, Ecclesiastes, Wisdom, Sirach (Ecclesiasticus), and the Song of Songs—a long poem in which human love symbolizes God's love for humanity. Some of these were written as late as 150 B.C.

In some bibles, Ecclesiastes is called by its Hebrew name, Qoheleth (ko-**hehl**-eth), "son of David."

Israel borrowed sayings and stories from her neighbors; as a result, many proverbs are purely secular—no more than practical suggestions to the court pages on how to get along in life, how to win friends and influence people, or how to accept frustration with grace. But the later books of Wisdom and Ecclesiastes show more depth. For example, the Book of Job asks such hard questions as: Why do the wicked so often succeed and the good fail? Why must we suffer?

■ How does suffering teach wisdom?

God, the Source of Israel's Wisdom

Personified means to be thought of or represented as a person.

Proverbs 8:22

Proverbs 1:7

Although it borrowed from the wisdom of other nations, Israel's wisdom was different, based on the belief that full wisdom belonged to God alone. For Israel, divine wisdom shone out in creation and was personified mysteriously as an eternal heavenly Being who accompanied God in all he did. "The Lord begot me, the firstborn of his ways," Wisdom says. This heavenly power is God's gift, bestowed on the talented and skillful, and "the fear of the Lord is the beginning of knowledge."

The Book of Wisdom divides the human race into two classes—the foolish and the wise. It regards youth as generally foolish, but capable of becoming wise. An adult without wisdom, however, is a hopeless fool, doomed to failure and earthly unhappiness. Mature wisdom is the acceptance of God's deeds in faith, especially calamities, accidents, and other misfortunes. The higher wisdom is the fulfillment of the Law.

Thus Hebrew wisdom goes far beyond the practical sayings of Benjamin Franklin. It teaches the lesson of

CALLED BY THE FATHER

the prophets: Unless you love God and do his will even in small things, your daily life will be without meaning or happiness.

Suggestions for a Sage

1. Search through the books of Proverbs, Ecclesiastes, Wisdom, and Sirach. Pick out five sayings that you like from each. After each, mark "N" if the saying is natural or "R" if it is religious in tone. Rewrite one saying in modern English. Why are some sayings about ordinary nonreligious affairs?

2. Chapter 3 of the Book of Proverbs is a father's advice to a child he loves. Rewrite it as a father or mother would speak to a son or daughter today.

3. In the Book of Proverbs, wisdom is sometimes personified as a beautiful woman who leads people to a full life. She is a spouse associated with the Spirit of God. Find a passage in Proverbs 1 and 8 that makes wisdom feminine. Madison Avenue has its version of a beautiful woman; read Proverbs 31:10–31 for Israel's ideal. Which qualities hold true for beautiful women even in today's age of women's rights?

Although Hebrew Scriptures refer to God's Spirit, the Israelites did not know of the Holy Spirit as a person (see Joel 3:1–2).

4. Write a modern version of the ideal wife, husband, child, teenage student, employee, employer, or diplomat based on Proverbs 31:10–31.

5. Read the passage from Ecclesiastes 3:1–8. What wisdom do you find in it?

6. Tell how these passages from the New Testament reveal that Jesus is the wisdom of God: Luke 21:14–15; Matthew 12:42, 11:28–30.

7. God's wisdom as revealed in Christ is different from human wisdom. What does Paul have to say on this subject in 1 Corinthians 1:17–20, 22–25 and in 2:1–8?

8. Browse through books of Oriental, Indian, Native American, Chinese, or African proverbs. Which sayings appeal to you?

Reflect

1. What does Solomon's request reveal about him? How do your desires both reveal your present qualities and shape your future self? What *is* the most important thing in life?
2. Solomon was rewarded for faithfulness. Are the good always rewarded and sinners punished? Read what Jesus said about this in Luke 13:1–5 and John 9:1–3. Is there usually a connection between wisdom and success?
3. Solomon celebrated his experience of God's nearness by giving a banquet for his friends. What Christian actions of the past and present does this remind you of?
4. From the story of the two women, how would you describe wisdom? What is an understanding mind? A listening heart? How could you acquire either?

SOLOMON'S SPLENDOR
(1 Kings 5:15–6:38, 7:1–12)

If you inherited a large sum of money, how would you spend it? Would any of it go to pay for something in your Church? Why or why not?

The glory of Israel for the glory of the Lord! This might have been the motto of the young Solomon as he took up his royal duties. He wanted to make Israel a respected nation. His plans included raising splendid buildings, insuring the nation's military defense, and expanding Israel's trade.

Solomon's dream took shape as a gigantic twenty-year building program to be financed by public taxes and carried out by the men of Israel. Local resources weren't enough for Solomon's ambition, as he needed fine woods, precious metals, and quarried stone. Native architects and skilled artisans were also lacking. For these he turned to advanced and prosperous Phoenicia, where his friend Hiram, King of Tyre, met his needs in exchange for grain and oil.

In ancient monarchies, able-bodied men could be pressed into royal service during inactive agricultural seasons.

Tyre was the principal seaport of the Phoenician coastal territory, which included the forests of Lebanon.

CALLED BY THE FATHER

The largest project was the king's own palace—a magnificent House of Cedar that required thirteen years to build. Larger than the Temple, it featured a luxurious grand ballroom with cedar pillars and ceiling beams. Solomon built a second palace like it for his most important wife, the pharaoh's daughter.

The Bible cites what might have been fragments of documents exchanged between the two kings in 964 B.C. as they made arrangements to erect Solomon's proudest achievement, the Temple. The elaborate details of the Temple and its furnishings are carefully chronicled in the first Book of Kings. From this time on, the Temple became the center of the world to the Israelites. It symbolized their unity and nationhood, and it attested to their faith. God's glory filled the Temple when the ark came to rest there.

See 1 Kings 5:17–23.

1 Kings 8:10–13

But in the middle of the many descriptive details there was this warning from the Lord to Solomon: "As to this Temple you are building—if you observe my statutes, carry out my ordinances, keep and obey all my commands, I will fulfill toward you the promise I made to your father David. I will dwell in the midst of

1 Kings 6:12–13

the Israelites and will not forsake my people Israel." In other words, God's presence with his people did not depend on the Temple, no matter how magnificent, but on whether his people were obedient to his will.

When the Temple was completed, Solomon ordered all the leaders of Israel to gather in Jerusalem for the dedication at the New Year Festival. Joyfully, the priests carried the ark of the Lord and the vessels of the meeting tent to the new Temple.

Today, this feast is called Rosh Hashana.

1 Kings 8:27

Solomon then led the people in a solemn prayer of dedication that contains some of the most beautiful lines in the Bible: "Can it indeed be that God dwells among men on earth? If the heavens and the highest heavens cannot contain you, how much less this Temple which I have built!" After the dedication, God appeared again to Solomon, renewing the covenant to David: "If you live in my presence . . . , I will establish your throne . . . forever."

1 Kings 9:4–5

■ Read Psalm 132. Why was it probably used for the Temple dedication?

Once the Temple and palaces were complete, Solomon extended the city walls to both enlarge and defend Jerusalem. Making use of the most advanced military weapons of the time, he built up a force of fourteen hundred chariots and twelve thousand drivers to constitute the main arm of his military strength. He stationed some in Jerusalem and the rest in six strategically fortified cities throughout Israel to discourage foreign invasions of the empire.

The key cities were Hazor (north); Meggido (at the mountain pass); Gezer, Beth-horon, and Baalath (lookouts on the west); and Tamar (south).

The king capitalized on what had always been a disadvantage to Canaan—its vulnerable positions between great empires. He maintained a monopoly on trade between the Nile and the Euphrates, which was forced to pass through his territory. Excavations of vast stables at Meggido, one of the "chariot cities," show that Solomon engaged in a profitable horse and chariot trade between northern and southern countries.

Hiring craftsmen from the Tyrean shipbuilding yards, Solomon built a fleet on the Gulf of Aqaba. These vessels, maintained by the Israelites under the direction

The numbers of Solomon's horses and chariots given in 1 Kings were once thought to be exaggerated. Excavations of numerous hitching posts and water troughs at Meggido, however, revealed that they were based on fact.

CALLED BY THE FATHER

of expert seamen from Tyre, brought back gold, precious stones, and sandalwood from Ophir. The king had another fleet that transported cargoes of gold, silver, ivory, and apes and monkeys from Arabia. In southern Palestine Solomon undertook the most extensive copper mining and refining known in the ancient Near East, and a "refinery" fleet carried the smelted metal to distant shores.

The famous exchange of gifts between Solomon and the Queen of Sheba (later referred to by Jesus as the Queen of the South) reveals the extent of Solomon's ambitions and fame. Not content to control the sea routes on the Red Sea, Solomon was also interested in land caravan trade with southern Arabia. All this must have had a devastating effect on the commerce of the Near East, and it is no wonder Solomon became the talk of the then-known world. But at home the wealth that poured into Israel shone as a symbol of God's approval. The Queen of Sheba summed it up in speaking to Solomon when she said, "Your wisdom and prosperity surpass the report I heard. . . . Blessed be the Lord, your God, whom it has pleased to place you on the throne of Israel."

1 Kings 10:7, 9

DETAILS OF SOLOMON'S TEMPLE

All the stones used in building the Temple were hewn to shape in the quarries, and the woodwork was prefabricated "so that no hammer, axe, or iron tool was to be heard in the Temple during its construction." It was a monumental feat.

The measurement of the Temple building was small by our standards: ninety feet long, thirty-five feet wide, and forty-five feet high. The main purpose of the structure was as the resting place of the ark, not as a gathering place for the people. Only the high priest entered its innermost sanctuary once a year. The measurements of the outer courts are unknown. Paved or lined with brick, they must have been vast to accommodate the worshippers who came from the length and breadth of Israel to make their offerings at the Temple they had helped to build.

Phoenician in design, the Temple was divided into three parts: *vestibule*; principal chambers, or *nave*; and rear chamber, or *Holy of Holies* (inner sanctuary). The building was fronted by a porch supported by huge bronze columns, probably representing the pillars of fire and cloud that guided the Israelites in the desert.

Double doors of olive wood led to the Holy Place, a high room that measured sixty-five by thirty-five feet. Its entire interior was paneled with cedar, which was carved with cherubim, palm trees, and open flowers. In this windowed room were kept all the rich apparatus for worship—the golden altar of incense, the table of shewbread, ten lampstands, and other sacred vessels. These treasures were often stolen and carted off to foreign lands during invasions.

Two double doors led into the Holy of Holies, or Most Holy Place, where the ark of the Lord (covenant) was kept in absolute darkness. This room, too, was paneled with cedar inlaid with gold. Two large cherubim of cedar stood over the ark, each fifteen feet high

182

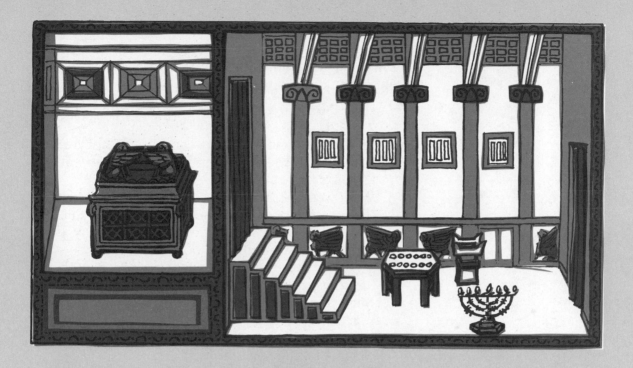

with a wingspread of fifteen feet. Storage chambers ran along the walls of the building. (A young king was once hidden in one of these chambers for six years.)

The bronze altar of sacrifice at which Solomon and the priests offered whole burnt offerings was in the court in front of the Temple on a platform. Large areas outside the Temple where the worshippers stood were paved or laid with brick.

Read and Recall

Read 1 Kings 7:1–12 (Solomon's building program); 1 Kings 5:6–38 (Solomon's temple); 1 Kings 10:1–29 (Solomon's trade empire and wealth).

1. Describe some features of Solomon's palace (1 Kings 7:1–12).
2. List the transactions between Hiram of Tyre and Solomon as well as Adoniram's tallies of workers (1 Kings 5:1–32).
3. What were the three parts of the Temple? What was the function of each? How long did it take to build it? Name and describe the purpose of any three things in the Temple.
4. What promise was made in connection with the building of the Temple (1 Kings 6:11–13)?
5. Make an inventory of the young nation's assets during this golden age (1 Kings 10:11–29). Did Solomon's wealth consist of practical things, luxury items, or basic necessities?
6. On a map of the ancient Near East trace the journey of the Queen of Sheba, naming places and things she must have passed. What did she offer Solomon? Which of his possessions made her breathless with admiration? What gifts did Solomon give her?

Reflect

1. In the Hebrew Scriptures wealth was a sign of God's favor. What attitude did Jesus take toward wealth in Luke 12:30?
2. In the Temple dedication prayer (1 Kings 8:27–30), Solomon said that the splendid dwelling of the Lord could not contain God. Catholics believe in Christ's special presence in the Eucharist. Does the Eucharist "contain" God, symbolize God's presence, or what? Do you believe that a church should be as fine as the local community can build? Why or why not?
3. At the completion of the Temple on high rock in Palestine, Jerusalem became the glorious City of God. What does the Book of Revelation say about

The rock upon which Solomon built the temple is still preserved in the Mosque of Omar—the Dome of the Rock.

CALLED BY THE FATHER

the New Jerusalem and the Temple in 21:2, 9–14 and 22–27?

4. Jesus referred to the temple of his body, and Saint Paul called Christians the temples of God (2 Corinthians 6:16). What do these statements mean to you?

5. Which words of the Queen of Sheba seem strange coming from the lips of a pagan Arabian queen? What is the sacred author saying?

SOLOMON THE COMPROMISER
(1 Kings 11)

If Saul was the brawn and David the heart, Solomon was the brain of Israel's kings. Yet when he was at the peak of his power there was a flaw in his success. In his new sophistication Solomon belittled the faith he had inherited from his father and equated his personal worth with magnificent buildings and a large court. His reputation before the foreign nations became more important to him than his real worth before God.

Under the pretense of tolerance, he allowed and even participated in the worship of foreign idols within the Holy City itself. He built temples to the false gods of his foreign wives to fill up the hollowness of his own inner temple.

For a while it worked. Solomon was flattered when the world powers treated him as one of their own. He was living in luxury as well as power, and Israel was being enriched by the arts and crafts of more sophisticated nations. But in the end, in compromising the faith of his childhood, Solomon set the kingdom on the road to destruction. It came not from the great nations whose advanced views he had adopted in order to be thought modern, but from his own people, whom he had taxed and forced into labor to achieve his cheap goals of display, self-indulgence, and greed.

His story is another version of Israel's teaching: true liberation comes not from wealth or scientific achievements or the arts, but from faith in the living God.

Read and Recall

Read the episode of Solomon straying from God in 1 Kings 11.

1. What two sins did Solomon commit?
2. Name the specific gods that Solomon endorsed, and their nations.
3. What punishment came to Israel through Solomon's infidelity? What kept the nation from total collapse?
4. Which Israelite vassal state was the first to rebel? Who became its king? How?
5. What startling revelation was made to Jeroboam? Why did Jeroboam flee to Egypt?
6. How long was Solomon's reign in Israel? Who succeeded him?

Reflect

1. Decide which of the following currently popular idols seem most attractive to you: sexual satisfaction, love, travel, freedom to do your own thing, good looks, popularity, athletic ability, drugs, alcohol, TV, freedom from pain, having "everything"— car, motorbike, stereo, clothes, money. Why did you make your choices? How can you develop the wisdom to use them in moderation?

2. If you've ever been ashamed of your faith or of performing some religious activity you thought might be mocked, what did you do? Why?

GETTING IT TOGETHER

The monarchy was at its best under its first rulers, each of whom began as a gifted person who listened to God and obeyed. Each also fell away from the high ideal that Israel set even for its kings. In their stories, Israel found materials for teaching its great truths.

The first king and giant warrior, Saul, initially directed his energies to fulfilling his call. He kept Israel's enemies—God's enemies—out of her backyard. But then, after conquering the Ammonites, Amalekites, and Philistines, he was himself conquered by pride, jealousy, and disobedience. As a king, a military leader, and a man, he was ultimately disappointing.

The third king, Solomon, also began with a listening heart. He prayed for wisdom rather than riches and ruled with justice and order. His first building was the Temple, but then the glories of architecture and the riches of commerce finally plugged his ears. He grew deaf to God as he worshipped idols to keep the favor of foreigners. He did not listen to his people, who carried the tax burden of his luxurious living, and he came to be despised for his worldliness.

Superficially, David's reign seems to follow the same pattern. Divinely chosen and anointed by the holy Samuel, David consulted the Lord before every undertaking. The capture of Jerusalem, the unification around the ark, the final conquest of the Philistines, the purchase of a temple site, and God's promise of an everlasting dynasty—these were David's achievements before he, too, sinned. But unlike the others, David was made more lovable as a result of his weaknesses. By sincerely repenting, humbly accepting God's punishments, and forgiving his enemies, he himself found forgiveness. His ears were never totally closed to God's word. If Saul was man's king, and Solomon a foreigner's king, David was Israel's true king.

REVIEWING THE CHAPTER

Linking Your Ideas

1. Jesus is the Wisdom of the Father. All creation is said to have its completion in him—nature, language, history, human life. In a composition, poem, or song, tell how Jesus is a fulfillment of any of these for you. You may wish to refer to Psalm 1, 8, or 72 for phrases and thoughts to help you develop your ideas.
2. By giving examples of particular traits, show that Solomon did or did not change during his kingship.
3. What did Jesus say about the Queen of the South (Sheba) in Matthew 12:42 to make her visit to Solomon meaningful to you?
4. Outline the achievements of Solomon.

Strengthening Your Grasp

1. How important is money to your idea of happiness? What do you think makes people genuinely happy?
2. Just as synagogues replaced the Temple for Jews, churches became the Christian "synagogues." What is the new Temple for Christians?

Expressing Your Conviction

1. What gifts did Solomon possess? How did he use his gifts? Draw symbols to signify your personal gifts. Write a prayer, poem, or song to express your gratitude and plans for using them.
2. Hold an interview with the Queen of Sheba in which she reveals her impressions of Solomon and Israel.
3. Write a prayer for wisdom, being specific about the particular things you need to become a wise person.
4. Create a prayer service honoring the temple of Christ's body and the temple of every Christian heart. Refer to what Saint Paul wrote in 1 Corinthians 3:10–17.
5. Write and present a skit set in a fast-food chain where, like Solomon, a teenager succumbs to idolatry in order to be accepted by the crowd.

REVIEWING THE UNIT

Patterns

1. Write headlines for the front page of Israel's major newspaper on what you judge to be the biggest day in the life of (a) Samuel, (b) Saul, (c) David, and (d) Solomon.
2. Make diary entries such as an ordinary citizen of Israel might have kept for three of the following occasions: the capture of the ark; the celebration of the return of the ark; Saul's and David's return from victory over the Philistines; the massacre of the priests of Nob; David's move to Jerusalem; Solomon's proclamation drafting laborers for Israel's new building projects; the dedication of the Temple; the dedication of the palace of the princess of Egypt.

Focal Points

1. Which leaders in Israel were the best hearers of God's Word? Which were the poorest? What result did each have on the nation? Who will be affected by your ability to listen to the Lord?
2. Compare and contrast any two characters of the monarchy during this period of Israel's history.
3. Interview any of the characters of the monarchy for the class, or prepare a feature article on one of them for a teen magazine.
4. Choose an animal, plant, food, or color to symbolize two of the people who figured in the account of the monarchy. Write short descriptions defending your choices.

Response

1. Discuss: How true is it today that God's favor rests on people who follow his commandments? Give examples to support your views.
2. Write a class celebration using appropriate psalms and other Scripture texts centering on the need to listen to the Lord or on the beauty of God's House.
3. Write a poem, song, prayer, psalm, or composition about any character, event, or insight that struck you during this study.
4. Dramatize a TV debate in which Saul, David, and Solomon discuss their goals as King of Israel, or have Samuel evaluate the three kings in an appearance on a TV talk show.

UNIT 4

Crisis and Growth:
Prophets, Priests, Kings

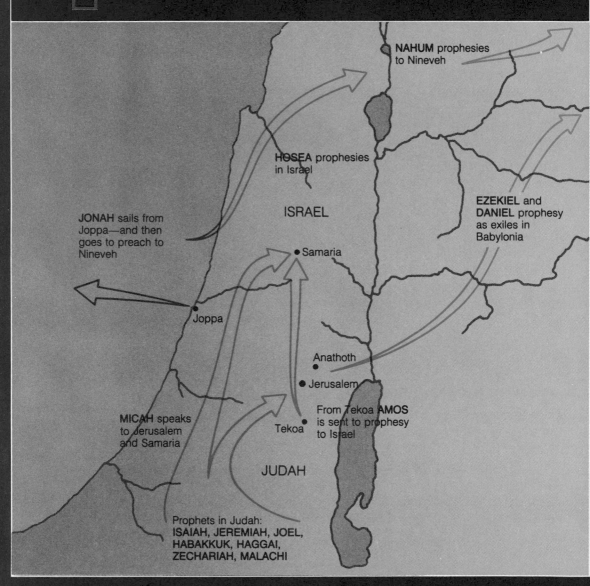

NAHUM prophesies
to Nineveh

HOSEA prophesies
in Israel

ISRAEL

EZEKIEL and
DANIEL prophesy
as exiles in
Babylonia

JONAH sails from
Joppa—and then
goes to preach to
Nineveh

Samaria

Joppa

Anathoth

Jerusalem

From Tekoa AMOS
is sent to prophesy
to Israel

MICAH speaks
to Jerusalem
and Samaria

Tekoa

JUDAH

Prophets in Judah:
ISAIAH, JEREMIAH, JOEL,
HABAKKUK, HAGGAI,
ZECHARIAH, MALACHI

Sources

1 and 2 Kings, 2 Chronicles, Amos, Hosea, Isaiah, Micah, Jeremiah, Lamentations, Baruch, Ezekiel, Nehemiah, Ezra, 1 and 2 Maccabees

- The Role and Lives of the Prophets in Israel

- The Decline and Fall of the Monarchy in Israel

- The Exile

- The Restoration

- The Maccabean Revolt

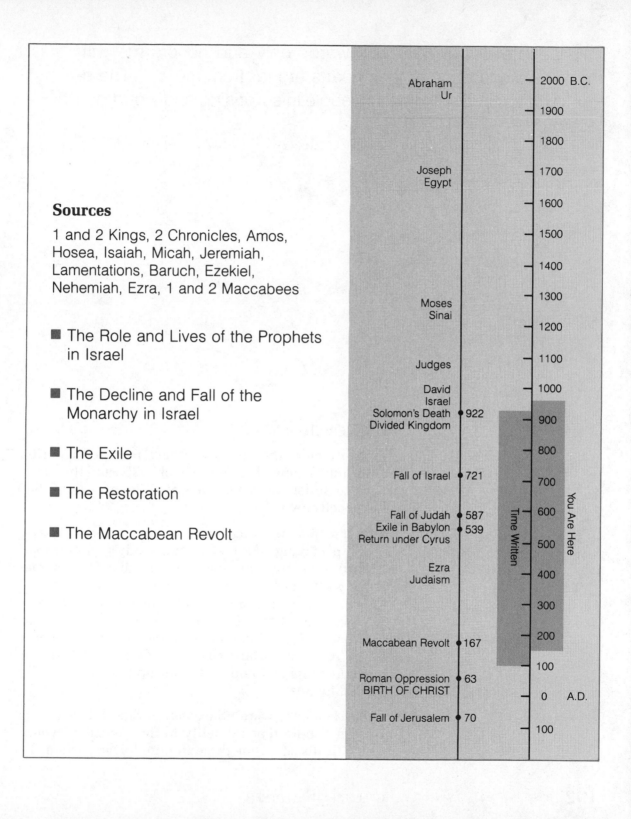

Abraham Ur	2000 B.C.
	1900
	1800
Joseph Egypt	1700
	1600
	1500
	1400
Moses Sinai	1300
	1200
Judges	1100
David Israel	1000
Solomon's Death ● 922 Divided Kingdom	900
	800
Fall of Israel ● 721	700
Fall of Judah ● 587 Exile in Babylon ● 539 Return under Cyrus	600 500
Ezra Judaism	400
	300
Maccabean Revolt ● 167	200
	100
Roman Oppression ● 63 BIRTH OF CHRIST	0 A.D.
Fall of Jerusalem ● 70	100

Time Written

You Are Here

This people draws near with words only and honors me with their lips alone, though their hearts are far from me. . . . Therefore I will again deal with this people in surprising and wondrous fashion.

ISAIAH 29:13, 14

UNIT OVERVIEW

Probably more than once you have regretted ignoring a warning. Human beings live recklessly, and then they have to suffer the consequences. Which of these has happened to you?

- You're playing rough, and your mom or dad says, "Stop playing like that or somebody's going to get hurt." You continue playing "like that," and somebody gets hurt.
- Someone gives you a cup of coffee or tea and says, "It's pretty hot. Let it cool or you'll burn your tongue." You drink it anyway and burn your tongue.
- You're in a car whose gas gauge is on "E." The driver ignores this fact and you wind up hiking down the road for gas.

The Israelites were no exception. God informed his Chosen People that infidelity to the Covenant would result in disaster. For three hundred years, when the

Israelites stooped to idol worship, immorality, and injustice, Yahweh sent messengers called prophets to rebuke them. But the Israelites, a stiff-necked people, chose not to hear. The result: God no longer trampled their foes. Israel split in two. The Assyrians destroyed the North in 721 B.C. and the Babylonians annihilated the South in 587 B.C., exiling the Israelites to Babylon.

During Israel's monarchy, forty-three kings reigned. The South had one line of kings, descendants of David, while the North had one dynasty after another. The author of Sirach says of Judah's kings, "Except for David, Hezekiah, and Josiah, they all were wicked; they abandoned the law of the Most High." The northern kings were no better.

The history of the three centuries between Solomon's reign and Israel's restoration revolves around the kings and the prophets. The prophets' role was to recall the great realities the Israelites had forgotten: the one God, the Covenant, and the Mosaic law. Although the prophets were heeded by only a few and were unable to prevent Israel's tragic fate, they did save her from extinction. Their word still has a saving effect on all who hear it.

The Israelites often adopted their neighbors' religions by combining pagan practices with their own. Loathsome Canaanite practices included child sacrifice and fertility rites that involved temple prostitutes.

Sirach 49:4

The prophets explained that only Israel's false hopes were demolished. The Israelites thought the Covenant was like a magic shield for them, but the prophets taught that Israel must live up to its covenant obligations or face the consequences. The Israelites thought that if they carried out the customs of formal religion, it didn't matter that their life was glutted with bad habits, perversions, and selfish injustices. The prophets declared instead that God wanted their hearts. The Israelites thought that the holy city of Jerusalem and David's dynasty were indestructible. The prophets explained that the prophecy concerning David's house pointed to a higher kingdom and to a future Messiah.

One day, after a lesson about the president of the United States, a first-grade teacher asked, "And what does the president do?" A little boy answered, "He flies in a helicopter." The tyke had focused on what was most fascinating to him. In the same way, people have emphasized the prophets' clairvoyant power and ignored their main function.

The prophets were spokesmen for God. Their messages were phrased in the diplomatic language used by

"Your house and your kingdom shall endure forever" (2 Samuel 7:16).

A *clairvoyant* is able to know things out of the range of the human senses.

CALLED BY THE FATHER

ambassadors: "Thus says the Lord." Prophets were called by God and compelled to declare his will in the current affairs of the people. In so doing, they made the past understandable, the present endurable, and the future hopeful.

In many cases the prophets' predictions were natural outcomes of the Israelites' actions. They were like a parent's advice to a young child: "If you run, you're going to fall." The prophets spoke to Israel like this: "If you join with the Egyptians, you will be crushed."

The prophecies that today are seen as foretelling the Messiah were not recognized as such by the prophets themselves. They spoke to their contemporaries and addressed local situations. For instance, Isaiah gave King Ahaz a sign that the house of David would endure: "The virgin shall be with child, and bear a son." This probably referred to the young unmarried woman who would be the mother of the future King Hezekiah. The Church now sees those words as pointing to the Virgin Mary. From our vantage point, we can see the words of the prophets verified as history unfolds.

Before the age of the classical prophets—those whose teachings are in the Bible—there were other prophets in Israel, like Elijah and Elisha, whose feats are leg-

The word *prophet* is from the Greek for "to speak in place of." The Hebrew word for prophet is *nabi*, which means "mouthpiece." *Nabi* is derived from another Hebrew word that means "to spring forth" or "to bubble up."

Isaiah 7:14

endary. Prophets in those days were usually counselors to the king. God worked through the culture of the times. Once the monarchy ceased, prophecy in the strict sense ceased.

The prophets were a diverse lot: Amos was a herdsman and keeper of sycamore trees, Isaiah was from the upper class, Jeremiah and Ezekiel were probably priests, and Hosea was a man married to an unfaithful wife. Although the prophets lived in different times and places, their message was the same: there is one God, you must trust him, and he demands justice.

■ Think of occasions when someone's words made you sad, or angry, or deliriously happy.

Words are powerful. They can wound or heal; they can even kill or give life. According to the mentality of the ancient Near East, God's word was himself—his active, dynamic presence. God described his word: "Is not my word like fire, . . . like a hammer shattering rocks?" Its might was evident at creation when, at God's words, the universe came into being. The New Testament affirms this: "God's word is living and effective, sharper than any two-edged sword. It penetrates and divides soul and spirit, joints and marrow; it judges the reflections and thoughts of the heart."

Jeremiah 23:29

Hebrews 4:12

You know how you feel when someone points out that you are less than perfect. As a result of their outspokenness in pointing out Israel's faults, the prophets were persecuted. They led uncomfortable lives that sometimes ended in martyrdom.

When Israel fell, the prophets were encouraging. They saw in the plight of Israel a New Exodus. Remembering God's fidelity, they foretold a New Covenant. God was still the Lord of History, controlling events to suit his new and always surprising future. After the Exile, a remnant returned to Jerusalem, where Governor Nehemiah and the priest Ezra directed the formulation of the restored faith of Israel. The religion called Judaism has its roots in this Age of Prophecy. Through mistakes and suffering, Israel arrived at a new maturity in the relationship with Yahweh.

A *remnant* is a leftover, a small surviving part. A census of the Jews during the Restoration in the Book of Ezra sets the population at less than fifty thousand, as compared with a million citizens during Solomon's reign.

CALLED BY THE FATHER

All was relatively peaceful in Israel as it passed from the rule of one foreign ruler to the next. Then in 167 B.C., the Syrian king, Antiochus IV, persecuted the Jews and desecrated the Temple. A Jewish family known as the Maccabees rose up to meet this challenge. After their victory, the Temple was rededicated.

Shortly after this rededication, and five hundred years after the last prophet, the greatest of all prophets came into the world: Jesus Christ, the Word made flesh. The people he encountered during his public life either accepted or rejected him. Since he and his Word still live, we in the twentieth century have the opportunity to hear him and respond to his covenant, his law, and his love. But keeping the Lord's law isn't any easier today; it requires courage, determination, and prayer. However, we have the advantage of the graces of the sacraments such as Baptism and Confirmation.

NINE

ELIJAH, AMOS, HOSEA, ISAIAH

God's Living Reminders

Sections

Elijah and Elisha: The Sound of God
   1 Kings 18:16–19:18; 2 Kings 4:8–37

Amos and Hosea: Trouble for Israel
   Amos 2:6–16; Hosea 2:15–22, 11:1–4

Isaiah and Micah: Ambassadors to Judah
   Isaiah (short passages); Micah 5, 6

God grant us the serenity
to accept the things we cannot change,
the courage to change the things we can,
and the wisdom to know the difference.

Put away your misdeeds from before my eyes; cease doing evil; learn to do good.

ISAIAH 1:16

CHAPTER PREVIEW

When God's people began walking the path to self-destruction, his love prompted him to send prophets to try to persuade them to give up their evil ways and return to the faith of Abraham and Moses.

■ How would you react if someone you loved was endangering his or her life by smoking, drinking, driving recklessly, or eating harmful foods? What would you do?

Solomon's death in 922 B.C. initiated a crisis: the kingdom split into two parts. The ten northern tribes rebelled against Solomon's son Rehoboam, who had made this threat: "My father beat you with whips, but I will beat you with scorpions." The tribes chose Solomon's foreman, Jeroboam, as king, and they became the separate Kingdom of Israel. The southern tribes of Judah and tiny Benjamin formed the Kingdom of Judah under Rehoboam. Fighting between these two kingdoms was almost continuous. After the split, when Israel was easy

1 Kings 12:11

The words "Jew" and "Judaism" come from the name "Judah." Most of the returned exiles had originated there.

to conquer, neighboring countries vied with one another for the territory.

In order to prevent his people from worshipping in Judah's holy city, Jerusalem, Israel's King Jeroboam established Shechem as the capital of Israel and made Dan and Bethel its holy cities. However, he erred by catering to false gods. The kings that followed were no better, and most of them were assassinated. The worst of them was Ahab, who married Jezebel from Tyre and adopted the worship of her god, Baal Melqart, as the court religion. The prophet Elijah and his successor, Elisha, campaigned against Ahab, Jezebel, and Baal. In the end, Elisha anointed a new king, Jehu, who overthrew Jezebel's family and gods. Paganism was not squelched, however.

By the time Jeroboam II came to power, Israel was again a flourishing empire, but internal deterioration had advanced. Amos and Hosea, the northern prophets, attacked the decay that was hastening the Day of Yahweh, when Israel would have to answer for her crimes. Jeroboam's reign was followed by anarchy. Twenty-five years later, when Israel refused to pay tribute to Assyria, its king, Sennacherib, stormed into the land and deported thousands of Israel's citizens. These people are referred to as the Ten Lost Tribes of Israel. The Israelites who remained became the Samaritans.

Meanwhile, Judah followed a course similar to that of Israel. The Israelites in the south survived their northern neighbors by more than a century. Depending on the king, idolatry was either upheld or purged. Jehoshaphat and Uzziah were two kings who initiated reform and brought Judah to a time of prosperity; under Ahaz, however, Judah became a vassal state of Assyria, and pagan practices were encouraged. Supported by the southern prophets Isaiah and Micah, Ahaz's son, Hezekiah, reversed this pattern. He made a valiant attempt to break free from the Assyrians by closing the shrines of Yahweh tainted with pagan practices and rallying the Israelites around the monarchy and the holy city of Jerusalem.

Jezebel was literally thrown out of a window to the dogs.

Anarchy is government without individual group leaders. It marks a time of chaos and danger.

An engineering feat of Hezekiah was the construction of a 1,750-foot water tunnel when Assyrians threatened to cut off the water supply. It connected the Spring of Gihon to a reservoir inside Jerusalem. Teams starting at both ends of the area chiseled through limestone until they met in the middle.

200

Hezekiah's reform was short-lived, however, as the prophets failed to stir the consciences of the majority. Judah was still a sinking ship. By the time Babylon, under Nebuchadnezzar, replaced Assyria as the leading world power, Judah was easy prey for it.

■ The Greek philosopher Socrates said, "The unexamined life is not worth living." Reflecting on your life's journey helps you to see in which direction you are heading and to correct false turns. Perhaps in your life you have even had some "prophet" to heed. In your journal, jot down your outstanding fault and two ways to control it.

Words to Know

Rehoboam (ree-eh-**boh**-ehm), Jeroboam (jer-eh-**boh**-ehm), Hezekiah (hez-eh-**kigh**-eh), Isaiah (igh-**zay**-eh), Ahab (**ah**-hahb), Jezebel (**jez**-eh-behl), Elijah (i-**ligh**-jeh), Elisha (i-**ligh**-sheh), Amos (**ay**-mehs), Hosea (hoh-**zay**-eh), Gomer (**goh**-mer), Jeremiah (jer-eh-**migh**-eh), Ezekiel (ee-**zee**-kyehl), transcendence

ELIJAH AND ELISHA: THE SOUND OF GOD
(1 Kings 18:16–19:18; 2 Kings 4:8–37)

Elijah was obviously a man of God. He was dynamic in combating the religious and moral policies of King Ahab and Jezebel, the king's pagan wife. When Ahab presented false charges against a man named Naboth and had him stoned to death because he wanted Naboth's vineyard for himself, Elijah rebuked Ahab and predicted a humiliating end for his family. A sign of Elijah's authenticity was that his predictions came true.

■ How do you recognize a "man of God" or "woman of God" today?

Although Elijah's words were not recorded, his spirit is alive in the Bible. As God's champion and Baal's greatest foe, Elijah became a legend in Jewish history.

Baal had a female consort named Astarte.

The fantastic stories about him and his successor, Elisha, reflect their reputation.

Elijah and Elisha belonged to a class of inspired prophets and reformers who upheld strict Yahwehism. They were personifications of the Mosaic tradition during a time when Israel had forgotten the meaning of the Covenant and had abandoned Yahweh for Baal. In a famous showdown with Baal's prophets, Elijah unmasked Baal as no-god. Furious, Jezebel sought to kill Elijah, who took refuge on Mount Horeb. There he encountered his God in the form of a whisper.

Yahwehism is the traditional religion of Moses, with no pagan additions.

At God's direction, Elijah threw his mantle of hair over Elisha to make him a sharer in the prophetic mission. Later, as Elijah and Elisha were walking together, a flaming chariot descended from the sky and whisked Elijah away. Elisha picked up Elijah's cloak and proceeded to carry out his aims. It was Elisha who anointed Jehu king in order to destroy the house of Ahab in 842 B.C.

All the symbolism behind the fiery chariot story is not known today. In any case, it emphasizes Elijah's important role in salvation history.

An indication of the impression Elijah made is that when Jesus preached, centuries later, the Israelites thought he was Elijah returned to earth. Even now an extra place is set at the Passover meal in expectation of Elijah's return.

CALLED BY THE FATHER

Read and Recall

Read 1 Kings 18:16–19:18 (the contest with Baal and the encounter with God) and 2 Kings 4:8–37 (Elisha and the Shunammite woman).

1. How do the adventures of Elijah and Elisha illustrate the traditional Jewish beliefs of the supremacy of God, his communication with humans, and his loving concern?
2. What was the prophetic mission of Elijah and Elisha?
3. What signs indicated that Elijah and Elisha were men of God?

Reflect

1. Why should we know about Jewish prophets?
2. Why is it appropriate that at the Lord's transfiguration Moses and Elijah appeared together?
3. How do you account for the many miraculous feats of Elijah and Elisha?
4. How is Elijah like John the Baptist?
5. Considering that the religion of Baal was associated with nature, why did God speak to Elijah in a gentle whisper rather than through strong wind, earthquake, or fire?
6. Why do people react violently to reformers?
7. The relationship between Elijah and Elisha is not unique. What other persons have taken up the work of a master or predecessor? How might you be one of them?
8. When Ahab adopted the religion of Tyre, the Israelites also accepted it. How can this be explained? What safeguards can you employ against losing your religion?
9. Jesus is the "new Elijah." Elijah called down fire from heaven in the contest with Baal, and he raised a boy to life by lying on the corpse. How was Christ even mightier than Elijah? (See Luke 12:49 and Matthew 9:23–26.)

AUTHENTIC PROPHETS AND IMPOSTERS

How do you feel when you find out someone has lied to you? Why? How do you react to flattery?

In this unit you are studying the *classical prophets*, those whose words were remembered and recorded in Scripture. The classical prophets responded to an urgent personal call from God to enter the public scene and convey the truth to people directly from God. They spoke in polished, poetic sermons set in traditional prophetic formulas. Because they stood for righteous living according to the Covenant and faithful worship of the one God, Yahweh, they often had to speak to their audiences in depressing, defeatist terms. They criticized the bad habits of their countrymen and women. They also frequently took issue with the state, so that a test of a true prophet was whether or not he or she was rejected by authority. The life of a true prophet was not easy.

A second type of prophet was the *professional* or *ecstatic prophet*, whose words were not preserved. Unlike the classical prophets, they lived and worked in groups and used special techniques—hypnotic music,

Christ remarked that no prophet is welcome in his own country (Luke 4:24).

CALLED BY THE FATHER

drink, or dancing—to work themselves into ecstasy, an emotional state or trance in which they would prophesy. Although classical prophets like Ezekiel sometimes had psychic experiences, in general they were not ecstatic. Elisha was probably a professional prophet. Once when he wanted to prophesy he called for a musician, and when the musician played, the power of the Lord came upon Elisha.

See 2 Kings 3:15.

Unfortunately, in Israel there were *false prophets* at work side by side with true classical and professional ones. These false prophets were often paid for their prophecies, and they spoke only the soothing, flattering words the Israelites wanted to hear. Their dangerous falsehoods and the fact that they prophesied for money disgusted the true prophets, who warned the people not to listen to them.

The difference between the true and false prophets is made clear in the Book of Kings. King Ahab asked four hundred prophets if he should attack Ramoth-gilead. They answered, "Go. The Lord will deliver it to you." Then Ahab reluctantly agreed to consult the prophet Micaiah, saying, "I hate him because he prophesies not good but evil about me." True to his call, Micaiah foretold a catastrophe and implied that the other prophets had lied. For his honesty, he was slapped in the face and thrown into prison.

Today the true prophets are recognized and appreciated for having reinterpreted Israel's vocation and given her new life. The false prophets, with their smooth words, have been forgotten.

A difficult responsibility people have is to rebuke one another. Just as your parents and teachers don't enjoy correcting you, you don't like to tell your friends that what they're doing is wrong. And yet, in conscience, you are obliged to do so in a kind, loving manner. It is good to pray often for the wisdom and courage to speak the right words to people, to say the "things that will really help them."

Ephesians 4:29

AMOS AND HOSEA: TROUBLE FOR ISRAEL
(Amos 2:6–16; Hosea 2:15–22, 11:1–4)

What kind of motivation works better: threatening punishment or appealing to love? Would the results be the same for children as for adults? Which motivates you?

To keep the North true, God used two strategies. He sent Amos with fire-and-brimstone prophecies and Hosea with words of love and promise.

During the reign of Jeroboam II, Israel experienced a rebirth. Her wealth and power equaled that of Solomon's time, but internal corruption was progressing like cancer. The privileged took advantage of the poor, and since judges were corrupt the poor had little hope. This situation existed because the people had lost their understanding of the covenant Law. Faith no longer touched their lives; it was merely a matter of religious rites, and even these rites had absorbed the evils of the pagan rituals. To this corrupt society Amos and Hosea announced condemnation and hope.

Amos was not a professional prophet. He was a herdsman and keeper of sycamore trees who lived in Tekoa on the fringe of the Judean wilderness. Yet he felt chosen by God to rebuke his people and their rulers for breaking the law of Yahweh. In the middle of the

Keepers of sycamores had to puncture the figs at the right moment to quicken their ripening.

CALLED BY THE FATHER

eighth century B.C., this stern man of the desert descended on the sophisticated city people and roared out the Lord's words like a lion. Amos dared to call the aristocratic ladies fat, lazy cows. He denounced immorality and luxury. When he lashed out his dire predictions for Israel, the priest enlisted King Jeroboam's help in banishing Amos from the Temple.

Although the Book of Amos ends with the promise of restoration, it is primarily a book of woe. It was Amos who gave new meaning to the "Day of the Lord," which originally meant the day when Yahweh would intervene to save his people. According to Amos it would be "darkness and not light," and he warned, "Prepare to meet your God, O Israel."

Amos 5:18, 4:12

Hosea, a contemporary of Amos, faced the same task and yet his approach was his own. He recalled God's love for Israel in his efforts to coax her back to him. In his marriage to the unfaithful Gomer, Hosea symbolically lived out the estranged relationship between Yahweh and Israel. Even his children had symbolic names. Gomer's adultery was like Israel's running after strange gods after it had vowed to be faithful to Yahweh. Hosea condemned Israel's priests and leaders. He called the country "an unturned hearth cake," burned on one side, not baked on the other.

The names *Hosea* and *Jesus* share the same Hebrew root meaning "Yahweh saves."

One child was named for the valley where the end of the king's dynasty had been foretold.

Hosea 7:8. The unturned hearth cake symbolizes the uselessness of the people and the difference between the rich and the poor.

Even though he was hurt and angered by Gomer, Hosea was willing to forgive her and take her back. Yahweh, too, would have taken back a repentant Israel. In the absence of contrition, however, Hosea predicted Israel's destruction.

Both Amos and Hosea preached that to break loose from God spelled annihilation. Deaf to the prophets and content without Yahweh and his demands, Israel rushed headlong into the fire.

Read and Recall

Read Amos 2:6–16. Notice that the formal opening of the prophecy repeats the opening of the preceding prophecies to the seven neighboring countries. Sum-

Verse 16 predicts the humiliation of being conquered. The victorious nations sometimes had their captives march naked.

marize the general form of the prophecy to Israel. Also read Hosea 2:15–22, 11:1–4. These passages are beautiful expressions of God's love for his people. Select the lines that appeal to you most.

1. What crimes of Israel did Amos and Hosea condemn?
2. How were Amos and Hosea the same? Different?
3. How did Amos and Hosea offer hope to the unfaithful Israelites?

Reflect

1. How are "Sunday Catholics" like the Israelites rebuked by Amos and Hosea? What attitudes can you cultivate to keep from becoming one of them?
2. What new meaning does the "Day of the Lord" have for Christians? Is it closer to the original meaning or to Amos's meanings?
3. Some people view the God of the Old Testament as a God of fear and the God of the New Testament as the God of Love. How would you refute this?
4. Why is evil so enticing to people?
5. If Hosea and Amos were to read today's newspapers, they would find that the human race hasn't changed much. What aspects of contemporary society would anger them?

ISAIAH AND MICAH: AMBASSADORS TO JUDAH
(Isaiah—short passages; Micah 5, 6)

Isaiah, a prophet from the South, attacked the very same evils as did the northern prophets, but from a different standpoint: the transcendence of God.

Transcendence is existence far above and beyond the normal state.

■ What is your conception of God? What is he like? Do you think of him in human terms—that is, just like us, but better?

To Isaiah, God was not merely a superman; he was totally other. God was holy: "As high as the heavens are above the earth, so high are my ways above your

Isaiah 55:9

CALLED BY THE FATHER

ways and my thoughts above your thoughts." The Hebrew word for *holy* means "cut off," separated from anything worldly or bad.

The Book of Isaiah indicates that he was a respected member of the royal court with access to the king. A vision of the holiness of God began Isaiah's career as a prophet. In the light of God's holiness, unfaithfulness and sin were hateful to Isaiah. He attacked the upper classes of Judah, predicting that the nation would be reduced to a remnant because of its pagan habits and immorality.

Isaiah was an adviser to the kings. When Assyria was the world power, however, Judah's King Ahaz ignored Isaiah's warning to have nothing to do with Assyria. Later, King Hezekiah heeded Isaiah's protest against attacking Assyria after Isaiah had demonstrated by walking through Jerusalem barefoot and stripped like a war prisoner. But Isaiah's later prediction that disaster would befall Judah if she opposed Assyria fell on deaf ears. Finally, when Isaiah encouraged Hezekiah to stand firm against Assyria, Judah was spared by a miraculous plague that wiped out Sennacherib's army of 185,000 Assyrians.

■ Did you ever sit down on a chair that collapsed? Did you ever set your alarm for six and have it ring at seven? Did you ever lend something only to have it lost or damaged? These are examples of misplaced confidence. You trusted in something or someone unreliable.

In all Isaiah's involvement in the political scene, he encouraged Israel to depend on the only One who is dependable. He said, "Woe to those . . . who put their trust in chariots . . . but look not to the Holy One of Israel nor seek the Lord!" The writings of Isaiah and of his disciples, including work done by followers known as Second and Third Isaiah, make up the Book of Isaiah.

Isaiah 31:1

Today Isaiah is best known for his Emmanuel prophecies. When Judah was destroyed, Isaiah spoke of a future Davidic king who would bring peace, and because of this prophecy the people were still able to

Chapters 40–55 are believed to be the work of Second Isaiah, and chapters 56–65 are probably from a later period.

hope and believe in God's promise. Isaiah also taught that the tragedies of the Israelites were not a sign that God really didn't exist, but were the result of their failure to believe in God's promises.

Another southern prophet, Micah, from the town of Moresheth, denounced his people more strongly than Isaiah had. Unlike other nations, Israel was to care for the poor, the oppressed, the widows and orphans. Micah promised ruin for Judah because of the social and economic abuses. He summed up what was necessary: "Only to do the right and to love goodness, and to walk humbly with your God." Although it is believed that Micah's words moved King Hezekiah to penitence and reform, Micah predicted doom for the kingdom. But he also anticipated a faithful remnant and a new ruler from Bethlehem.

Micah 6:8

All in all, Isaiah and Micah in the South were no more successful than the northern prophets in halting the avalanche of evil.

Read

As you read the passages in the left-hand column, from Isaiah, match each one with a theme from the right-hand column that is characteristic of him.

1. 11:1–4	a. God eventually will restore his people to happiness.
2. 35:4–6	
3. 5:1–7	b. Only a remnant of Israel will survive.
4. 10:20–22	
5. 3:8–26	c. God is holy.
6. 6:1–9	d. A future Davidic ruler will bring justice and peace.
	e. Judah will be destroyed for its wickedness.
	f. God, who took such good care of Israel, has received nothing in return.

Find verses in Micah 5 and 6 that reflect the same themes.

CALLED BY THE FATHER

Recall

1. What message did Isaiah and Micah deliver for God to Judah?
2. Explain whether or not Isaiah and Micah were successful prophets.
3. In a few words, what is the characteristic theme of Isaiah? Of Micah?

Reflect

1. In Isaiah's first vision, when God asked for a messenger, Isaiah responded, "Send me." What do you think made the difference between his enthusiasm and the reluctance of such other people as Moses or, later on, the prophet Jeremiah?
2. The prophets probably didn't know that passages of theirs referred to a future messiah. Why doesn't this detract from their reputation as prophets?
3. Although God is transcendent, the prophets assured the people that he was also immanent—that is, very near to them. When would it be good to concentrate on God's transcendence? On his immanence?
4. A visitor talking to Lincoln said, "Let us have faith, Mr. President, that the Lord is on our side in this great struggle." Lincoln replied, "My constant anxiety and prayer is that we are on the Lord's side." How does Lincoln's response apply to Israel and Judah during the time of the prophets?
5. What does Micah 6:8 mean when it says, "Walk humbly with your God"?
6. Why is it dangerous to make God in our image or to suggest solutions to him for our problems?
7. What are five things you can trust God for today in the spirit of Isaiah?

GETTING IT TOGETHER

A story tells about a sparrow lying on its back in the road. A horseman stopped and asked him why he was lying there. "I heard the heavens are going to fall," replied the sparrow. "Oh," said the horseman, "do you really think your spindly legs can hold up the heavens?" "One does what one can," said the sparrow.

The prophets were like this valiant sparrow: they did what they could when the odds were against them. They fought the corruption that made Israel easy prey for Assyria and Babylon. Elijah confronted hundreds of Baal's prophets and singlehandedly revealed them as fake. In the North, Amos and Hosea denounced the rich for oppressing the poor. In the South, Isaiah and Micah attacked immorality. Even at the zero hour God would gladly have forgiven Israel, but she stubbornly clung to her evil ways. Thus the prophets predicted only bad news: the Day of the Lord.

Through the gloomy picture painted by the prophets, a glimmer of hope shone out: Israel could look forward to a new King of Judah, one whose reign of peace and justice would have no end.

This king who came was also a prophet. He challenged people to work for improvement. Robert Kennedy once said, "Each time a man stands up for an ideal, or acts to improve the lot of others, or strikes out against an injustice, he sends forth a tiny ripple of hope. And crossing each other from a million different centers of energy and daring, these ripples build a current that can sweep down the mightiest walls of oppression and resistance."

As a follower of Christ, you are called to bring about his kingdom by influencing the world around you. The prophets, working separately, were able to make it happen together and saved the faith of Israel. Christians could cause a good revolution if each one would take up Christ's challenge. But, Robert Kennedy continued, "Moral courage is a rarer commodity than bravery in battle on great intelligence. Yet it is the one essential vital quality for those who seek to change a world that yields most painfully to change."

CALLED BY THE FATHER

REVIEWING THE CHAPTER

Linking Your Ideas

1. Make a chart listing each prophet in this chapter, the time and place of his message, his chief characteristics, and his themes.
2. Explain how the national fortunes and the religious fidelity of the Israelites went hand in hand during this period.
3. Choose a contemporary problem and write a statement from each prophet that reveals how he would characteristically react to the problem. Possible topics: the arms race, economic problems, unemployment, widows, orphans, refugees, the unborn, senior citizens, the disabled, race relations.

Strengthening Your Grasp

1. Put yourself in the shoes of a prophet. What would be the hardships of your life? Your joys?
2. Think of contemporary persons who are doing the work of a prophet. What is their goal? What obstacles do they encounter? How do different groups react to them? Why are they doing what they do?
3. Find modern folk songs that are related to prophetic themes.
4. Some people look at things through rose-colored glasses. Other people are blind to certain problems. Someone with prophetic vision sees things as God sees them. Write a news commentary by a prophet that focuses on a couple of world events or world conditions today.

Expressing Your Convictions

Prophets saw work for the poor as work for God and his people. How can you help the poor? In an essay, discuss the pros and cons of your present opportunities to put your faith into action.

Extending Your Interest

1. Ask various religious organizations which social-justice activities they engage in. Report or chart your findings.
2. Interview the people in your parish who are behind activities of social justice.

TEN

JEREMIAH AND EZEKIEL

Voices in Exile

Sections

Jeremiah: The Martyr Prophet
   Jeremiah 1–42
Ezekiel: The Mystic Prophet
   Ezekiel 34:1–5, 34:11–15, 36:25–31, 37:1–14

My God, my God, why have you forsaken me,
   far from my prayer, from the words of my cry?
O my God, I cry out by day, and you answer not;
   by night, and there is no relief for me. . . .
Be not far from me, for I am in distress;
   be near, for I have no one to help me.

PSALM 22:2–3, 12

The days are coming, says the Lord, when I will make a new covenant with the house of Israel and the house of Judah.

JEREMIAH 31:31

CHAPTER PREVIEW

Pompeii, Sidon, Hiroshima, Jerusalem—what do these cities have in common? Pompeii was destroyed when the volcano Mount Vesuvius erupted, Sodom was destroyed by an earthquake and fire, Hiroshima was destroyed by the atomic bomb, and Jerusalem was destroyed by the Babylonians.

After Assyria had destroyed the Northern Kingdom, it made Judah a vassal state, but soon Assyria was engaged in a power struggle with Egypt, Babylon, and the Medes. When the Assyrian empire collapsed, the rival powers prepared to take Judah as part of the spoils. First Egypt conquered Judah. Then Nebuchadnezzar of Babylon fought both Egypt and Judah. The invasion of the Babylonians and the destruction of Jerusalem in 587 B.C. ended Judah's independence. Thus the holy city the Israelites had thought was guaranteed to last forever was no more. Even worse, they were taken from the Promised Land and exiled in Babylon.

Onto this scene of doubt and confusion came a pair of prophets who declared that the catastrophe was the result of Israel's failure to keep the Covenant and to

The Babylonian Captivity ended almost fifty years later, in 538 B.C.

Josiah had the people renew the Covenant. He cleansed the country of pagan cities, reinstated the feast of Passover, and repaired the Temple.

obey God's prophets. Because of Jeremiah and Ezekiel, the people in exile retained their religious convictions and their longing for their homeland.

Jeremiah's career as a prophet spanned the reigns of five Judean kings. The first of these, Josiah, undertook a religious reform supported by Jeremiah and spurred on by the discovery of the long-lost Book of Deuteronomy in the Temple. This renewal was short-lived, however. Another king, Joakim, was violently against Jeremiah, and the last king, Zedekiah, was too weak to oppose the nobles and support Jeremiah.

Jeremiah's vocation was not at all to his own liking. He was so tormented and persecuted during his ministry that he is known as "the man of sorrows." He was unpopular because he said that the Jews should be resigned to their Babylonian conquerors. King Zedekiah temporarily silenced Jeremiah by imprisoning him, and then he formed an alliance with Egypt against Babylon. This act led to the destruction of Jerusalem.

The remainder of Jeremiah's life was spent calling to repentance the Israelites who had fled to Egypt, taking him with them against his will. He prophesied that the end of Jerusalem was not the end of the people. According to legend, Jeremiah was stoned to death by his own people.

Ezekiel was called to prophesy while in exile. The Babylonian conquest came in two waves. First the king and about forty-seven hundred of the leaders of the country were deported. Then Jerusalem was leveled and the people as a whole were taken into captivity. Ezekiel, being of a priestly family, was exiled in the first deportation.

Like Jeremiah, Ezekiel warned of the approaching fall of Jerusalem. After it occurred, he restored hope by prophesying a new temple, a new covenant, a new king, and a new Jerusalem.

Ezekiel also predicted that the Israelites would be given a "new heart" and that they would confess their faith by means of tradition and law. Because he emphasized law and ritual, Ezekiel is sometimes called the founder of Judaism.

CALLED BY THE FATHER

Under the prophets, the Exile became a healthy purge that gave direction to Jewish faith and religion. During this time the Israelites re-edited the historical books of the Bible, preserved the sayings of the prophets, collected the priestly code, and developed the priestly theology of the history of the world. Thus out of catastrophe came new insights and deeper wisdom.

- Disaster and failure are never easy. What attitudes can you develop toward suffering that would contribute to your mental health and holiness?
- In your journal, draw up a list of things to remember when times are hard.

Words to Know

Jeremiah (jer-eh-**mi**-eh), Judaism (**ju**-dee-izm), Ezekiel (eh-**ze**-kee-ul), Baruch (**bear**-uhk), Josiah (jo-**zi**-eh), anawim (**ah**-neh-wim), Zedekiah (zed-eh-**ki**-eh)

JEREMIAH: THE MARTYR PROPHET
(Jeremiah 1–42)

Jeremiah's life was given over to doing God's will; being a witness was his top priority. From his call to be a prophet (probably at the age of eighteen) until his death, he risked all, even personal happiness, for God's cause.

First, Jeremiah's message was painful because he had to foretell disaster for the people, the Temple, and the country he loved. Second, Jeremiah suffered like Saint Paul: he was scourged, put in stocks, and imprisoned for the sake of God's Word. Furthermore, Jeremiah's personal life was so tied up with his prophetic role that it was marked by tragedy and disappointment. When Jeremiah exhorted his people to turn from their evil ways, they mocked him. When he advised them to submit to the Babylonians and later to settle down in Exile, he was branded a defeatist and a traitor. When he warned the Jews not to flee to Egypt, they not only went but took him with them.

It was as though all the world were singing in the key of C and God had Jeremiah singing in B flat. Never-

theless, through all the unpleasantness, physical suffering, and mental anguish, Jeremiah was faithful. In the Book of Jeremiah, passages known as Jeremiah's "confessions" reveal his despair as well as his belief in the need for perseverance and faith in God.

Basically, the Book of Jeremiah is a collection of speeches Jeremiah dictated to his friend and secretary, Baruch. (Baruch probably added the bibliographical sections.) The Book of Lamentations is a collection of laments, or expressions of grief, about the sad state of Jerusalem. This book, too, is attributed to Jeremiah.

Jeremiah introduced new ideas into Jewish theology. The concept that religion is a personal affair between God and the individual originated with him. The family would not be punished for the crimes of one member as before. No more would sons be cursed for the sins of their fathers. Jeremiah also taught that salvation was not for the proud and powerful but for the *anawim*, the poor and lowly who relied on his help.

CALLED BY THE FATHER

Jeremiah is known as the Prophet of the Covenant. It was his mission to revive the spirit of the Covenant and to predict a new one in place of the broken Sinai covenant. In this new covenant, external actions were less important than the sincerity of one's heart.

But Jeremiah's strongest message was the one portrayed by his life. For fifty years he was a martyr, God's suffering servant, and as such he is a type of Christ. The Church applies to Christ many words that Jeremiah used of himself. After Jeremiah's death, his stature increased. His influence is felt in the New Testament, where he is referred to and quoted. Today he is considered a prophet and a member of the quartet of major prophets: Isaiah, Jeremiah, Ezekiel, and Daniel.

Sometimes the Lamentations of Jeremiah are chanted during Holy Week.

Read and Recall

Read these verses from Jeremiah and prepare a profile of the prophet: 1:1–10, 7:1–7, 8:23, 10:1–7, 10:10–14, 16:1–4, 16:14–15, 17:1–8, 20:8–15, 28:1–8, 29:4–15, 31:31, 36:20–26, 38:4–6, 42:19–43:7. Include his hometown, his response to God's call, his message, his life style, his attitude toward his role, the people's reaction to him, the fate of his prophecies, the end of his life.

Reflect

1. It is not easy to "go against the tide" and do what you know is right. Where did Jeremiah get his courage? How can you prepare for such occasions?
2. How is Jeremiah a type of Christ?
3. Jeremiah complained to God about his frustrating job. What does this reveal about him? About his relationship with God?
4. In the Book of Jeremiah, God deals with people more on a one-to-one basis than as a community. What does this mean? How does he work to save us today?
5. At what points did Jeremiah have to exercise deep faith? When might you be called upon to demonstrate similar faith? How would the sacrament of Confirmation be a help to you in such a situation?

SYMBOLIC ACTIONS

In the 1960s, to make a point at a United Nations meeting, Soviet premier Nikita Khrushchev took off his shoe and pounded the table with it. Harold Macmillan, the British prime minister, turned to an interpreter and said, "I would like a translation of that." Khrushchev's dramatic action really needed no translation. Moreover, it made a strong impression on the people present as well as on the millions watching the scene on TV.

■ How have you used actions that enabled you to speak louder than words?

Symbolic actions were frequently used to convey prophetic messages. During Solomon's reign, the prophet Abijah informed Jeroboam of the division of the kingdom with a dramatic action. He took his own new coat, tore it into twelve pieces, and offered ten of them to Jeroboam, the future king of the northern tribes.

See 1 Kings 11:29–37.

Jeremiah and Ezekiel continued to prophesy in this audiovisual tradition. The major messages and their manner of presentation are listed here.

Decay and Uselessness of Judah

A *loincloth* is material a man drapes around his waist.

Jeremiah bought and wore a loincloth, and then hid it in a cleft of a rock. After a time it became rotten (Jeremiah 13:1–11).

Destruction of City and Temple

Jeremiah dashed an earthern flask to the ground (Jeremiah 19:1–11). Ezekiel drew a map of Jerusalem on a clay tablet and acted out the siege of the city (Ezekiel 4:1–3).

Ezekiel cut his hair and beard with a sword. Then he burned a third of it in fire, hit a third with his sword, and strewed the last third in the wind and chased it with his sword. This signified that some people would die of hunger and disease, some would be killed, and the rest would be scattered and pursued (Ezekiel 5:1–11).

Ezekiel did not mourn or weep at the death of his beloved wife (Ezekiel 24:15–23).

Exile

Ezekiel took his baggage outside during the day and at night he dug a hole in the wall of Jerusalem and went out (Ezekiel 12:1–16).

Submission to Babylon

Jeremiah made a yoke and wore it himself in front of the people (Jeremiah 27:1–3).

A *yoke* is a crossbar with two U-shaped pieces that encircle the necks of animals used for work. It is a symbol of slavery.

The Restoration After the Exile

Jeremiah bought real estate in Anathoth of Judah (Jeremiah 32:6–13).

Ezekiel took two sticks. He marked one "Judah and related Israelites" and the other "Ephraim and related Israelites." Then he joined the sticks together to make one (Ezekiel 37:15–22).

Visual images did much to heighten the message of God to his people, but not enough. The Israelites were not only deaf but blind to the truth.

- When did Christ, the greatest prophet, use symbolic action? When does the Church use it to enrich her liturgy and the lives of her members?

A *mystic* is a person who aims at union with God through deep meditation.

An angel spoke to Saint Joseph in a dream (Matthew 1:20, 2:13); Saint Peter had a vision which revealed that salvation is also for gentiles (Acts 11:1–18); Daniel interpreted dreams (Daniel 2:24–30).

EZEKIEL: THE MYSTIC PROPHET
(Ezekiel 34:1–5, 34:11–15, 36:25–31, 37:1–14)

There are some occurrences in everyday life that cannot be explained by known laws. The word of psychic powers or extrasensory perception (ESP) is a mysterious, unexplored field of science. In God's dealings with people, he communicates through ordinary means, such as dreams and thoughts, or through extraordinary means, such as visions and mystical trances.

■ Did you ever dream something that later came true? Tell about it.

Of all the prophets, Ezekiel was the most unusual. He was a colorful person whose imagination was constantly on fire. His strange experiences and seemingly

CALLED BY THE FATHER

strange personality are still puzzling. No one knows if the events in his book were normal psychic experiences, supernatural experiences, or literary devices. In any case, God used this person to make his will known. The Spirit took Ezekiel as he was and made use of him just as a flute player breathes into a flute to produce sound.

Ezekiel the priest became Ezekiel the prophet while in exile in Babylon. He had a mystical vision of God's majesty similar to Isaiah's vision, but more spectacular. In it he saw winged creatures with human bodies, each with the face of man, a lion, an ox, and an eagle on different sides of its head. They stood beside sparkling wheels that could turn in any direction. Above these, Ezekiel envisioned God in human form seated on a sapphire throne.

The faces represented the highest forms of these creatures; they were later adopted as symbols for the four evangelists—Matthew, Mark, Luke, and John.

In this marvelous trance, God commissioned Ezekiel to speak to the rebellious house of Israel and warned him that the task would be like sitting on scorpions. Ezekiel showed his willingness to deliver God's nourishing word by eating a scroll containing the words "Lamentation and wailing and woe." How did the word of God taste? It was as sweet as honey.

A *scorpion* is a spiderlike creature with a poisonous sting.

To foretell the collapse of Jerusalem and the Exile, Ezekiel was commanded to perform bizarre symbolic actions. For instance, he was told to lie on his left side

for three hundred ninety days to bear Israel's sins and on his right side for forty days for Judah's sins. In addition, Ezekiel was led by an angel through a series of visions. In one of them Ezekiel saw God leaving the Temple in Jerusalem in the same form in which he had seen him in the first vision.

Ezekiel used a variety of scorching images to condemn Israel for its infidelity: a faithless spouse, a withered tree, dry land, rust on a pot. But the prophet also predicted punishment for Israel's foes: one after another, Israel's neighbors would be doomed. The reason for God's harsh action is stated no fewer than seventy times in Ezekiel: "You shall know that I am the Lord."

■ What excuse for wrongdoing do you find yourself using most? Everybody's doing it? That's the way I was brought up? The devil made me do it?

CALLED BY THE FATHER

Like Jeremiah, Ezekiel emphasized personal responsibility. Each person would be judged for his or her own offenses. Faith was between an individual and God.

Although Ezekiel condemned, he also consoled. The book ends with visions of a new Israel, a new law, a new temple, and a new city. The sign of the new people, according to Ezekiel, was fidelity to the Law. More than any other prophet, Ezekiel stressed tradition and law, promoting the Sabbath, circumcision, and ritual cleanliness. But Ezekiel also echoed Jeremiah's teaching that faith was an affair of the heart, not a dead formalism. Finally, Ezekiel had a vision of the glory of the Lord re-entering the Temple. The name of the new city Ezekiel described was "The Lord is here."

Jewish laws governed the cleanliness of utensils, food, and persons. People who touched a corpse, ate meat with blood in it, were lepers, or had sexual relations were considered "unclean" until they performed a cleansing ritual.

Read and Recall

Read these popular passages from the Book of Ezekiel, which show God acting to renew his people: 34:1–6, 34:11–15, 36:25–31, 37:1–14. Each is based on a particular image. Tell what the image is and why it is appropriate.

1. How did Ezekiel receive his call to be a prophet?
2. What aspects of Ezekiel's prophecies make them very colorful?
3. Did Ezekiel condemn or console God's people? Explain.

Reflect

1. The Israelites looked on the possibility of the destruction of Jerusalem the way some people today think of a nuclear war: it will probably never happen. What danger lies in this attitude?
2. Why does God ask hard things of certain people?
3. Ezekiel's vision of God's majesty sustained him when life became difficult. What other people have had an experience that they could always recall to help them persevere? What memories do you have of God acting in your life?
4. Where else is the shepherd theme found in Scripture?

5. What is the role of the Spirit in the parable of the dry bones? Where else does the Spirit bring forth life in the Bible? In the Church?

GETTING IT TOGETHER

You might ask, "Why read Jeremiah and Ezekiel? They were men of their times. I'm not an Israelite." True, these two prophets served a purpose in Israel's history. They advised kings and rebuked the citizens for their sins. During the suffering of the Exile they offered hope for Israel by means of a new vision. More than this, though, the fact that their writings are in Scripture—God's word for all time—means that they have a message for all people, including you.

■ How do you feel when you realize you've been "used" by someone?

Most people resent being manipulated by others. An exception is when God is the user, for then being used is a privilege. Both Jeremiah and Ezekiel are models for putting your life at God's disposal. Merely to admire the long-suffering Jeremiah and to marvel at the strange Ezekiel is not enough. Their cooperation with God in shaping his kingdom calls for imitation. They are saints of the Hebrew Scriptures.

Another fact that makes Jeremiah and Ezekiel relevant is that their words are eternal. They told of the God of the Israelites, who is the God of Christians as well. They revealed that he is a loving God of faithfulness who keeps his promises, and that he is the one mighty God who asks for undivided loyalty and obedience. Most of all, they led the Israelites into a new dimension of faith where God made known his personal love for each individual. The "I–Thou" relationship between God and a person, described by Jeremiah and Ezekiel, was intensified with the coming of Jesus Christ. Now every one of us can say with Saint Paul, "God . . . loved me and gave himself up for me."

REVIEWING THE CHAPTER

Linking Your Ideas

1. How did the messages of Jeremiah and Ezekiel overlap?
2. Show from the lives of these two men that being a prophet is no easy task.
3. Write a letter from Jeremiah to Ezekiel or from Ezekiel to Jeremiah, cleverly including what you have learned about them.

Strengthening Your Grasp

1. Read the following psalms and note which aspects of this period of Jewish history they refer to: Psalms 42, 74, 79, 126, and 137.
2. Like Jesus, Ezekiel taught in parables. The people said of him, "Is not this the one who is forever spinning parables?" (Ezekiel 21:5). Choose one of the six parables in Ezekiel 15, 16:1–43, 16:44–63, 17, 19, and 23 and explain its message.
3. How would prophets today communicate their message to people? What images and symbolic actions would they use?
4. Why would the *anawim* (the poor and lowly) be the ones to be saved?
5. Draw dramatic scenes from the life of either Jeremiah or Ezekiel.

Expressing Your Convictions

Both Jeremiah and Ezekiel disturbed people's smugness and revealed their mediocrity. They declared that God desired his people's whole hearts. This is stated in strong language in the last book of the Bible: "Because you are lukewarm, neither hot nor cold, I will spew you out of my mouth!" (Revelation 3:16). In a composition, explain how this deadening mediocrity can creep into your life. Discuss its causes, symptoms, and cures.

Extending Your Interest

Jeremiah, Ezekiel, and all the prophets counseled Israel so that it would be not just a nation, but a holy people. Rudyard Kipling was a British poet, not a prophet, but he wrote a prophetic poem called "If," a blueprint for developing into a mature human being. Read it and select the piece of advice you consider most valuable for you. Then write an "If" poem for girls modeled on Kipling's "If" for boys.

ELEVEN

SECOND ISAIAH, NEHEMIAH, EZRA, MACCABEES

Call to Renewal

Sections

Isaiah: The Innovator
   Isaiah 40–66
Nehemiah and Ezra: The Renovators
   Nehemiah 8:1–9; Ezra 9:1–10:15
The Maccabees: Champions of Judaism
   1 Maccabees 2:1–30, 4:36–59; 2 Maccabees 7:1–6, 7:18–40

*Our Father who art in heaven, hallowed be thy
name. Thy kingdom come; thy will be done on
earth as it is in heaven. Give us this day our daily
bread and forgive us our trespasses as we forgive
those who trespass against us. And lead us not into
temptation, but deliver us from evil. For thine is
the kingdom and the power and the glory, now
and forever. Amen.*

> As a mother comforts her son, so will I comfort you.
>
> ISAIAH 66:13

CHAPTER PREVIEW

Toward the end of the Exile, a prophet known only as Second Isaiah foretold the return of the Israelites to their homeland. He consoled them by announcing that the time of punishment and penance was almost ended: the one true God would re-enact the Exodus and bring them to a new and glorious city. This dream came true when the Persians conquered the Babylonians and the Persian king, Cyrus, allowed the Israelites to return to Jerusalem in 538 B.C. The Israelites then anticipated an age when Yahweh would establish Jerusalem (Zion) as a universal empire.

He is named after Isaiah because he wrote in the spirit of that great prophet.

■ Recall an occasion when you had to redo a project. Perhaps you lost your composition and had to write it over, or maybe your dog chewed up your entry for a science fair and you had to begin again. How did starting over compare with the first time you undertook the task?

Back in Jerusalem, however, the dream turned into a nightmare. Not every exile returned to Palestine, and

Sixteen years later, the total Jewish population of Judah was not much more than twenty thousand people, who were sprinkled over a strip of land twenty-five miles from north to south.

making a living was easier in the fertile land of Babylon than in rocky Palestine. The tiny remnant in Jerusalem faced the task of rebuilding a city. Furthermore, both nature and their neighbors worked against them. Most disheartening, the Persian Empire was growing, threatening Israel's independence.

The work on the Temple proceeded slowly and was then abandoned. Two prophets, Haggai and Zechariah, took advantage of the troubles in Persia in 522 B.C. to spur the Israelites on to finish the Temple by reminding them of their destiny to be a light to all nations. In 515 B.C. the Temple stood completed, thanks to the money and protection of the Persians under King Darius.

It wasn't until a hundred years after the first exiles returned to Jerusalem that the city walls were rebuilt. The King of Persia authorized Nehemiah, a Jew, for the task and appointed him governor. Although beset by problems, Nehemiah not only fortified the province of Judah but also began a reform that gave Judah political status and an honest administration.

Whereas Nehemiah reorganized Judah's secular life, it fell to Ezra the priest to reform its spiritual life. The discouragement of the people had given rise to religious and moral laxity. The King of Persia empowered Ezra to enforce the sacred Law. Ezra began by reading to the

CALLED BY THE FATHER

people from the Book of the Law. Then they joined in a covenant that bound them to live by the Law, which was Israel's constitution, and became a community of the Law. It was their faithfulness to the Mosaic law that would bind the Jewish people together no matter how scattered they were.

Little is known about Israel during the two hundred and fifty years after Nehemiah, beyond the fact that it existed under foreign rule until a rebellion in 165 B.C. won a temporary independence. During these "dark ages" Israel passed from the rule of the Persians to that of Alexander the Great, who considered it his mission to spread Greek culture. Many Jews emigrated to Egypt, where Alexandria became a center of Jewry.

At Alexander's death, his generals divided his empire. Rule in Palestine transferred from the Ptolemies of Egypt to the Seleucid kings of Syria in 200 B.C. Under Antiochus IV, the Jews faced a new crisis.

Antiochus promoted the worship of the Greek gods and plundered the Jewish Temple. When the Jews resisted his attempts to identify Yahweh and himself with Zeus, Antiochus forbade all practice of Judaism. Many Jews were tortured and put to death for refusing to comply. In 167 B.C., Antiochus ordered that swine be offered to Zeus, whose idol had been erected on their altar in the Temple. To the Jews this was detestable.

Antiochus named himself Epiphanes, which means "the god manifest." He appears on coins in the likeness of Zeus, the chief god of the Greeks.

The sacrifice was horrible because the Jews considered pigs and pork unclean. They called the act an "abomination of desolation."

This persecution was a low point in Jewish history, but it rallied flagging spirits and called forth some of Israel's most famous military heroes, the Maccabees. Mattathias and his five sons began a guerrilla war against the Seleucids and traitorous Jews. Under the third son, Judas, nicknamed Maccabeus (the hammer), the enemy was defeated and the Temple rededicated. The feast of Hanukkah commemorates this event.

■ The Israelites were forced to look to Yahweh for strength in times of distress: during the Exile, the restoration, and the persecutions. Make a list of your worries and problems. Check each one that you have prayed about specifically by name. Your checkmarks indicate how much you are relying on God and his love for you.

Hanukkah, the Feast of Light, lasts for eight days in December. Tradition says that there was enough oil in the Temple lamp for only one day. By a miracle it burned eight days, until new oil could be made. Each night of Hanukkah a candle is lit in the Jewish nine-branch candelabra (menorah). The center candle is used to light the others.

Words to Know

Second Isaiah, Zerubabbel (zer-**u**-bub-el), Ezra, Nehemiah (nee-heh-**mi**-eh) Maccabees (**mak**-ah-beez), Antiochus IV (an-tee-**ohk**-us), Epiphanes (eh-pi-**fane**-us), Hasmonaeon (has-**mon**-ee-un)

ISAIAH: THE INNOVATOR
(Isaiah 40–66)

Isaiah 48:6

Second Isaiah, the great unknown who authored chapters 40 to 55 and influenced chapters 56 to 66, declared, "From now on I announce new things to you." One of the startling new things found in his writing is the concept of servanthood. This concept blends well with the dominant theme of Second Isaiah, which appears in his opening verse: "Comfort, give comfort to my people, says your God." Second Isaiah's book is known as the Book of Consolation.

Isaiah 40:1

Isaiah explained that it was the meek and humble servants of the Lord—those who suffered and sacrificed without complaining—who carried out the divine plan. The idea of Israel serving God by suffering gave meaning to the trials of the Jews in exile.

The Servant Songs are 42:1–9, 49:1–7, 50:4–11, and 52:13–53:12.

The "suffering servant" is described in four poems Isaiah called the Servant Songs. No one knows exactly to whom they were meant to refer. Perhaps they per-

sonified Israel. The Apostles saw them as descriptions of Christ, who achieved glory through suffering and death. For instance, they recognized the crucified Christ in these words: "I gave my back to those who beat me, my cheeks to those who plucked my beard; my face I did not shield from buffets and spitting." These prophecies opened up the new understanding that salvation comes through suffering.

Isaiah 50:6

Isaiah harkened back to the Exodus to confirm that Yahweh would love and save his Chosen People, and he foretold a new exodus. Cyrus, the conqueror of the Babylonians and the one who had freed the Jews, was a tool God would use to lead them again to their Promised Land. When their time of purification was completed, they would travel from slavery to freedom, from death to life. But salvation would have a new twist, according to Isaiah. God was king of the gentiles, too, and in creating a new heaven and a new earth, God would extend his salvation to all people. It was Israel's task to be a light to all people and to all nations.

A *gentile* is a non-Jew.

Along with his fresh ideas, Second Isaiah repeated in a vigorous and beautiful way the theme of monotheism: Yahweh is one God and the only God. He is the all-powerful Creator and no image will ever represent him.

Monotheism is the belief in only one God.

The Book of Isaiah is referred to in the New Testament more than any other Old Testament book. This is logical because Isaiah stood on the threshold of a new era. His writings prepared for the interpretation of the supreme saving act of God in Christ. God in Jesus Christ would experience an exodus from death to life in his dying and rising.

In the Acts of the Apostles (8:36–40) an Ethiopian was reading one of the Servant Songs (Isaiah 53:7). The deacon Philip used it to lead into the explanation of Jesus, which in turn led to the pagan's baptism.

Read and Recall

Tell which key ideas are repeated in these consoling verses from Isaiah: 40:31, 43:1, 43:3–5, 49:15–16, 60:19, 62:5, 64:7.

1. What new notions are in Second Isaiah? What old notions?
2. How did Yahweh console his people through Isaiah?

THE MESSIAHS AND THE MESSIAH

Every so often someone announces: "The end of the world is near! The Messiah is coming!" Awaiting a messiah is a very old pastime.

The hope for a messiah is one of the themes of the Hebrew Scriptures. In the story of the garden of paradise, there is a hint of a promised savior (Genesis 3:15). God's blessing was promised to the world through the patriarchs and their descendants, particularly the tribe of Judah. When the prophet Nathan spoke of an eternal dynasty for David of Judah, some Israelites began to hope for a royal messiah to establish God's reign on earth. Some people expected two messiahs—one military, one spiritual. The core of Israel's belief, then, was faith in Yahweh's will to save his people by direct intervention in their history.

Christians believe that Jesus, the promised Savior, has come—not the military conqueror but the one who, shedding no blood but his own, conquered evil and won eternal life. Early Christians spiritualized the Jewish notion of kingship, teaching that Jesus was the very

Jesus himself avoided raising false hopes of his political leadership.

Son of God whose full messiahship would be revealed only at his Second Coming.

After the resurrection, the evangelists drew upon the Hebrew Scriptures to express their belief that Jesus was indeed Lord and Christ.

Following are some Old Testament passages used by the evangelist to announce Jesus's messiahship. What events of Christ's life do they suggest? Read the New Testament passages that are cited to see how the Old and New Testaments complement each other.

Birth of the Messiah

"The virgin shall be with child, and bear a son, and shall name him Emmanuel." (Isaiah 7:14)

"A shoot shall sprout from the stump of Jesse." (Isaiah 11:1)

Jesse was David's father.

"A child is born to us, a son is given us; . . . They name him . . . Prince of Peace. His dominion is vast and forever peaceful, from David's throne." (Isaiah 9:5–6)

"But you, Bethlehem-Ephrathah . . . from you shall come forth for me one who is to be ruler in Israel." (Micah 5:1)

"All from Sheba shall come bearing gold and frankincense, and proclaiming the praises of the Lord." (Isaiah 60:6)

Life and Mission of the Messiah

"Lo, I am sending my messenger to prepare the way before me." (Malachi 3:1—referred to in Matthew 3:3)

"The root of Jesse . . . the Gentiles shall seek out." (Isaiah 11:10)

"The spirit of the Lord is upon me, because the Lord has anointed me; he has sent me to bring glad tidings to the lowly, to heal the brokenhearted, to proclaim liberty to the captives and release to the prisoners." (Isaiah 61:1—referred to in Luke 4:18–21)

"He shall judge the poor with justice, and decide aright for the land's afflicted . . . and with the breath of his lips he shall slay the wicked." (Isaiah 11:4)

"Then will the eyes of the blind be opened, the ears of the deaf be cleared; . . . then the tongue of the dumb will sing." (Isaiah 35:5, 6—referred to in Matthew 11:3–6)

Death of the Messiah

"Shout for joy, O daughter Jerusalem! See, your king shall come to you; a just savior is he, meek, and riding on an ass." (Zechariah 9:9)

"Like a lamb led to the slaughter . . . he was silent and opened not his mouth." (Isaiah 53:7)

"The Lord said to me, 'Throw it in the treasury, the handsome price at which they valued me.' So I took the thirty pieces of silver and threw them." (Zechariah 11:13)

"He was pierced for our offenses, crushed for our sins; . . . by his stripes we were healed." (Isaiah 53:5)

"My God, my God, why have you forsaken me?" (Psalm 22:2—referred to in Matthew 27:46)

Reflect

1. Does suffering, especially on the part of the innocent, have meaning? How can it be given meaning?
2. Why do you think God chose the Israelites rather than another people to bring salvation to the world?
3. How does God comfort and console his people today? How have you experienced it?
4. What does being a servant involve? In Mark 10:45, why does Christ say, "The Son of Man has not come to be served but to serve"? When does he serve? How can you imitate Christ in his servanthood?

NEHEMIAH AND EZRA: THE RENOVATORS
(Nehemiah 8:1–9; Ezra 9:1–10:15)

A *renovator* is one who renews or restores something.

Even though you have the best intentions, sometimes you slow down or even go backward in your progress as a Christian. You constantly have to be recharged or redirected because the unavoidable challenges of living make you frustrated, discouraged, or just plain tired. When this happens, it is good to have someone give you a little push toward the ideals you hold in your heart.

■ Write down the names of three persons who have helped you by being good Christians. On how many lists of other Christians would your name appear?

The odds against the exiles who returned to Jerusalem were such that they accomplished little during the first century of their homecoming. Crop failures, poverty, hostile neighbors, and opposition from the Jews who had not been in Exile—especially the Samaritans—dampened their spirits. Furthermore, since the Persian Empire was being extended into Egypt, it seemed that Israel would be controlled by the Persians for a while longer.

Zerubbabel, the governor under whom the Temple was built, refused the help of the Samaritans. This widened the split between the exiled Jews and those who had remained in Samaria. The Samaritans interfered with the building project, and they offered sacrifices at their own temple on Mount Garizim. The Jews saw them as heretics.

In the face of these obstacles, the work of rebuilding the Temple—the bond of unity for the people—slowed and then stopped. At last, at the prodding of the prophets Haggai and Zechariah, and with the support of the Persians, the Judeans completed the Temple in 515 B.C., twenty-three years after their return.

But the people once again lost sight of their obligations and their destiny. They fell into immoral practices and intermarried with the gentiles. Providentially, two men appeared to remedy the situation: Nehemiah and Ezra. Nehemiah, a Jew who was cupbearer to the Persian king, was sent to Jerusalem as governor. He began by rebuilding the city walls, which had been demolished in the war. The walls were put up in record time, even though the former governor of Samaria organized plots to break down Nehemiah's morale. Nehemiah was quick-tempered, opinionated, and too blunt, but he got the job done. His first term as governor lasted twelve years, and he was sent back for a second.

It took fifty-two days to build the walls, according to Scripture. But the historian Josephus wrote that it took two years and four months to complete.

Even though Nehemiah overhauled the political and social situation of Judah, he exercised little influence over the moral and religious life of the nation. About 428 B.C., the scribe-priest Ezra was appointed to enforce the sacred law. He launched his mission by reading the Law to the people all morning from a platform in the public square. He continued this daily during the seven days of the revived Feast of Tabernacles. Fasting, praying, and pleading with much emotion, Ezra prompted the men to divorce their foreign wives. The people then

The Feast of Tabernacles (booths), or Succoth, is a nine-day harvest celebration commemorating the time when the Israelites lived in temporary huts in the desert.

CALLED BY THE FATHER

confessed their sins and sealed a covenant binding themselves to follow the Law. It seemed that, within a year, Ezra had achieved his goal; he had organized the Jewish people around the Law and had given their faith a lasting form. It is Ezra's Judaism that is the religion of the Jewish people today.

Read and Recall

Read Nehemiah 8:1–9 (the reading of the Law) and Ezra 6:2–5 and 10:1–15 (Ezra's rebuke and the people's conversion).

1. What contribution did Nehemiah and Ezra each make to the development of the Jewish people?
2. What physical and spiritual obstacles had to be overcome before the Jews attained the stage of restoration the prophets had predicted?

Reflect

1. How can you provide times of renewal for yourself?
2. Why did the Jews have to divorce their foreign wives? What are some habits that God might ask someone your age to change?
3. It is said that the road to hell is paved with good intentions. What does this mean? What can you do to avoid this road?
4. How can you combat discouragement?

The books of Nehemiah and Ezra may be the last part of first and second Chronicles, which contain Israel's history from Saul to the return from exile.

THE MACCABEES: CHAMPIONS OF JUDAISM
(1 Maccabees 2:1–30, 4:36–59; 2 Maccabees 7:1–6, 18–40)

When the Syrian king, Antiochus IV, tried to unite his empire by decreeing a national religion, he asked for trouble. Many weak Jews, influenced by Greek culture, complied with ordinances outlawing the practice of the Jewish religion. But outraged Jews clung to the faith of their fathers despite punishment and even death.

Sabbath observance and circumcision were punishable by death.

■ To what extent are you willing to fight for what you think is right?

The Maccabee family was joined by the Hasidim (pious ones), who were strongly opposed to the royal edict.

Under the leadership of a family called the Maccabees, the Jews rebelled. The two books of the Maccabees contain a detailed record of the struggle, which won not only religious freedom but political independence for the Israelites. At the death of Mattathias, the original rebel, his son Judas took his place in the conflict. Although it is Judas who was called "Maccabee" (the hammer), the term "Maccabee" was extended to all the family members. Now it refers to any of the Jewish

240

heroes of that period. When Judas was killed in battle, his brother Jonathan assumed the leadership, and when Jonathan was killed, his brother Simon became ruler. Simon was assassinated, but his descendants ruled as priest-kings until the Roman conquest of Palestine put an end to Israel's independence in 63 B.C.

Many traditional Old Testament themes run through 1 Maccabees: Israel is chosen by God, and God is the Israelites' helper; they must worship him alone and abide by his laws. The second book of Maccabees covers roughly the same history, but gives a theological interpretation of the events, including some new ideas: the resurrection of the just, the intercession of the saints for people on earth, and the power of the living to help the dead through prayers and sacrifice. All this is taught by the Catholic Church today. The Church sees herself as composed of three distinct groups that are interdependent: the people in heaven (all saints), the just who die before the Second Coming but do not attain heaven (all souls), and those on earth (all sorts!).

Jonathan also acted as high priest, although he was not of the line of Zadok. Some Jews were angered by this, and yet the practice of combining the role of high priest with king continued throughout the Hasmonean dynasty. (Hasmonean was the Maccabees' family name.)

Catholics accept 1 and 2 Maccabees as inspired books of the Bible but Jews and Protestants do not, because these writings were not on the canon, or original list, of biblical books drawn up by the Jews at the end of the first century.

Read

Read the explanatory note first and then the highlight of the Maccabean period referred to.

Origin: 1 Maccabees 2:1–30. The Maccabees were heroes who helped to liberate and preserve the law. They were in direct contrast to the Jews, who abandoned their religion to follow the Syrians. Eleazar, a Maccabean brother who never ruled, died heroically in battle while attacking an elephant which he thought carried the enemy king.

Jewish Martyrs: 2 Maccabees 7:1–6, 18–40. Second Maccabees includes a description of Jewish heroes much like the stories of the martyrs and saints in the Christian tradition. This is one of them. The Jewish mother and her seven sons refused to eat pork and all of them were murdered.

Rededication of the Temple: 1 Maccabees 4:36–59. The height of insult and an abomination occurred when Antiochus offered swine to Zeus in the holy Temple of Jerusalem. It was a great day when Judas purified the Temple and rededicated it to Yahweh. The Feast of Hanukkah commemorates this event today.

Recall

1. How do 1 and 2 Maccabees recall the Exodus? The Book of Judges?
2. Why was the rededication of the Temple the climax of the revolution?

Reflect

1. What do the teachings of 1 and 2 Maccabees have in common with your beliefs?
2. What do you consider worth dying for?
3. The Temple was a sacred place. What traditions or practices set churches apart as special buildings?
4. The Maccabees disobeyed government laws. Do you know any other group that had done this in conscience? When might you be obliged by your conscience to break government laws?

CALLED BY THE FATHER

5. What has preserved the Jews through the centuries despite bitter persecution?
6. What Church practices are derived from her belief in the afterlife? From her belief in the three divisions of her members and their interdependence?

GETTING IT TOGETHER

The exile of the Jewish people before their restoration was like Lent, which precedes the celebration of Easter: it was a time of turning back to the Lord, for making up for failings, and for renewing faith. The resurrection of the Jews as a people was promised by Second Isaiah in lovely imagery. Through the efforts of Nehemiah, Ezra, and the Maccabees, this promise became a reality when the Jewish nation was brought back to life. In the process, the Jewish people arrived at new insights and a new understanding of their role in salvation. Through their suffering, their servanthood, and their loyalty to the Law, all people would come to know God. The faith of the Jews withstood even bloody persecutions until the Jewish people gave birth to the Messiah, himself a suffering servant.

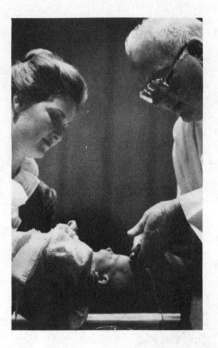

Because of the death and resurrection of Jesus Christ, King of the Jews and Savior of the world, you can hope for resurrection. Through baptism, periods of penance and renewal, and a steadfast loyalty to God in all the challenges of life, you can live forever in a new creation. This is your faith. It is either true, or it isn't. Are you willing to stake your life on it?

REVIEWING THE CHAPTER

Linking Your Ideas

1. Show how each of the following brought about a renewal in the lives of the Jewish people: Second Isaiah, Nehemiah, Ezra, the Maccabees.
2. How did Nehemiah, Ezra, and the Maccabees live the role of the suffering servant?

Strengthening Your Grasp

1. Look up the four Servant Songs (Isaiah 42:1–9, 49:1–7, 50:4–11; 52:13–53:12). List the information each one supplies about the servant of God.
2. Design a poster or card based on one of Isaiah's verses.
3. Find passages in Isaiah 40–55 that speak of the power and the glory of God.

Expressing Your Convictions

1. The Exodus theme recurs in salvation history. Write an essay or poem about it in connection with the escape from Egypt, the restoration, the death and the resurrection of Christ, your own baptism, or death and resurrection.
2. Recall the meaning and purpose of Christian Confirmation. How does it help you to be an Isaiah, an Ezra, a Nehemiah, or a Maccabee? Prepare a slide show or a booklet that illustrates the graces of Confirmation at work in a Christian today.

Extending Your Interest

Do research on the period of the Maccabees. It will help to read some sections of 1 and 2 Maccabees that were not assigned in class: 1 Maccabees 1:41–63, 3:38–4:35, 6:17–63, 7:26–50, 12:1–23, 12:39–13:30, 16:11–24; 2 Maccabees 6:18–31, 12:38–46.

REVIEWING THE UNIT

Patterns

1. God continued to form his people into a holy nation after the split of the kingdom. Explain the tactics he used.
2. Strong, faithful individuals kept the heritage and hope of the Jewish people alive. Who were some of them? What did they accomplish?
3. Show from the parts of the Bible studied in this unit that God desired both love and obedience from his people.
4. What is the significance of each main word in this unit's title?

Focal Points

1. How is the Church today the servant described in Isaiah?
2. Find a key passage from one of the prophets. Practice saying it, and then deliver it to the class in the manner of the prophets.
3. Write an interview with one of the prophets encountered in this unit, or an entry from his diary.
4. Compose a ballad in honor of the Maccabees.
5. Make a poster, banner, collage, sticker, or button that conveys the message of the prophets.

Response

1. Read a song of trust in God in Habakkuk 3:17–19 and then write an updated personal version of it. For instance, "Though I live under the threat of nuclear war . . ."
2. Create a prophetic speech that one of the prophets could deliver to certain people today. What would Amos say to the heads of organized crime? How would Jeremiah advise the president? What would Isaiah say to oppressive governments? How would Ezekiel address the Ku Klux Klan? What would Hosea say to the students in your school?
3. The poor and the weak are favored in God's sight. Refer to both the Old and New Testaments to show this. Who are these people in your neighborhood or school? What should be your response to them? Plan and carry out one project in which you minister to an individual or group who needs help.
4. Write a prayer service around a theme found in the prophets: the call of God, the love of God, the forgiveness of God, the majesty of God, loyalty to God, the Law, justice, the undivided heart.
5. Write an essay telling who your favorite prophet is, and why.

Reflection and Hope: Theologians and Poets

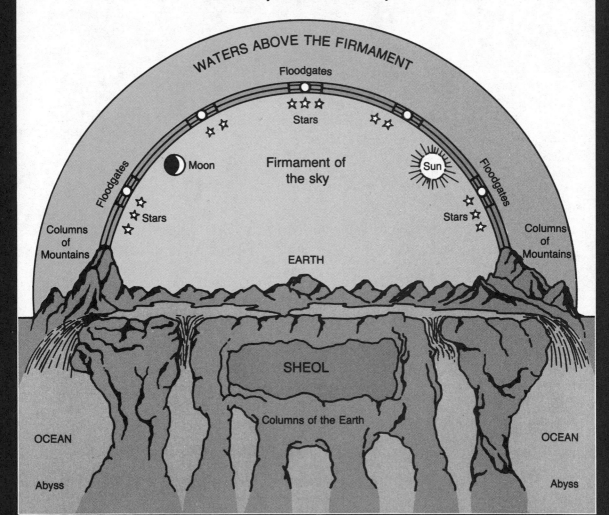

Heavenly Seat of the Divinity

WATERS ABOVE THE FIRMAMENT

Floodgates

Stars

Floodgates

Stars

Moon

Firmament of the sky

Sun

Floodgates

Stars

Columns of Mountains

Columns of Mountains

EARTH

SHEOL

Columns of the Earth

OCEAN

OCEAN

Abyss

Abyss

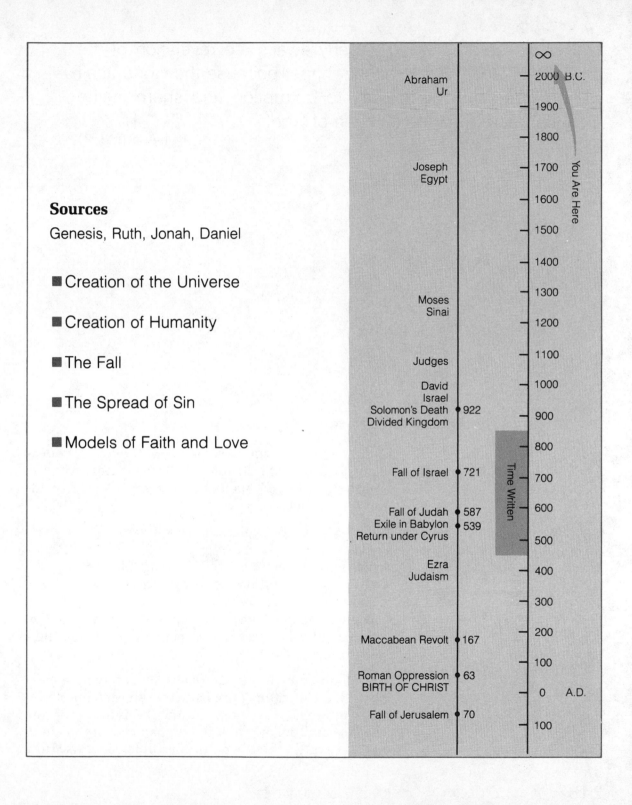

Sources

Genesis, Ruth, Jonah, Daniel

■ Creation of the Universe

■ Creation of Humanity

■ The Fall

■ The Spread of Sin

■ Models of Faith and Love

∞

Abraham
Ur — 2000 B.C.

— 1900

— 1800

You Are Here

Joseph
Egypt — 1700

— 1600

— 1500

— 1400

— 1300

Moses
Sinai — 1200

— 1100

Judges

David — 1000
Israel
Solomon's Death ◆ 922
Divided Kingdom — 900

— 800

Time Written

Fall of Israel ◆ 721 — 700

Fall of Judah ◆ 587 — 600
Exile in Babylon ◆ 539
Return under Cyrus — 500

Ezra — 400
Judaism

— 300

Maccabean Revolt ◆ 167 — 200

— 100

Roman Oppression ◆ 63
BIRTH OF CHRIST — 0 A.D.

Fall of Jerusalem ◆ 70 — 100

The whole created world eagerly awaits the revelation of the children of God . . . not without hope, because the world itself will be freed from its slavery to corruption and share in the glorious freedom of the children of God.

ROMANS 8:19–21

UNIT OVERVIEW

In the days of Solomon, someone in the South endeavored to record the history of the Israelites from the beginning of time. This was an awesome task, considering these facts:

- The Milky Way galaxy is roughly 16 billion years old.
- The earth is about 4.6 billion years old.
- Homo sapien did not appear on the scene until about forty thousand years ago.
- Written records have been kept for only the past five thousand years (less than 1 percent of humankind's existence).

Undaunted by these handicaps, an anonymous Jewish writer, called the Yahwist, wrote an account of prehistoric times. His story of the beginnings of the universe and the origin of the human race are in chapters 2–11 of the first book of the Bible, Genesis. How

If the last 4 billion years of the universe's existence were compressed into one year, human beings would arrive shortly before midnight on December 31, and all of recorded history would occur in the last ninety seconds.

CALLED BY THE FATHER

did he do it? The Yahwist worked with the same source material that other writers of epics used: the oral traditions of the people. Tales about the first man and woman, a great flood, and the beginnings of different tribes were told around Israelite campfires and at tribal gatherings, recited at shrines, and sung by minstrels. As nomads, the Israelites came into contact with other peoples and no doubt swapped stories. Because Abraham originated in Mesopotamia, Genesis is similar to Mesopotamian stories.

■ Are there any stories that have been passed down for generations in your family?

The stories recorded by the Yahwist are known as the J tradition. They speak familiarly of God and as though he had a manlike body. In the sixth century B.C., a version of Israelite history—known as the Elohist, or E, tradition—was composed in the North. In 400 B.C., after the Exile, scribes blended these two traditions and added features from two other traditions: the Deuteronomic (D) from 600–550 B.C. and the Priestly (P) from 500–450 B.C. This piecing together of four traditions

The Yahwist is named for his use of the word *Yahweh* for God. Some think that he was a member of Solomon's court.

The "J" is derived from the German for Yahweh—*Jahweh*.

In the Elohim tradition, God is called by the majestic term *Elohim*.

Four Traditions

TRADITION	CHARACTERISTICS	SUBJECT
Jahwist (J) 850 B.C. (South)	Uses "Yahweh"; God is close to humanity; God referred to in manlike terms; concrete, vivid language	Primitive legends and patriarchal history
Elohist (E) 750 B.C. (North)	Uses "Elohim"; God is far above humanity; God is majestic	Primitive legends and patriarchal history
Deuteronomic (D) 600–550 B.C.	Sermonlike rather than narrative style	The Law: Ten Commandments and regulations
Priestly (P) 500–450 B.C.	Dry, statistical style; use of genealogies	Law and liturgy; opening of Genesis; priestly rituals

explains the repetition and contradictions found in Scripture, such as the two versions of creation. In general, though, the Yahwist account dominates.

The primitive history before Abraham was written by the Yahwist from a religious motive and under God's inspiration. As Israel's first theologian, the Yahwist made his account a confession of the one God—the Lord of the Covenant, of the universe, and of the human race. The pagan gods were nothing. The Yahwist also viewed the Exodus and the promise of a new kingdom as central to Jewish history. But to the Israelites, every event is linked, so the Yahwist shows that Yahweh is a saving God from the start. Creation is his saving act. The God of the Exodus is the God of Eden.

Eden is the ideal garden where the first couple were placed.

In addition to confirming these basic Jewish beliefs, the primitive history stories serve another purpose. From the time they learn to talk, humans ask why. Why do we live? Why do we die? Why is there suffering and evil? Why are there different languages? The Israelites

250

wove their answers into stories, an effective teaching technique.

Besides Genesis, other books contain the fruit of centuries of reflecting on the mysteries of the human condition and the covenant promises of God. The Book of Job is a literary classic on the question of suffering. The Book of Daniel emphasizes the necessity of keeping God's law despite opposition, and it predicts the eventual triumph of good in God's kingdom. The books of Ruth and Jonah both deal with God's concern for Jew and gentile alike and his willingness to save everyone who is virtuous, or at least repentant.

The same problems that faced the Israelites confront you as a member of the human race and a believer. You might find that the answers presented in God's holy Word as conveyed by the Israelites are not completely satisfying or understandable, and they may only lead you deeper into mystery. But doesn't the glory of being human involve using your mind and heart to delve into the mystery of the universe until that day when you come to the ultimate Mystery face to face?

TWELVE ADAM AND EVE

Creation and Catastrophe

Sections

In this vast universe
There is but one supreme truth—
That God is our friend! . . .
Knowing thou art within thy Father's house,
That thou art surrounded by His love,
Thou wilt become master of fear,
Lord of life, conqueror even of death!

JOSHUA LOTH LIEBMAN,
"GOD IS OUR FRIEND"

Give thanks to the Lord, for he is good, for his mercy endures forever.

CHAPTER PREVIEW

You only have to look at today's newspaper to realize that you live in a troubled world. The crazy pattern of evil, suffering, and death that mars life is a mystery.

The Israelites, too, read these signs in their lives. During the Exile they had the opportunity to ponder these mysteries. They saw in their own history the elements of sin, covenant, forgiveness, and promise. They did not, like other philosophers, call the situation hopeless. They concluded that everything God had made was good, but he had endowed human beings with a power that made them superior to all other creatures: the power of decision.

This power enables human beings to mar the gift of a perfect universe in that they can refuse to follow the laws that govern their nature. God's plan, however, is not foiled by his own gifts. In keeping with his loving nature, God always gives people a fresh start and the promise of a glorious future, but he lets them suffer the consequences of their evil deeds.

The medium the Israelites used for their interpretation of the mysteries of the human race was the story. Some profound mysteries can be expressed only through symbolism. Sacred realities cannot be described directly and completely in human language, but they can be presented in myths in a way that can be grasped by human beings. In simple, vivid terms the Yahwist put the belief of the Israelites into the folktales that precede the history of Abraham. Some of these stories are unrealistic: you read of a talking snake; a woman made from a rib; men who live to be nine hundred and sixty-nine years old. Some of the stories resemble the folk histories of other peoples. The flood tale of Noah, for instance, was related in a Babylonian myth down to the detail of sending a bird to look for land. The important thing is the story's theme. The question is not "Did this really take place?" but "What insights into eternal truths does this story contain?"

Through the instrument of people and their traditions and customs, God spoke his Word. The creation stories were told from the world view of the people of Israel, who did not know that the world was round (Columbus, 1492), that the earth revolved around the sun (Copernicus, 1563), or that humankind probably evolved from lower animals (Darwin, 1859). These are comparatively recent discoveries.

■ What would you say to someone who wanted to ban all fairy tales because the animals in them talk? Or to someone who taught English using a grammar book published in nineteenth-century England?

A person who uses the Bible as a science book or as a history book is missing the point. Science and religion both search for truth, but by different paths. The Bible is a book of religious truths. Some things are beyond the scope of science. How do you prove that a sunset is beautiful?

Some groups have so identified the Bible with their scientific view of the world that when that view is changed, their faith is shaken. Saint Augustine warned that the Bible does not tell us how the heavens go, but how to go to heaven.

In the face of the theory of evolution, the Church is struggling with questions. What is original sin? What was the state of human beings before they sinned? Did one or many couples begin the human race? It was not the intent of the inspired writers of the Bible to explain these things, although information on such matters can be derived from Scripture. Theologians who work on the topic of our origin explore ways of understanding Church teaching in the light of scientific discoveries.

In all things, you can exclaim with Saint Paul, "How deep are the riches and the wisdom and the knowledge of God! How inscrutable his judgments, how unsearchable his ways!" That is, if you take time to think. The tempo of American life is so fast that sometimes you bounce from one activity to another like a ping-pong ball, with no chance to catch your breath, much less to relax, reflect, and relish the joy of being alive.

■ You can always make time to do the things you want to do. In your journal, plan some pockets of silence in your week to "waste time" being more human. Use this time to ponder important questions or to appreciate the wonders of your world.

The theory of evolution states that complex organisms develop from simpler ones. Current theory suggests that the modern human species and apes developed separately but could have had a common ancestor—a prehistoric apelike creature.

Romans 11:33

Words to Know

Yahwist, Elohist, Genesis, evolution, original sin, cosmology, protoevangelium, intellect, free will, sanctifying grace, anthropomorphism, concupiscence, integrity

CREATION: THE GIFT OF A GOOD GOD
(Genesis 1:1–2:4)

The more we discover about the universe, the more we stand in amazement and awe. What a mighty and wonderful One must have fashioned so glorious a cosmos for humankind! This was the Israelites' conclusion even though their experience of the world was limited.

The Israelites and their neighbors thought the world was flat and covered by a solid bowl-shaped firmament, the sky, which held back the waters above the earth. This firmament had gates that released the waters in

The word *genesis* means beginnings. The opening words of the book are "In the beginning."

To experience the poetic beauty of Genesis in the sound of Hebrew words, try saying the first verse in the original: "*Bere*shith ba*ra* Elo*him* eth hasha-ma*yim* weth ha*a*rets."

the form of rain. The sun, moon, and stars were set like ornaments in this firmament to give light. The earth was supported from below by columns. Under the earth there was more water.

Against this primitive concept of the world, the Israelites composed what is still the most majestic, the most well-known, and the best-loved description of the origin of the universe. It is the story of creation as told in the first pages of the Book of Genesis. Because of the poetic structure of the story, scholars believe it was a liturgical song, part of the priestly tradition.

Genesis compares God, the architect of the universe, to a common Jewish laborer who works for six days and then rests on the Sabbath. In the course of relating each day's activity, the writer uses the poetic devices of parallelism and repetition. The description of each workday begins with a command—God's Word calling something into existence—and ends with the refrain: "Evening came, and morning followed—the . . . day." On the first three days God prepared the house, and during the next three days he furnished it:

1—light	4—sun, moon, stars
2—sky, water	5—birds, fish
3—land, plants	6—animals, man

CALLED BY THE FATHER

For those who take it literally, the Bible's creation account poses problems. It took billions of years for the universe to arrive at its present form, not six days. Consider how there could be light on the first day if the sources of light weren't created until the fourth day. Problems like these disappear when you remember that the Bible is not meant to be a science book.

The message that Genesis proclaims is that God has *created*. The Bible leaves the question of *how* God created as a puzzle for humankind to solve. By saying that all created things were brought forth by the Spirit (power) and the Word of God, the inspired writer made the point that God existed before the world and attacked pagan religions that worshipped mere creatures (the sun, the moon, and animals).

One truth that can't be missed is that God intended his creation to be good. God appraised his handiwork seven times and saw how good it was. All things were part of his plan of salvation. In creation God "saved" all beings from nothingness and incorporated them into a magnificent scheme. The end result of God's great design remains to be seen, but you can rely on Saint Paul's observation that "Eye has not seen, ear has not heard, nor has it so much as dawned on man what God has prepared for those who love him."

To the Israelites it would have been natural to create light first: who can work in the dark? Light is also symbolic of spirit, and God's Spirit infuses the world.

Genesis describes God bringing order out of a confused, unorganized state of matter. Strictly speaking, *create* means "to make out of nothing."

1 Corinthians 2:9

Read

Read Genesis 1–2:4. Poetry suggests more than it says. As you read the opening verses of Genesis, use the thoughts below to help you visualize the dawn of creation.

First day (Genesis 1:1–15). In the midst of a vast, swirling darkness, a glow appears. It is an eerie light like the early morning before sunrise.

Second day (Genesis 1:6–8). Surging tons of water are thrust in two by a solid, curved blue wall. With thunderous crashing sounds, the watery chaos splits.

Third day (Genesis 1:9–13). Rushing blue water drains off the land and settles into the ocean basins. Gigantic waves pound against the cliffs and break into

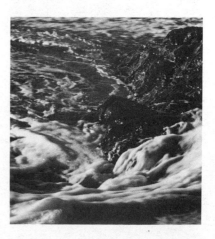

spray. In some places gentle waves lap the sandy sea-shore; in others the water is calm and smooth as glass. The dark earth takes on color as the first tiny green tendrils shoot forth, unfold, and then burst into bloom. Trees creak and groan as branches extend and push up toward the sky. Lush forests cover the hills and fill in the valleys.

Fourth day (Genesis 1:14–19). The brilliant sun rises for the first time, its rays playing on the waters. It lends beauty to everything it touches, then sinks behind the mountains in a blaze of orange, red, and purple. Against the velvety blackness of the night, thousands of sparkling stars fill the sky. The full moon, with its cold, white light, hangs a little above the horizon. All is still.

Fifth day (Genesis 1:20–23). The waters come alive with millions of creatures. Gigantic whales silently glide through murky depths. Tiny fish dart in and out of rocks in shallow streams. The air is filled with the twittering, the calls, and the songs of birds and the sound of flapping wings. The ostrich, the hummingbird, and the swan search for food.

Sixth day (Genesis 1:24–31). Herds of buffalo thunder across the plains, sleek panthers prowl the forests, lions roar, snakes slither across the desert sands, lambs bleat. Finally, the first human being inhales his first breath and stands up.

Recall

1. What indications are there that the opening account of creation was once a liturgical song?
2. According to the Bible, in what order did God create?
3. What truths underlie the Genesis creation story?
4. How does the inspired author teach each essential truth?

Reflect

1. Why doesn't Genesis open with a more realistic account of creation—more in line with those proposed by today's scientists?

CALLED BY THE FATHER

2. How do modern scientific theories of cosmology and evolution enhance rather than detract from the greatness of God?

Cosmology is the science that deals with the origin of the universe.

3. One translation of Psalm 46 reads, "Be still, and know that I am God." How can quiet reflection on the world lead you closer to God?

4. G. K. Chesterton explains, in *Orthodoxy*: "Because children have an abounding vitality, because they are in spirit and free and fierce, therefore they want things repeated and unchanged. They always say, 'Do it again . . .' It is possible that God says every morning, 'Do it again' to the sun; and every evening, 'Do it again' to the moon . . . that God makes every daisy separately, but has never tired of making them." Creation is ongoing. What signs are there that things are still becoming?

5. How do people share in the creative power of God?

6. What is creativity? Why is it good to be creative? How can you be a creative person?

7. How big a God do you believe in?

8. In Genesis, the word for God's spirit that brings being and life out of chaos is *ruah*, the same word that means "breath" in Hebrew. Where else do you find the Spirit bringing forth life? Why is God's power identified with his breath?

MAN AND WOMAN: CREATION'S CROWN
(Genesis 1:26–2:25)

One gem found in Shakespeare's play *Hamlet* praises human beings:

> What a piece of work is man! How noble in reason! how infinite in faculty! in form, in moving, how express and admirable! in action how like an angel! in apprehension how like a god! the beauty of the world! the paragon of animals!

Shakespeare's words are not extravagant when you consider human beings as God created them. After fashioning the kingdom of the universe and myriads of animals, God created the crown of creation, man and

woman. These creatures, who in size were about half-way between an atom and a star, walked upright and had beautiful bodies. Best of all, when God's love brought them into existence, he made them in his image and likeness with the power to think (intellect) and the power to choose (free will). Because they reflect God, human beings are God's masterpieces.

In pagan creation stories the world was an accident, a whim of the gods, or the result of conflict between good and evil. In the Babylonian account, people originated from the blood of a dead rebellious god, and they existed only to wait on the gods and goddesses. The Israelites knew from experience that Yahweh was a saving, loving, and forgiving God; therefore, they wrote of a Creator who offered his love and friendship to his creatures. Yahweh treated Adam and Eve as his children and showered them with gifts: a beautiful home (the garden of Eden), health, happiness, and a share in his own life (sanctifying grace). The first people were totally preoccupied with God, joined to him, and overwhelmed by him. In return, God asked for their love to be shown by doing what he commanded.

The goal of the human race, then, is to live in eternal bliss with God, loving him and being loved by him. This was the covenant God offered humankind. Be-

Irenaeus, an early Church Father, stated, "God creates so as to have someone on whom to confer his goodness." He creates not to gain something for himself, but for the gain of his creatures.

CALLED BY THE FATHER

cause intimacy with God is our deepest drive and the ultimate goal of our lives, the closer we are to God the happier we are.

- Saint Ausustine prayed, "Our hearts are restless, O Lord, until they rest in thee." What evidence is there that this is true?
- God doesn't make junk. Do you realize what a wonderful gift you are? What do you do to cherish yourself? To develop youself? How do you share youself as a gift to others?
- Other persons are gifts from the Father to you. Who are the gifts in your life? How have you let them know you appreciate them? Who in your life is an unopened gift? What can you do about it?

The unique design of your thumbprint is a reminder that you are one of a kind.

Psalm 8 celebrates the dignity of being human:

> When I behold your heavens, the work of your fingers,
>> the moon and the stars which you set in place—
> What is man that you should be mindful of him;
>> or the son of man that you should care for him?
> You have made him little less than the angels,
>> and crowned him with glory and honor.
> You have given him rule over the works of your hands,
>> putting all things under his feet.

Psalm 8:4–7

Not mentioned in Psalm 8 is a truth that adds to our glory: God himself became a man. He crossed the gulf that separates humanity from divinity. Jesus Christ, the Son of God, walked the earth with human feet and worked with human hands. He spoke human words and shed human tears. Finally, he died a human death. Because God became man, a million stars are nothing compared to us. We have more worth than all the animals and we are the envy of the angels.

Furthermore, Jesus was the first person to experience the resurrection promised to his followers. The risen Christ anticipated our destiny. Knowing that he exists glorified, we can look forward to an unbelievable life in the new creation foreseen in the garden of Eden.

FINISHING TOUCHES ON CREATION

An ancient Jewish text reads, "On the sixth day, having created man, God said to him: Heretofore I have worked, now you shall continue." It is your privilege and responsibility to be a creator and to bring the world to completion. Human beings have already harnessed the powers of the earth, tamed some of its jungles, and added to its beauty by agriculture and architecture. More challenging is the task of renewing the earth by working to establish justice and peace.

To create a better society, you have to begin with yourself. As wonderful as you may be, you are not a finished product. You can develop the gifts God gave you to become your best self. Potentially, you can make a unique contribution to the world. Martin Luther King advised, "Set yourself earnestly to discover what you are made to do, and then give yourself passionately to the doing of it. This clear, onward drive toward self-fulfillment is the length of a man's life."

The three animal stories that follow illustrate steps for bringing God's creative power to bear on the world and on behalf of other people.

Step 1: Know Yourself

An Indian brave put an eagle's egg in a prairie chicken's nest. When the eagle hatched, he thought he was a prairie chicken, and all his life he did what prairie chickens did. He scratched in the dirt for food, he clucked, and he never flew more than a few feet off the ground, with much thrashing of his wings. One day when he was very old, this eagle saw a majestic bird riding the powerful wind currents with scarcely a beat of its golden wings. "What's that?" the eagle asked his neighbor. "An eagle, the king of birds. Too bad we can't be like him," the neighbor replied. "Yes, too bad," said the eagle. And he died thinking he was a prairie chicken.

A popular saying is, "What I am is God's gift to me; what I become is my gift to God."

262

- What are your talents, skills, and interests? What are the strong points of your personality and character? How can you discover more about yourself?

Step 2: Be Realistic

Once a frog in a pond wished he could be as large as the ox in the field nearby, so he took a deep breath and blew himself up to twice his normal size, but he wasn't as big as that ox. The next day he tried again, inhaling even more air. He still wasn't the size of the ox. On the third day, he was determined to be as big as the ox. He took a very deep breath and BANG! The frog was no more.

- Considering your strengths, weaknesses, abilities, opportunities, and situation, what goals can you set for the coming year? For the next four years? For life? What strategies can you use to achieve these goals?

Step 3: Persevere

Two frogs fell into a pail of cream. One of them gave up and drowned. The other swam around and around, churning the cream until he made a lump of butter. Then he jumped onto the butter and hopped out of the pail. The difference between champ and chump is *U*.

- How can you motivate yourself to keep going when you feel discouraged and ready to quit?

A good motto is "Don't just live, grow!" Develop your gifts and use them for the betterment of all people. Then at the end of your life you will be happy to answer when God asks "What did you do for love of me?"

- Begin to carry out Step 1 by compiling a "Who I Am" booklet. Devote pages to your personality, idiosyncrasies, talents, interests, likes and dislikes, favorite things, strengths, weaknesses, fears, and dreams.

Read

In Genesis 1:26–2:25, read about the creation of man and woman, stopping after each section to read the notes, and the underlying truths, below.

Genesis 1:26–31

Notes: Humans were given dominion over the earth in that they were to care for it like a good king, but this doesn't mean that they can exploit the earth. The author might have in mind the ideal rule of David as opposed to the rule of Solomon, who used his people for his own gain. God commanded human beings to reproduce.

Truths: Human beings are above the animal world because of their minds and wills. People are basically good. Sex is good because it originates with God.

Genesis 2:4–7

Notes: One sentence takes care of the universe; the focus is on human beings. God is cast in the role of a potter. The Israelites knew that people stopped breathing at death and their bodies turned to dust. This process was reversed when God made the first man. *Adam* is the word for *man* in Hebrew and is related to *adama*, meaning "to ground."

Truths: God brings human beings into existence in a special manner. All human beings are united. God admits human beings into his friendship.

CALLED BY THE FATHER

Genesis 2:8–9

Notes: No one knows the location of Eden; the term means "a delightful place." The tree of life is a symbol of living forever that occurs often in ancient stories. The tree of the knowledge of good and evil stands for the right to decide for oneself what is right or wrong. It is this power, rather than a god of evil, that allows the possibility of evil.

Truths: God's plans for us include an ideal situation, a supernatural state above our nature. God didn't intend for us to die. Human happiness depends on listening to God.

Genesis 2:10–17

Notes: The four rivers emphasize the richness of Eden for the Israelites, who had lived for so long in the desert. Two rivers (the Tigris and Euphrates) are known. Two are unknown.

Genesis 2:18–25

Notes: Naming the animals shows Adam's power over them. The first surgery—the removal of Adam's rib—is rich in symbolism. For one thing, Arabs today say of their friends, "He is my rib." In the original, the Bible says that Adam "stamps his foot for joy" when he beholds Eve. The relationship of man and woman is expressed in the words "woman" (*ishsha*) and "man" (*ishah*). Nakedness meant disgrace and defeat to the Israelites. War captives were often stripped. Nakedness without shame in Eden is a sign of innocence.

Truths: Eve has the same nature as Adam. She is equal to him. They are partners, but she is dependent on him in certain things. The mysterious attraction between man and woman is rooted in their being.

In the Gilgamesh epic, Gilgamesh swam to the depth of the sea to get a bough from the tree of life, but a jealous snake god devoured it when Gilgamesh stopped to bathe in a pond.

Recall

1. What are the basic messages in the Genesis account of the origin of the human race?
2. How were man and woman the crown of creation? How were they both material and spiritual? How were they stamped in the image and likeness of God?

3. What was God's intention for human beings?
4. What is the meaning of some of the symbolism in Genesis?

Reflect

1. The remarkable gifts of intellect and will have a corresponding responsibility. What is it?
2. Give some examples of human beings forgetting their dignity and acting like animals.
3. Your intellect seeks knowledge; your will seeks love. How do you know that neither is satisfied on earth? Why won't they ever be satisfied in this life?
4. What does dominion over all the world involve?
5. In what ways is the universe a gift of God to you? How can you show appreciation for this gift?
6. Tell how these Scripture passages confirm the basic dignity of human beings: Deuteronomy 5:17, Matthew 6:26, Hebrews 2:16–17, Ephesians 1:3–6.
7. Why is it great to be alive?

THE FALL: A REFUSAL OF LOVE
(Genesis 3:1–24)

Have you done anything recently that you could "kick yourself" for? Said something that you wish you could take back? Hurt someone by your anger? Given in to a bad habit when you didn't want to?

CALLED BY THE FATHER

If you feel tension between what you would like to be and what you actually do, you are normal. Saint Paul spoke for everyone: "Even though I want to do what is right, a law that leads me to wrongdoing is always ready at hand. My inner self agrees with the law of God, but I see in my body's members another law at war with the law of my mind; this makes me the prisoner of the law of sin in my members."

Romans 7:21–24

The plight of the human race today is a far cry from the paradise God had in mind for Adam and Eve's family. Genesis provides a key to the mystery. The first parents made a fatal mistake that marked their descendants: they rejected God's love; they sinned. The nature of their disobedience is not clear, but the Bible outlines the prehistoric happenings in colorful symbolism.

Not content with God's love, his presence within them (grace), and his gifts, Adam and Eve wanted more. The devil appealed to their pride by telling them they would be like God if they listened to him and not to their Creator. They risked all—and lost. The friendship between God and humankind was shattered.

The Church teaches in the dogma of the Immaculate Conception that Mary was preserved from all sin, even original sin. Her state of sinlessness was won by her Son's redemption and applied to her in an extraordinary way because of her role in salvation history as Mother of God.

Clearly, the inspired author was not an eyewitness to the Fall; he was relaying the basic truths through folk history. The drama of the first people's refusal to cooperate with their loving Creator is told simply but vividly. It presents a psychological study of sin that is valid today.

The nature of its symbols makes the Hebrew story an argument against pagan religions. The villain, for instance, is cast as a snake. To the Canaanites, the snake was sacred; it was a sign of fertility and was represented in an upright position, usually twined around a staff. In the Bible, the snake was ordered by God to crawl on his belly and eat dirt, a sign of total defeat.

In ancient times, a conquered king had to bow his head to the dust with the victor's foot on his neck.

Alone, Adam and Eve found themselves a broken people. Their rebellion left their intellect and wills (the source of their nobility) injured. They were drawn toward evil and would more easily succumb to temptation. They became ashamed of their nakedness, and they acted in conflict, each blaming the other for the sin. Even the world turned against them. Although they

Blame is passed from one party to another: Adam blames Eve; Eve blames the serpent.

were originally destined to live forever, Adam and Eve had to face death.

Ever since then, the human race has suffered the consequences of that catastrophe. Adam and Eve's failure to respond to God's love—the first sin—introduced into the world all the companions of evil: violence, suffering, pain, and death. It also paved the way for more sin because, separated from God and goodness, human beings are weak.

The effects of Adam and Eve's original sin are many. Sin pervades the world. Countries are ravaged by natural tragedies like earthquakes, fires, and plagues, as well as by tragedies caused by or allowed by human beings: war, violence, famine, and fraud. Genesis indicates that all discord is rooted in the heart of humanity. Our pull toward evil is connected with all evil—natural or human. Furthermore, we come into life without the benefit of God's sanctifying grace; we are born alienated from God instead of in the state of holiness and justice. In order to do good, we must struggle against dark impulses.

The term "original sin," then, has several meanings. It refers to the first sin of Adam and Eve, the root of sin; it stands for the atmosphere of sin and evil in the world; and it also means the inclination toward evil. Sin is a universal condition, and it is human beings who are responsible for it.

The Israelites believed in "collective guilt": if a member of a family sinned, the tribe could be punished. Adam represented the entire human race, so when he lost his gifts, his descendants were also deprived of them.

The inclination toward sin is called *concupiscence*. Adam and Eve had an inclination to goodness, called *integrity*.

The sacrament of Baptism, however, reinstates human beings as sons and daughters of God and fills them with divine life.

CALLED BY THE FATHER

Imagine the despair of the human race if the relationship between God and humankind had been completely severed at the Fall. But God extended another opportunity for happiness to his fallen creatures. In cursing the serpent, God hinted at a Savior who would conquer Satan. He said to the snake: "I will put enmity between you and the woman, and between your offspring and hers; he will strike at your head, while you strike at his heel."

Human beings can hope for communion with God because he sent his only Son to repair the damage done by sin. On Calvary, good and evil engaged in cosmic combat, and Easter Sunday proved God victorious.

God made the Fall the occasion of the fullest expression of his love. Through the life, death, and resurrection of Jesus Christ, divinity became humanity and was invited to share divinity. Living according to the way of Jesus unites us with the good, loving Father who gives life and lets us hope for the intense joy that no one can ever take from us.

Genesis 3:15. This passage is called "protoevangelium," which means "first good news," because theologians later understood it to be the first promise of the Redeemer. They interpreted the woman's "offspring" to be Jesus Christ.

Read

As you read the account of the Fall in Genesis 3:1–24, analyze it in the light of the psychological pattern of any sin, as expressed in the "Seven Steps to Sin and Sadness":

1. Allurement of the senses
2. Questioning the command
3. Toying with the idea in the imagination
4. Concentration on the "benefits" of the sinful act
5. The free and responsible choice of sin
6. Shame
7. Alienation from God

In Greek mythology it is Pandora, the first woman, who is responsible for evil. Pandora's curiosity led her to open a chest against the gods' commands, and all kinds of wicked creatures were let loose upon the world. At the very bottom of the chest there was a tiny creature called Hope.

Recall

1. What is sin? What is original sin?
2. How does Genesis explain suffering and evil?
3. What punishment was meted out to each person connected with the Fall?

4. How did God show himself "the tremendous lover" in the opening scene of humankind's history?
5. What is the present condition of the human race? What kind of future can it hope for? Why?
6. How were pagan peoples involved in the telling of the Adam and Eve story?

Reflect

1. God is a God of surprises. How has he surprised the human race so far? What surprising things has he done in your life?
2. Why does the Easter liturgy call original sin "O happy fault"?
3. How has Christ's suffering given meaning to all suffering?
4. You would hardly believe that the little green stalk that shoots up from the ground could bear a lovely flower, that the acorn could turn into an oak, or that the furry caterpillar could emerge from its cocoon a butterfly. What will life after death be like for those who love God?
5. Who is Satan? What other sources of evil exist?
6. Eve made Adam an accomplice in her crime. Was he any less guilty? Why or why not?
7. Does God will evil? Explain.

TALES OF WOE: A SIN-SCARRED RACE
(Genesis 4:1–22, 25, 26; 6:5–9, 18; 11:1–9)

Divorced from God, people fell repeatedly into sin. The original sin started a chain reaction of wickedness and rebellion that swept through the human race like a disease. Three stories in Genesis record the progress of sin as the great separator. They show that not only does sin divide people from God, but it also divides people from one another. In the story of Cain and Abel, sin split apart the first family. Then in the tale of Noah and the flood, sin reached such immense proportions that God almost erased all humanity from the face of the earth. Finally, in the account of the tower of Babel, sin divided

all human beings from each other when God had each person speak a different language.

■ What examples can you think of to illustrate Sir Walter Scott's famous saying: "O what a tangled web we weave, when first we practice to deceive"?

The pattern in these three stories is the same. People sin and are punished, and then God demonstrates his forgiveness. Since the time of these original tales, many more stories with the same pattern could be told. You are familiar with those in the Book of Judges and those from your personal life. How can God show such patience with the human race? Patience is exercised in love. God loves his creation.

Read and Recall

Read the three tales of woe. For each one be able to tell (1) the crime, (2) the motive, (3) the punishment, (4) the sign of forgiveness (except for Babel).

Cain and Abel (Genesis 4:1–22, 25, 26). Cain was a farmer like the Canaanites, Israel's enemy. Abel was a shepherd. The mark on Cain placed on him by the slaying of his brother is a mystery. Notice that the Genesis 4:7 sin is compared to a crouching animal ready to pounce on someone. Another son, Seth, was born to Adam and Eve to replace Abel.

To remember which brother is the murderer, think of a "cane" being used to beat someone.

Today there are over three thousand languages in the world.

Noah (Genesis 6:5–9:18). God brought the world back to the watery chaos that existed before creation. The flood story might be based on a historical flood that covered a large part of the world as the people long ago knew it. A worldwide flood occurs in a number of ancient tales; one of the oldest versions (dated about 2000 B.C.) is from the Sumerians. Although the Israelite account is very similar, it differs in that it relates the story to sin and divine punishment.

The long lists of ancestors before and after the Noah story are genealogies. Their purpose is to show the passage of time and explain the origins of different peoples. Genealogies are characteristic of the priestly tradition.

Tower of Babel (Genesis 11:1–9). The tower the people endeavored to build was probably a ziggurat or sacred tower like those the Babylonians used for worship. It was meant to stand for the first mound of creation that appeared out of the chaos at the beginning of time. *Ziggurat* comes from a word meaning "to build high." The story presents a reason for the many languages in the world: pride.

Reflect

1. How does sin have harmful side effects today? Give specific examples.
2. What means do you have to become reunited with God after sin? With your fellow men and women?
3. One of the popes said that the greatest evil in the world today is the loss of a sense of sin. What is a "sense of sin"? Do you agree that people today do not have it? Why or why not? Why should you preserve a sense of sin? How can you?
4. How can you be your brother's keeper?
5. How does every deed you do involve other people?
6. Why is the rainbow a good sign for the covenant between God and humankind?
7. Some people think of God as someone who is out to get you. How does the Bible counteract this idea?
8. Describe a world in which people stopped sinning.

CALLED BY THE FATHER

GETTING IT TOGETHER

The Exodus and the Exile experiences provided the Israelites with the knowledge to construct a theology. Genesis is the result of their reflection on the human condition. In the first eleven chapters, present problems were explained through past events in such a way that Israelite theology became the foundation for what is believed today, over two thousand years later.

The great human gifts of knowledge and freedom make us Godlike and raise us above the animal kingdom. Instead of using their gifts to serve God, men and women—beginning with the first couple, Adam and Eve—misused these gifts and turned against their greatest benefactor. They used their freedom to become prisoners of sin. Created in the state of grace, they *dis*-graced themselves. Thus sin, the willful resistance to God's will, spread throughout the world. The legends of Genesis are the very ones we live today.

But because the Creator is a saving God, he pulled humankind out of the mire of contradiction, opposition, hatred, fear, and the meaninglessness brought on by disobedience. Jesus Christ, the God-man, a representative of the human race—a new Adam—made up for the hideous crime against the infinite God. With him, sin and death were conquered. All things were set right, and God and human beings were one again. Men and women were empowered to love one another. Even the confusion of Babel was resolved at Pentecost, when once more the Spirit moved over the face of the earth. The new creation God promised had begun.

But the scars of the rebellion remain. Life is full of hardship and pain, and the root of evil lies deep within. The temptation to quit responding to God is ever-present, threatening your future. Again, it is Jesus who saves. Those who put their trust in him, who cultivate a friendship with him, have all they need to come through victorious. With God's help, you can become more fully human and help to create a better world.

Saint Thomas More said, "God created the flowers to be beautiful, the mountains to be majestic, the animals to be and to move, but God made men to serve him in the wit and tangle of his mind."

REVIEWING THE CHAPTER

Linking Your Ideas

1. How does Genesis show God's power? His kindness? His closeness?
2. Something in the nature of human beings and in the world is out of control. What in the Genesis narratives illustrate that this is due to humanity itself, and not to God?
3. The predicaments people find themselves in today are no different from the predicaments of prehistoric man and woman. Present one of the stories in Genesis in the form of a soap opera.
4. Chart the progress of sin from the Garden of Eden through the ages to the present. (Don't forget the years of Christ's life.) Then consider the future. What will happen at the end of time?
5. Respond to this statement: "God must not be taking care of the world since there is so much suffering."
6. Read chapter 8 of Romans for insights into the plan of God for humankind in Jesus Christ and through the Holy Spirit. How does baptism fit into the scheme presented in this chapter?

Strengthening Your Grasp

1. Anthropomorphism is speaking of God as if he were human and had a body. God's walking in the garden in the cool of the evening (Genesis 3:8) is one example of anthropomorphism. Find others.
2. A poem by Gerard Manley Hopkins begins, "The world is charged with the grandeur of God./It will flame out, like shining from shook foil." Different things in creation reflect different aspects of God's glory. For instance, the mountains tell of his majesty, the flowers speak of his beauty. Make a photo essay based on this aspect of nature.
3. Represent the work of the six days of creation in an art medium.
4. Write a modern version of any of the sin stories in Genesis.
5. Do research on the theory of evolution. As a Catholic, how can you accept it?
6. Find out more about the theories of the origin of the universe.
7. Read the prayer "The Canticle of the Sun" by Saint Francis of Assisi, in which he praises God for "brother sun," "sister moon," and all of creation. Write your own Hymn of Praise to the Creator.

CALLED BY THE FATHER

Expressing Your Convictions

1. Compose a poem or a reflective essay on one of the lines of this short prayer:

   O God, for all that has been—thanks!
   For all that shall be—Yes!

2. Write an editorial attacking some form of sin that is prevalent in today's society.

3. Plan and carry out a Celebrate Life Day. Everyone in the class should contribute by presenting slides on the wonders of life, singing a song, distributing bookmarks, planning a prayer service, and so on.

Extending Your Interest

Find verses from the psalms that carry the themes of creation, fall, and redemption. Compile them into a booklet illustrated with your own drawings or with magazine pictures.

THIRTEEN RUTH, JONAH, JOB, DANIEL

Old Testament Saints

Sections

Ruth: The Devoted Daughter
  Ruth: 1:1–4:22

Jonah: The Runaway Prophet
  Jonah 1–3

Job: The Trusting Sufferer
  Job 1–42

Daniel: The Zealous Lover of God
  Daniel 1–14

O Lord, you have been our refuge
  through all generations.
Before the mountains were begotten
  and the earth and the world were brought forth,
  from everlasting to everlasting you are God. . . .
Fill us at daybreak with your kindness,
  that we may shout for joy and gladness all our days.

PSALM 90:1–2, 14

Everything written before our time was written for our instruction, that we might derive hope from the lessons of patience and the words of encouragement in the Scriptures.

ROMANS 15:4

CHAPTER PREVIEW

Several books of the Bible center around individuals who are models for God's people. Each of these heroes or heroines excels in a quality that should characterize anyone involved in a covenant relationship with God.

You will meet Ruth, whose loyalty to Naomi, her mother-in-law, makes her the epitome of faithful love; Job, whose trust in the Lord remained unshaken even during the bitterest trials; and Daniel, a model of obedience to God's law.

You will also enjoy the story of Jonah, the Bible's comic-relief character. As a type of antihero, this prophet demonstrates what witnessing for the Lord is *not*. After first trying to run away from his mission, he grudgingly preached to Nineveh. Then, when his audience repented, he complained because he would rather have seen them destroyed.

The stories of Ruth, Job, Daniel, and Jonah are significant. They are the fruit of centuries of reflection on the relationship between God and humanity and on the

The books of Ruth, Job, Jonah, Esther, Judith, and Tobit are short stories. The Book of Daniel is a collection of stories about Daniel.

hard questions of life. God inspired the Jewish authors to write about outstanding Jewish persons as vehicles of his revelation. By means of a good story, the unchanging truths of the Jewish faith—our heritage—are presented simply and clearly for easy transmission through the ages. God revealed through the books of Ruth and Jonah that he was not just one of many gods and not the God of the Hebrews alone, but the universal God who loves every man and woman. It was Israel's vocation to bear witness to a God whose salvation reaches to the ends of the earth.

The story of Job explores the question "What is the meaning of my life?" It views suffering and human existence from the perspective of the relationship between the Creator and the created. The Book of Daniel underlines the necessity for a courageous faith that is unyielding in the face of severe opposition. Through the combined wisdom of all biblical writings, you learn what it means to love and to be loved by God.

■ What one characteristic would you like people to associate with you? In your journal, write three suggestions for developing that quality in your life.

Words to Know

Ruth, Boaz (**bo**-az), Naomi (nay-**o**-mee), Jonah (**jo**-nuh), Nineveh (**nin**-u-vah), Job (johb), Daniel, apocalyptic

RUTH: THE DEVOTED DAUGHTER
(Ruth 1:1–4:22)

Liberation. Self-fulfillment. Identity. Pleasure. These are the clarion calls of an ego-centered world. Rather than concentrating on herself, Ruth lived for others, and thus she attained true freedom, fulfillment, and joy. Ruth was a Moabite, not one of the Chosen People, yet God rewarded her goodness. She became the ancestress of King David and, ultimately, of Jesus Christ. The Book of Ruth describes how, out of loyalty to her mother-in-law, Naomi, Ruth gave up her home, country, and religion. The courage of Ruth in going with Naomi to Jewish Bethlehem is evident: as a pagan stranger, she was regarded with suspicion, if not hostility. Her decision was a leap in the dark.

Ruth found her equal in Boaz, a good, kind, and wealthy relative. According to Jewish law, the closest relative of a dead man had the right and the duty to

Clarion means "shrill and clear."

Much later, when the Jews returned to the land of their fathers for a census, Mary and Joseph went to Bethlehem, the town of their ancestor King David. *Bethlehem* means "house of bread."

marry the widow and buy back the family land if it had been sold to pay debts. The first male child would then be the legal son of the deceased husband. However, there was an obstacle to the marriage of Boaz and Ruth: Boaz was not Ruth's closest relative.

Although the story of Ruth is set in the time of the judges, it must have been written much later because the closing verses trace Ruth's descendants down to David. Obed, the son of Ruth, was the father of Jesse, David's father. Scholars think that the story originated during the time of Nehemiah and Ezra to counteract nationalism and the belief that salvation was only for the Jews. Under Ezra, the Jews had divorced their foreign wives. In Ruth, however, God found a foreigner who was pleasing because of her loyalty and faith. Later, through Ruth, God granted his greatest favor to humanity: he sent his Son. The introduction of Ruth, a gentile, into the family tree of the Messiah foreshadowed that he was to be the Savior of the whole world, Jew and gentile alike.

Read and Recall

Use the following questions to guide your reading of Ruth 1–4.

1. Why did Elimelech, Naomi, and their two sons leave Bethlehem to live in the pagan land of Moab?
2. What did Naomi urge her daughters-in-law to do after their husbands died?
3. What words of Ruth demonstrate her loyalty to her mother-in-law?
4. How did Ruth meet Boaz?
5. How did the rich Boaz show favor to Ruth? Why?
6. What did Naomi advise Ruth to do to put herself in Boaz's care?
7. Why didn't Boaz agree to marry Ruth immediately?
8. What symbolic act, comparable to a handshake today, sealed a Jewish bargain?
9. What relation was Ruth, the Moabite, to the great Israelite king, David? To Jesus?
10. What does this story show?

IN PRAISE OF WOMAN

The women's rights movement of this century challenges irrational and unjust notions about women. Actually, women have come a long way when compared with the degrading position they held in ancient societies. In most nations, women were little better than slaves whose main purpose was to serve men and eventually bear male children. Women had no schooling or careers. Their husbands could divorce them at will. They lacked legal and property rights. They could be killed at birth simply because they were female.

Certain features of the Bible, however, stand in contradiction to this antifeminine world. Woman was in her rightful place at the side of man (not behind him) from the very beginning in Genesis. She was bone of his bone and flesh of his flesh, a "suitable partner" for him. Poet Gordon Higham interpreted the symbolism of the use of Adam's rib in the creation of Eve:

Genesis 2:18

> Woman was created
>   from the rib of man
> Not from the head to be higher
> Nor from the foot
>   to be trampled upon.
> But from the side
>   to be equal
> Under the arm
>   to be protected
> And near the heart
>   to be loved.

Biblical women were sometimes exalted as saviors of their nation. Judith and Esther are known not only for their great beauty, but also for their valor. Deborah, Rahab, and Jael were also praised for their roles in salvation history. Although Boaz was a good man, it was his wife, Ruth, who was the main character in the book named for her.

To review the deeds of these remarkable heroines, see the Book of Judith, the Book of Esther, Joshua 2–6 (Rahab), and Judges 4 (Deborah and Jael).

The hymn to the worthy wife found in Proverbs 31:10–31, which was edited during the fifth century B.C., is unequaled in any other literature of that period. The woman's significant place in society as detailed by Proverbs was unusual, if not revolutionary. She is depicted as a good provider as well as the heart of her family and the strength of her husband.

Womanhood was crowned in Mary, a Jewess who became the Mother of God. Her faith and openness to God made possible the redemption of the human race. Mary is the woman of Genesis whose offspring crushed Satan underfoot. She is the woman of Revelation, "clothed with the sun, with the moon under her feet and on her head a crown of twelve stars," whose son is "destined to shepherd all the nations."

Revelation 12:1, 12:5

In choosing to save the world through the cooperation of a woman, God has not only undone the harm of the first woman, Eve, but has raised woman to a new and glorious dignity. For all ages, she will be called blessed in the person of Mary.

■ In what ways is Mary the perfect model of womanhood? What qualities should the movement for women's rights emphasize?

Reflect

1. The loving Ruth constantly made good decisions. What were some of her praiseworthy actions?
2. How was Boaz just and righteous?
3. Ruth was not bound to stay with Naomi, and Boaz, who was not Ruth's closest relative, did not have to marry her and assume her husband's land problems. Why did Ruth and Boaz do what they did?
4. The relationship between Ruth and Naomi was ideal. What attitudes should the young have toward their elders? How should older people regard the young?
5. It is not easy to be different. Besides being a Moabite among Jews, Ruth was virtuous in an age of immorality—the period of the judges. Where did she find strength to persevere in goodness?
6. Why is prejudice dangerous and evil?

JONAH: THE RUNAWAY PROPHET
(Jonah 1–3)

When God commanded Jonah to march into Nineveh, the capital of Assyria, to prophesy, Jonah boarded a ship headed in the opposite direction. This was cowardly, but it was also very human and understandable, because Assyria was a powerful enemy of Israel. Thus Jonah did not follow the tradition of Israel's great prophets. He didn't even argue with God; he simply refused the dangerous mission. But God just as firmly refused Jonah's refusal.

After he was miraculously transported by God to the wicked city of Nineveh, Jonah foretold its destruction. The people repented, and God repealed his sentence against them. Instead of rejoicing at his success and at God's mercy, Jonah resented being deprived of seeing his foes punished. Jonah pouted as he said, "Is not this what I said? . . . I knew that you are a gracious and merciful God, slow to anger, rich in clemency, loathe to punish." This "complaint" is a beautiful expression of faith in God. Using nature, God then taught Jonah a lesson about his love.

Since the prophet Jonah is mentioned in 2 Kings 14:26 as the son of Amittai, it is likely that the story of Jonah is based on the life of a real person.

Isaiah volunteered, "Here I am, send me" (Isaiah 6:8); Samuel responded, "Speak, Lord, for your servant is listening" (1 Samuel 3:10); and although Moses and Jeremiah offered excuses, they cooperated.

Jonah 4:2

The Book of Jonah is an example of God's use of a literary form to teach humanity. Jonah is not a historical book, but a short story that relates a prophetic truth. Although its colorful details and unique situations have made Jonah a famous "fish story" and the most humorous book of the Bible, it has a serious message. While laughing at Jonah's narrow-mindedness, the reader is reminded that God is concerned about all people, including the detested Assyrians. Even though the book was probably written in the fifth or fourth century B.C. during the post-Exile period when many Jews were strongly nationalistic, its theme is timeless and its call to holiness is universal.

Read and Recall

Read Jonah 1–3:11 and then sketch four stick-figure drawings that tell the story.

Reflect

1. What are some of the strong visual images in the story of Jonah that make it interesting and funny?
2. The British poet Francis Thompson wrote a poem that called God the Hound of Heaven. How does God live up to this name in the Book of Jonah?
3. Why do people run from God? How?
4. God is a main character in the Jonah story. What do his words and actions reveal him to be?
5. How did Christ warn against the selfishness of Jonah in the parables of the prodigal son (Luke 15:28) and of the employer and his workers (Matthew 20:15–16)?

JOB: THE TRUSTING SUFFERER
(Job 1–42)

If you are human, you have problems. Even within your immediate family, chances are that some painful circumstance is causing suffering.

■ In how many ways can you complete this sentence: I'd be perfectly happy if only . . .

Since the Jews of the period believed that the good are rewarded and the bad are punished during life, they interpreted suffering as a punishment for sin. This, however, is not a completely satisfactory explanation, for it does not help us understand why innocent people suffer. This perplexing question is the subject of the Book of Job, a literary masterpiece. Written between the fifth and third century B.C., Job's story analyzes the question, but it does not offer a definite answer. Rather, it encourages us to accept suffering as a test of fidelity and cautions us not to challenge the all-wise providence of God. It was Christ who finally promised what was not revealed in the Old Testament until the very end. Like the progressive Jewish rabbis of his time, Jesus taught belief in a personal resurrection, and by his own death and resurrection he gave us eternal life, in which the good will be rewarded. Thus suffering becomes redemptive when offered to God in union with the Suffering Savior, the innocent victim. By patient suffering, people can purify themselves and build up the people of God.

The mystery of the suffering of innocent people is explored in the Book of Job through the story of a good man's utter ruin. Job was prosperous and had an ex-

One of the beatitudes of Christ (a guideline for perfection) is "Blest are the sorrowing; they shall be consoled" (Matthew 5:4).

In the Morning Offering prayer, Christians offer to God their joys and suffering of the day.

cellent reputation. God allowed Satan to try him, and in no time Job lost everything, including his health. Although he agonized over why he, a good man, had to suffer, Job's trust in God was steadfast. He declared that he would still love God even if God killed him.

The bulk of the book is the record of a debate the suffering Job had with three friends and a young man named Elihu, who represent the wise men of Israel. They sympathized with Job, but they insisted that since God is just, Job must have done wrong, maybe even unconsciously, to deserve such rough treatment in life. Job affirmed his innocence and, finally, he uttered this challenge: "Let the Almighty answer me." God stepped in and addressed Job. He settled the arguments by reminding Job of his power and wisdom. Job's complaints were silenced, his friends stood corrected, and God rewarded Job with twice as much prosperity as he had formerly enjoyed.

The author of the book is unknown. Job himself was an Edomite sheik. From the structure of the book, it appears that an Israelite sage living near Edom used a folktale (the opening and closing narrative) as a frame for his reflections on life (the poetic speeches). In writing the story of Job, the author challenged Israel's traditional explanation for suffering, insisting that God cannot be manipulated by our actions or omissions but is bigger than our fears and disasters. No matter what life brings, we can be sure that "God makes all things work together for the good of those who have been called." Job's suffering is a learning experience for him and for every person who reads his story.

Read and Recall

The Book of Job falls into five acts. After you read each section, summarize its events in a sentence.

> Act I—1:1–12
> Act II—1:13–2:10
> Act III—2:11–3:4, 4:1–9, 6:28–30
> Act IV—38:1–41
> Act V—42:1–17

Both *sympathy* and *compassion* mean "to suffer with" someone.

The Edomites to the south of Palestine were a threat to the Israelites.

Romans 8:28

Archibald MacLeish used the story of Job in a contemporary setting in his successful play *J.B.*

CALLED BY THE FATHER

CREATION: A MYSTERY STORY

"Where were you when I founded the earth?" God challenged Job. Since neither Job nor any other mortal was present at the birth of the universe, no one knows how it came about. Humanity's fascination with the mystery of the origin of things is reflected in its literature.

Job 38:4

In Enuma Elish, the Babylonian creation story, Mardok, the city god of Babylon, defeated the she-monster Tiamet, the symbol of chaos, and then built the universe out of her carcass. One half formed the earth, the other half the sky. Thus the world was only a by-product of a war between angry gods, and material things were basically evil.

Enuma Elish (e-**new**-mah e-**leesh**)

According to Greek and Roman mythology, Chaos had children—Night and Erebus (the depths where death dwelt). From them came Love, who created Light and Day. Mother Earth and Father Heaven then arose and bore giant monsters: the one-eyed Cyclops, the Titans, and three creatures with a hundred hands and fifty heads each.

Erebus (uhr-**ee**-bus)

■ How is the Jewish account of creation in Genesis more appealing than pagan accounts?

Genesis is not the only book of the Bible that tells the story of creation. Read the following passages: Job 38–40, Ezekiel 28:11–19, and Psalm 104. What characteristics of God do they emphasize?

The Bible ends with a description of a new creation that balances the story of creation at the beginning of the Bible.

■ Read Revelation 21:1–22:5. How was the new creation related to the old? What role did Jesus Christ have in it? You might enjoy composing your own creation story in prose or poetry.

Reflect

1. What reasons do you have to trust God?
2. How can suffering be good for a person?
3. What natural and supernatural aids can help someone endure the hardships of this life?
4. One of the spiritual works of mercy is to comfort the sorrowing. How can you comfort someone who is living through a time of suffering?
5. How can trials make you either bitter or better? How do you personally react to crisis?
6. Prove that God doesn't spare even his best friends from suffering.
7. How is Job like Christ?
8. What could be the value of suffering when you fail an exam; are not accepted by a group; are ridiculed for your efforts, ideas, voice, or appearance; lose your temper; realize there is a poor spirit in your class or your school?

DANIEL: THE ZEALOUS LOVER OF GOD
(Daniel 1–14)

Daniel was saved from being cut into pieces and from being devoured by lions. His friends were saved from fire.

During the Macabbean period, the Jews were subjected to persecution for practicing their faith. They were threatened with death if they lived out the prescriptions of the Mosaic law. The Book of Daniel was written during this period (167–164 B.C.) to encourage and strengthen the persecuted Jews. It is a compilation of legends about Daniel, a staunch Jew whose faith and love were put to the test during the Babylonian Captivity, sometime before 538 B.C.

Daniel's miraculous deliverances and herioc exploits were not the result of science or luck; they were the natural destiny of a man who put all his trust in God. Undaunted by the laws and punishments of pagan kings, Daniel zealously followed the law of God. When Daniel faced danger, God saved him and endowed him with the power to interpret dreams, prophesy, and read the writing that miraculously appeared on the wall.

CALLED BY THE FATHER

Although the villainous characters in the story historically were Babylonian kings, the Israelites saw them as symbols of their present persecutors. Just as Daniel and his companions were able to hold out against their enemies, so the Jews, although oppressed by the Syrian kings, should also remain faithful. The visions of Daniel offered hope by foretelling the end of the persecutions and the eventual triumph of the kingdom of God, when the faithful would be rewarded.

In Daniel's vision, four consecutive empires are represented by different beasts.

In reality, the author of Daniel traced contemporary history in the symbolic language of these visions. On another level, this writing refers to the end-time, the Day of the Lord, and thus belongs to the form of writing called *apocalyptic*.

Apocalyptic writing flourished from 200 B.C. to A.D. 200 and was based on the imminent coming of the Kingdom of God. The style of apocalyptic literature is marked by symbolism, supernatural happenings, and predictions of events that had already occurred. Whereas the prophets taught that salvation would come in *this* world once the Messiah brought peace, apocalyptic writing encouraged reform in order to prepare for the New Age that would begin with the Day of Judgment.

The last book of the Bible is sometimes called the Apocalypse, and in its prophetic visions it uses some of the same symbols that are found in the Book of Daniel. For more apocalyptic writings, see Zechariah 2:1–11, Joel 4:1–21, and Mark 13.

One of the most famous apocalyptic passages is Daniel's description of someone who was like a son of man and whose kingship was universal and eternal. It has its parallel in chapter 1 of the Book of Revelation. The fact that Christ fulfilled this prophecy is suggested by his own use of the title "Son of Man" when referring to himself.

Jesus was the only one who used this title in relation to himself. It occurs eighty-three times in the New Testament.

Although the last two chapters of Daniel are not part of the Jewish canon, the Church accepts them as inspired. The first tells the story of Susanna, an upright woman who was saved from the evil accusations of false witnesses when a young man named Daniel had the courage to speak up for her. The final chapter records how Daniel revealed the falseness of the Babylonian gods, Bel and the dragon. These later stories blend in with the rest of the book because they echo its theme—the triumph of those who love and follow the one true God.

Read

Read Daniel 1–14. First read chapters 1 and 2, which combine many of the elements characteristic of the Book of Daniel. Then choose two of the following selections from Daniel to read.

> Chapter 3—the fiery furnace
> Chapter 4—the dream of the tree
> Chapter 5—the writing on the wall
> Chapter 6—the lions' den
> Chapter 7—the vision of four beasts
> Chapter 13—Susanna
> Chapter 14—Bel and the dragon

Recall

1. Explain how each of the selections you read is characteristic of the Book of Daniel.
2. Which aspects of the Book of Daniel would persecuted Jews have found helpful?

Reflect

1. According to Daniel, what is required to belong to God's kingdom at the end of the world?
2. Which other heroes and heroines lived out their convictions despite opposition?

3. You can witness to your faith by a martyr's death, but you can also do it by faithful day-to-day living. What are the similarities and differences between these two modes of witnessing?
4. You constantly face opportunities to be good or to be bad. Which requires more courage?

GETTING IT TOGETHER

You are a mere mote on a spinning speck called earth, which is one of billions of heavenly bodies. Until a few years ago, you did not exist. A hundred years from now, you will no longer be alive. As Scripture says, "Man's days are like those of grass; like a flower of the field he blooms; the wind sweeps over him and he is gone, and his place knows him no more." Psalm 103:15–16

What is the meaning of life? Perhaps you have already wondered about this, at those times when you've come face to face with the mystery of life. Most of humankind yearns to know the purpose of existence. Some would say, however, that the universe is an accident, a chance combination of elements, while others would say life is nothing but a cruel joke and that it has no meaning.

To the Jewish believers, life was a gift from an almighty but loving Father. All of creation was permeated with his glory and his goodness, and human beings—the splendor of creation—were his children. Everything was centered on the relationship between people and God. In the span of a lifetime, one either strengthened the love covenant with God or shattered it.

The literature of the Jews is built on this mentality. Books like Ruth, Job, Jonah, and Daniel demonstrate how to live the most meaningful life. Ruth tells you to be virtuous and faithful in love. Job tells you to trust God through everything. Jonah tells you to witness to God's love for all people, and Daniel tells you to be steadfast in observing God's law. These same principles underlie the Christian faith.

■ Your outlook on life makes all the difference in the world, both day by day and at the end of your journey. What do *you* think life is all about?

REVIEWING THE CHAPTER

Linking Your Ideas

1. What do Ruth, Jonah, Job, and Daniel contribute to your understanding of what it means to be a good person?
2. Discuss the patterns of the lives of Ruth, Jonah, Job, and Daniel. When did they act? How? How did they make decisions and follow through? How did they allow God to enter everyday life?
3. Of the four people in this chapter, who was the best Jew? The closest to God? The most human? The most successful?

Strengthening Your Grasp

1. What symbols would you select to represent Ruth? Jonah? Job? Daniel? Explain your choices.
2. Make a collage representing the life of one of the characters in this chapter.
3. Write a personal letter to Ruth, Jonah, Job, or Daniel that summarizes what their lives have taught you.

Expressing Your Convictions

1. Write a short story that has an outstanding Christian teenager as its hero or heroine.
2. Dramatize one of the stories in this chapter.
3. Create a cartoon strip of a modern Job, Ruth, Jonah, or Susanna.

CALLED BY THE FATHER

REVIEWING THE UNIT

Pattern

1. What experiences of the Jews shaped their thinking in such a way that, in the period of their maturity, they were able to write the books of Genesis, Ruth, Jonah, Job, and Daniel?
2. What light does each book of the Bible studied in this unit shed on the covenant relationship between God and humankind?

Focal Points

1. List the themes of the books studied in this unit.
2. Write a children's version of one of the Bible stories. Make the theme obvious.
3. Write an unwritten chapter of a Bible story—Adam and Eve's reaction to the murder of Abel; Noah's explanation to his family about building the ark; Ruth's first day in Moab—or choose your own event.
4. Make a portfolio of five character portraits from this unit. Attach a brief description of each person.
5. Write an imaginary diary for one of the people studied.

Response

1. Compose and hold a paraliturgical service for this unit.
2. Explain which Jewish concepts underlying on the content of the books in this unit are valid for Christians today.
3. Write a prayer thanking God for the gifts of life, of other people, and of the world.

FINAL REVIEW

1. To find a complete review of the main characters and events of the Old Testament, read Sirach (Ecclesiasticus) 44–50 and make a list of all the people mentioned. What lines in 51:1–12 apply to any of those characters? Which apply to Christ? Which to you?
2. Compose one statement about each of the Old Testament characters named in Hebrews 11.

Epilogue: Jesus Christ

In the beginning was the Word;
the Word was in God's presence,
and the Word was God. . . .
Through him all things came into being,
and apart from him nothing came to be. . . .
To his own he came,
yet his own did not accept him.
Any who did accept him
he empowered to become children of God.

JOHN 1:1, 3, 11–12

A little more than a hundred years after the last words of the Old Testament were written, the longed-for Messiah appeared. For believers he brought to completion all the expectations that Abraham's faith had set in motion. He was a liberator like Moses and the judges, but greater. He was the king of peace and justice foreshadowed by David and foretold by the prophets, but greater. Jesus Christ, the Savior of the World, was the Son of God himself.

Never in their wildest imaginings had the Jews ever guessed God's plan. They believed in his love for them, and for centuries they safeguarded and trusted the promise of a God-sent messiah. But God's love went far beyond any Jewish hope. He came in person—as one of us—to save us, and he loved us to the point of death.

CALLED BY THE FATHER

In Jesus Christ, God's people—as the result of a growth process that had gone on for thousands of years—reached the peak of their development. Through Christ's new, universal covenant, his infinite sacrifice, and the gift of his Spirit, we can become a new creation—sons and daughters of the Father, alive with the life of his Son and bonded in the love of the Spirit. We can cooperate in building the kingdom of love that will have no end. In Jesus, humanity is already glorified and at the right hand of the Father.

In Christ's first coming, humanity was opened once and for all to a relationship with God. It remains for each individual to respond to God's offer of salvation until Christ's Second Coming in majesty at the end of the world. Then God's love and life will permeate all peoples and the entire universe, so that God will be all in all. In the words of the Jesuit theologian Teilhard de Chardin, "At all costs we must renew in ourselves the desire and hope for the great Coming."

Eucharistic Prayer II confesses the essence of Christian faith and contains the only response appropriate for all the marvels the Lord has done for his people:

> Father, it is our duty and our salvation, always and everywhere, to give you thanks through your beloved Son, Jesus Christ.
>
> He is the Word through whom you made the universe, the Savior you sent to redeem us.
>
> By the power of the Holy Spirit he took flesh and was born of the Virgin Mary.
>
> For our sake he opened his arms on the cross; he put an end to death and revealed the resurrection.
>
> In this he fulfilled your will and won for you a holy people.
>
> And so we join the angels and the saints in proclaiming your glory . . .
>
> Jesus Christ yesterday, today, and forever!*

* *Vatican II Weekday Missal* (Boston, Mass.: Daughters of St. Paul), 1975.

A Jewish Update

Spiritually we are all Semites.

PIUS XI

Some people forget that Jesus was a Jew. His parents and grandparents were Jewish. He spoke, prayed, and dressed like a Jew. His closest friends were all Jews. Jesus lived and died a Jew.

The Jews during Jesus's time spoke Aramaic.

Respect and love for Jesus has inspired modern Christians with new interest in the Jewish people. Vatican II emphasized that Judasim is the root of Christianity and that Jewish and Christian relations should be improved. Saint Paul taught that because God called the Jews to a close covenant with himself, and because God's gifts are never taken back, the Jews will always be God's Chosen People.

Although you have studied the Hebrew Scriptures, which prepared the way for Christ, you may not be familiar with modern Judaism. The history of the Chosen People in the Bible ends with the stories of Jesus and the early Church, but there have been developments in the Jewish faith since then.

Romans 11:28–29

The Great Destruction

All who hold the Jewish faith are members of the Jewish religion. Although traditionally said to be Semites (descended from a common ancestor, Shem), the Jews come from some eighty-five racial/ethnic stocks.

The Jews were a people without a country for two thousand years. Driven out of Palestine shortly after Jesus's death, they remained without a land of their own until the 1940s, when Israel became a nation.

When the Romans rolled into Judea under General Pompey in 63 B.C., a Galilean rebel organization called the Zealots began an underground movement that ended in an unsuccessful revolt in 6 B.C. This group reorganized and struck out for independence again in A.D. 67. Finally, in 70, a Roman army sealed off Jerusalem, trapping the thousands who had come from all over Palestine for the Passover. Escapees fell into the arms of waiting soldiers, who promptly had them crucified. For a hundred days, no food or water passed into the city.

Then the Romans resorted to fire. Flaming brands tossed into the city transformed Jerusalem into a mammoth cauldron of fire. When all was over, the once magnificent cream and gold Temple of Herod stared with hollow eyes on a charred and desolate landscape.

About a thousand refugees fled to the rock fortress of Masada in the upper city. There, in A.D. 73, they committed mass suicide rather than surrender.

An entire way of life went up in smoke in that fire. It was as if some gigantic bomb had wiped out Washington, D.C., while a national convention on religious life was being held there, killing not only the president and all of Congress but the nation's religious leaders as well. With the destruction of all but one wall of the Temple, the daily sacrifices, which had once been central to Jewish worship, came to an end. Home and synagogue worship took their place.

Jewish Refugees

Most of the Jewish people who had not been in Jerusalem during the siege fled to Babylonia, Syria, Asia Minor, and throughout the Mediterranean world. This flight was called the Great Dispersion, and the Jews since then have lived in the Diaspora, the term describing communities outside of Palestine. After a final uprising in A.D. 165, the Jews were forbidden to set foot in their beloved Jerusalem.

The leader of this rebellion against the Emperor Hadrian was a messiah figure, Bar Kochba.

Survival in the Diaspora

Today, two thousand years later, close to 15 million Jews witness to the remarkable power of the Jews to survive. One thing kept them united: their faith. Despite their wide separation from one another, they established schools for rabbis; they built synagogues in every community; and they faithfully followed their religious laws and festivals.

Any man or (in some branches of Judaism) woman who studies the Law can be a rabbi, a specially trained lay person who is neither anointed nor appointed. In some foreign countries, chief rabbis play a role akin to that of a bishop.

The Pharisees—the laymen educated in the law who had grown influential after the Maccabean wars—immediately assumed leadership. They established rabbinical schools in Jamnia near Galilee, and there, together with scholars in the older school of Babylon, they worked for sixty years to gather the oral teachings of the rabbis and to organize and adapt Jewish law to fit the new situation of the Diaspora. The book containing this rabbinical teaching is the Talmud.

Deprived of the Temple, the people of the Diaspora built the same kind of plain buildings without altars that had served them during the Babylonian Exile. In these synagogues, or "meeting places," the people worshipped, kept in touch with their leaders, were educated in the faith of Israel, and maintained their own social life apart from their neighbors.

Each synagogue has an ark (a tabernacle) in which are kept the sacred biblical scrolls. Today, morning and evening services, the Sabbath and community feasts, and social events are held in the synagogue.

The feasts and ceremonies of Judaism also gave the people an opportunity to express, learn, and live their faith and to hand it down to their children. The Jewish people still celebrate the religious events of their history through an annual cycle of feasts. By means of specific traditional ceremonies, each individual's life is blessed from cradle to grave. (See chart, "Jewish Life Sanctified," page 312.)

■ If the Catholic Church everywhere were suddenly forced underground, what essentials would insure its survival?

THE BAD TIMES

The Holocaust

You have seen films and books about the Holocaust—Nazi Germany's systematic extermination of more than 6 million Jews in the gas chambers of European concentration camps during World War II. It also included the annihilation or subjugation of 5 million members of certain other groups: Gypsies, Slavs, and the mentally and physically disabled. The special character of the Jewish suffering must not be forgotten. Between 1939 and 1945, under the dictatorship of Adolf Hitler, one-third of the total world population of Jews was wiped out of existence, and thousands of others were forced to flee. Reviving the medieval use of the yellow star of David to mark the Jews, the Nazis shipped them in crowded boxcars to the camps, where they were starved, used in scientific experiments, forced into hard labor, and gassed at the rate of twelve thousand a day.

Some people blame Hitler alone for this incredible slaughter. Although the Nazi philosophy was rooted in fundamentally anti-Christian beliefs, the anti-Semitism promoted in the Christian countries of Europe just prior to the war had prepared the soil to receive the seed. Hitler only carried the prejudice of the people to its logical conclusion. He cloaked their hatred in misguided versions of Darwin's theory of the survival of the fittest, insisting that only fair-skinned people like the northern Germans were "the fittest." Hitler also twisted the teachings of German philosopher Friedrich Nietzsche (1844–1900) to justify his claims that the "master race"—the Aryans, or gentiles—was superior to the laws of morality governing everyone else.

Although some Christians died defending Jews, no public voice was raised in defense of the Jewish victims, to the eternal shame of the Christian Church and other world leaders. The word *holocaust* has the religious meaning of an offering made to God by complete destruction of the victim. Today some Christians and Jews look upon Israel's sacrifice as somehow related to

The six-pointed star of David is said to have been the insignia on David's shield. Ninth-century Muslims segregated Jews by forcing them to wear it.

Anti-Semitism is hostility toward or discrimination against Jews as a religious or ethnic group.

CALLED BY THE FATHER

Isaiah's Servant figure who suffered for the salvation of the world.

During his underground existence between 1943 and 1945, Jewish theologian Jules Isaac wrote: "The glow of the Auschwitz crematorium is the beacon that lights and guides all my thoughts. Oh, my Jewish brothers, and you as well, my Christian brothers, do you not think it mingles with another glow, that of the Cross?"

Auschwitz was one of the Nazi concentration camps. A *crematorium* is a furnace for reducing bodies to ashes.

- What evidence of prejudice against Jews are you aware of?
- What is your reaction to the Holocaust?
- What can an average person do to prevent such a thing happening again?

Roots of Anti-Semitism

A quick overview of the sources of anti-Semitism shows that for centuries Christians and others strayed far from Christ's command of love.

Non-Jews Before the Time of Christ. Israel's neighbors disliked the Jews because the Jews insisted on the right to religious freedom and held themselves separate from nonbelievers.

New Testament Christians. The criticism of Jewish leaders that is found in the Gospels and epistles was given out of concern for the spiritual welfare of the Jews. After all, Jesus was one with the Jews. Like the prophets, his criticism was delivered to make his own people better, not to stir up hatred. The authors of the New Testament were steeped in a Jewish tradition which held that people needed strong words to keep them faithful. However, some of the gentile converts who read the New Testament also read into it their own pagan-influenced prejudices.

Early Christian Fathers. Some of the early Christians preached against the Jews as the people who had crucified and rejected Christ. In reality, only the Jewish Council, and not even all of its members, condemned Jesus. Today we know that the Jews neither collectively nor individually are to blame for Jesus's death.

Although they were members of the Jewish Council, Nicodemus and Joseph of Arimathea were sympathetic to the cause of Jesus.

Medieval European Christians. During the Middle Ages, Christian teaching mistakenly held that Christians who punished Jews were God's instruments. Jews were seen as resisting grace and corrupting society; accordingly, they were increasingly attacked, robbed, and even murdered in the name of Christ. When Jews withdrew to worship in seclusion, they were dragged into courts and charged with treason and conspiracy. Open massacre was followed either by expulsion (in England, France, and Germany) or segregation in disease-ridden ghettoes around which were built walls that were locked every night. Jews were forbidden to own land, attain higher education, or participate in government. Kept by law out of agriculture, industry, and certain crafts, they were forced into finance and small trades.

Russian Christians. Eastern non-Orientals confined the Jews to shtetles, villages they could not leave without police approval. Periodically, the Jews were the victims of pogroms, or organized massacres.

Spanish Catholics. When Muslim armies conquered much of Spain in the early eighth century, the Jews, who shared Semitic roots with the Arab Muslims, fared well under Muslim rule in Spain. However, by the thirteenth century, Christian princes were successful in driving out the Muslims. When the Spanish Inquisition hunted down the Moriscos (Muslims converted to Christianity), Jews were also persecuted.

Protestants. When Martin Luther, the father of Protestantism, first recognized the Jewish roots of Christ, he wrote a book in which he called the Jews "the blood brothers of Jesus." But when the Jews wouldn't convert to Christianity, Luther grew bitter toward them.

The Enlightenment. As a result of renewed struggles for the universal right of human freedom during the American and French revolutions in the eighteenth century, Napoleon abolished the ghettoes and granted Jews full citizenship in France. In America, they enjoyed constitutional freedom. These reforms, however, did not stem the tide of anti-Semitism.

Catholic Liturgy. Before Vatican II, the solemn intercessions for the Jews recited on Good Friday prayed

Shtetles rhymes with *kettles.*

Pogrom is pronounced peh-**grum**.

The Inquisition was a Roman Catholic court set up in the Middle Ages to suppress heresy.

Vatican II opened in 1962.

CALLED BY THE FATHER

that God might "tear the veil from their hearts so that they also may acknowledge our Lord Jesus Christ." It was asked that Jews be "brought out of all darkness." When the Council openly denounced anti-Semitism, the prayer was updated to read, "Let us pray for the Jewish people, the first to hear the word of God, that they may continue to grow in the love of his name and in faithfulness to his covenant."

Today's Christians. Anti-Semitism isn't dead yet. In 1980 a leading American Christian minister said at a national convention, "God doesn't hear the prayers of a Jew," while in various European countries bombs are being exploded in front of some Jewish synagogues and other gathering places. In this country, some synagogues are being vandalized and desecrated.

■ Someone has stereotyped Catholics as fisheaters who are always fingering their beads and who have large families. What truth do you find in these images? How would you describe a Catholic? How fair do you think any stereotypes are?

THE GOOD YEARS

The Golden Age

Granted freedom of education under the Moors (Spanish Muslims) in Spain, Jewish scholarship enjoyed a golden age from about A.D. 700 to 1250. The great Jewish scholar Moses Maimonides reorganized, updated, and translated the Talmud and made the Hebrew Scriptures available in Arabic. He is often compared to Catholicism's Thomas Aquinas because he tried to show the reasonableness of the Faith.

Maimonides (1135–1203) was a Spanish rabbi, philosopher, and physician. Saint Thomas Aquinas (1255–1274) was an Italian philosopher; his great work is the *Summa Theologica.*

A group who objected to "reasonable faith" explored the mysticism of the teachings of Israel. They worked out a system of theology known as the Cabbala. Along with number symbolism and magical formulas in their main book, *The Zohar* ("bright light"), Cabbalist theories about God's closeness to the world have influenced contemporary Jewish and Christian thinkers.

The Zohar was written in 1280 by Moses de Leon in Spain.

Jewish Holy Ones

Although the Jews do not have a doctrine of saints who intercede with God and form a Mystical Body with people still on earth, they have high respect for persons who give evidence of special closeness to God.

A group known as the Hasidim (the "pious ones") followed such a special person—Baal Shem Tov, known as the "Kindly Master." This humble Polish claydigger received a divine vision in which he became convinced that God was everywhere and in everything. He taught that even the poorest, most illiterate person could grow close to the spirit of God.

The Hasidim are strict Orthodox Jews. Following the ancient traditions of Judaism, each community is formed around a holy messiah figure, the *rebbe* (rabbi). Ecstatic songs and dancing form part of their response to his preaching. For Hasidim, holiness is a relationship with God rather than a mindless conformity to rules or extensive study. They were pioneers in establishing private schools for their children.

■ Prepare a report on these Jewish holy men: Martin Buber, Isaac Luria, Moses Chaim Luzzatto.

Tzaddik (or Savior-Rabbi) Baal Shem Tov lived from 1699 to 1761.

A Great Day

Every family has its own special days. May 14, 1948, was such a day for the Jews, for it was on that day that modern Israel was born. After two thousand years of alienation and persecution, the Jewish people again possessed a homeland in Israel, formerly Palestine.

Because the revolutionary ideas of the Enlightenment failed to dispel prejudice in Europe, and Russia conducted periodic pogroms against the Jews, many Jews became convinced of the need of a Jewish national state. In 1896, the Jewish statesman Theodor Herzl's book, *The Jewish State*, gave rise to a movement called Zionism. Zionism originally aimed to restore Palestine as the national homeland of the Jews; since the establishment of Israel, it has been concerned with the development and defense of the homeland.

CALLED BY THE FATHER

During World War I, Britain made an official statement known as the Balfour Declaration, encouraging Zionism. Thousands of Jews immediately flocked to Palestine. Next, the League of Nations gave Britain a mandate to administer Palestine, and the Jews laid a foundation for their state.

The tragedy of the Holocaust brought the issue to a head. After World War II, in a spirit of reparation to the Jews (who were already immigrating to Palestine in considerable numbers), in November 1947 the United Nations Assembly voted to have the British withdraw and to partition Palestine into a Jewish state, an Arab state, and a small internationally administered area that included the city of Jerusalem. The Jews accepted this arrangement, but the Arab Palestinians felt that Palestine should be granted independence with Jews allowed to live there as a protected minority. Even so, the Jewish people had at long last acquired a homeland.

More than just a political achievement, the re-establishment of Israel is to the Jewish people a new development in their covenant relationship with God, and some believe it compares with the first Exodus. If Auschwitz stands as a symbol of Christian failure in this century, the State of Israel symbolizes the unexpected rescue of the Jews. It is a resurrection of the Suffering Servant of Isaiah, who was sacrificed so that the world might be saved.

But the Arabs, who had called Palestine their home for many years, felt dispossessed. Several Arab countries joined the Palestinian Arabs in a war for domination early in 1948 as the British withdrew. They were unsuccessful, and the Jews officially declared the existence of the State of Israel on May 14, 1948. Arab refugees fled to the Gaza Strip, Jordan, Syria, and Lebanon and formed political and military groups dedicated to regaining their homeland in Palestine (now Israel). To this day each side struggles for possession of the land.

You may wonder whose side to be on—that of the Jews or that of the Palestinians. While recognizing the religious meaning of the Israeli state, neither Christians nor Jews can afford to glorify that state. It is not in existence primarily because once, long ago, the Jews conquered the territory, or even because the Bible promised it to them. It arose as a vehicle to protect the Jews from murderous anti-Semitism, and it was legally established by the peoples of the world represented in the League of Nations and later in the United Nations. Israel is a nation like any other. If Israel violates the rights of others, she must expect criticism and defensive action. She is also responsible for working toward peace in the Middle East.

■ Where Jews have enjoyed equal rights, they have excelled in many fields. Name the contributions made by the following: Sigmund Freud, Samuel Goldwyn, Adolph S. Ochs, Arthur Rubinstein, Jonas Salk, August von Wassermann, Robert Oppenheimer, Julius Rosenwald, Albert Einstein, George Gershwin.

SHORT ANSWERS TO THE MOST-ASKED QUESTIONS ABOUT JEWS AND JUDAISM

Why don't the Jews accept Jesus?

One rabbi said, "It's a matter of faith in Jesus. You have it. We don't." The Jews had many ideas of a messiah. Some Jews had nothing more than vague hopes for a glorious future age. Others looked forward to an ideal king like David. At times the Jews expected two messiahs, one a priest like Aaron, the other a prophet.

When Jesus lived, the atmosphere was charged with the expectancy of a military messiah. Unlike the Zealots, Jesus usually avoided any connection with political kingship or military takeover, though he did criticize the system when he invaded the Temple. But the main role of Jesus was to be a suffering messiah, the idea of which even his followers could not grasp until after the resurrection.

Today Jews remain divided about a messiah. Even those who believe in resurrection cannot accept the

In general, messianism includes those ideas that represent the Israel of the future as identical with God's kingdom, a time of peace and justice.

CALLED BY THE FATHER

scandal of Jesus's saving death. "The world is no better for Jesus's coming," they say, "so how could he be the Messiah?" But the Jews' most serious objection to Christianity is rooted in their idea of God's greatness; they cannot imagine a completely holy (other) God becoming a man.

They blame Saint Paul, who abolished the Sabbath and circumcision, for separating Christians and Jews. They reject his claim to having been divinely commissioned to preach that only faith in Christ (and not the Law) would bring salvation.

■ There is a growing movement called Messianic Judaism. Research these "Jews for Jesus" as to origin, purpose, and meaning, and make a report to the class.

What do Jews think of Jesus?

Jews regard Jesus as one of their own—a Jew preaching the Jewish faith of love for God and neighbor, especially the poor. In his book *Basic Judaism*, rabbi Milton Steinberg wrote:

> To Jews . . . Jesus appears as an extraordinarily beautiful and noble spirit, aglow with love and pity for men, especially for the unfortunate and lost, deep in piety, of keen insight into human nature, endowed with a brilliant gift of parable and epigram, an ardent Jew, moreover, a firm believer in the faith of his people: all in all, a dedicated teacher of principles, religious and ethical, of Judaism . . . and always there is his own personality, a superb achievement in its own right.

Parable and *epigram* are techniques of teaching.

Jews do not see Jesus as a prophet because they say he preached more about the "other world" than about this world, and in the Jewish view it is through *this* life that God is glorified. They see Jesus as being indifferent to social affairs—the tyranny of the Roman Empire, for instance. They do not regard him as the *ideal* human being because they say he showed no interest at all in the human concerns of philosophy, science, government, or art. They feel that his outbursts of temper in

the Temple, over the unfruitful fig tree, and toward the scribes and Pharisees—and his prejudice against such non-Jews as the Syro-Phoenician woman—show a flawed character (see Mark 7:24–30). On the other hand, they criticize him for accepting evil too patiently and passively.

Jews find the four diverse portraits of Christ in the Gospels and the different images of him in the various branches of Christianity confusing. For instance, there is the severe Christ of the Calvinists; the mystical, divine Christ of the Eastern Orthodox; and the Christ of Catholics who becomes present to his people in the sacraments. They ask which of these is the true Christ.

Jews feel obliged neither to pronounce a judgment on Jesus nor to convert the world to Judaism. They feel their mission is to make known the God who spoke on Sinai. They regard it as a mystery that billions have come to know the true God through Christians, who have spread the Jewish Scriptures throughout the world.

▪ Write a careful description of your views of Jesus as you might present it to a group of Jewish teenagers. Your purpose is to inform, not to make converts.

Are there different branches of Judaism?

Perhaps on Saturday you have seen Jewish families walking to their synagogues, the boys wearing yarmulkes (skullcaps), the bearded men looking dignified in their somber long coats, the women in dark-colored dresses. These are Orthodox Jews, the traditional Jews who strictly follow the six hundred and thirteen laws of Judaism.

You may have heard the expression, "That isn't kosher." The word *kosher*, which means "fit to eat," originates with the Orthodox Jews' obligation to kill and prepare animals in the exact way prescribed by Mosaic law. Other dietary rules prohibit the eating of pork, taking milk and meat together, and mixing dishes used in preparation of milk and meat. Because of this law some Jewish families have two separate sets of dishes.

The original reasons are lost, but these and other dietary laws make every family meal in the Orthodox Jewish home a religious practice.

CALLED BY THE FATHER

When the men pray, they don a prayer shawl (*tallith*). At morning prayer, except on the Sabbath and on festivals, males strap to their forehead and to the arm nearest their heart two small boxes (*tefillin* or *phylacteries*); each contains a part of Scripture. Like all observing Jews, Orthodox Jews celebrate the Jewish festivals and kindle the Sabbath lights. In addition, they practice ritual washing and other prescribed actions, and they regard written revelation as their sole guide.

Orthodox Jews firmly believe in a coming messiah, but they do not expect him to be divine. For thousands of years, all Jews were Orthodox. The novel *The Chosen*, by Chaim (hi-ehm) Potok, presents the struggles a young person has in trying to remain faithful to strict Judaism in the modern world. With the recent freedom of Western and American Jews to mingle with people of other faiths, Judaism has divided into two other branches. One (called Conservative) is modified traditional; the other (called Reform) is entirely open to change.

In the last century, a movement called Reform Judaism was organized to modernize Jewish laws and customs. This most liberal branch of Judaism abbreviated the Sabbath services. Although recently there has been a trend to reinstate the use of Hebrew, Reform Jews hold services mainly in the vernacular. They introduced the use of the organ during worship even though, out of mourning for the destruction of the Temple, musical instruments had been forbidden since the Exile. They also abolished many other time-honored practices. Some even considered giving up the Sabbath as a holy day!

In 1845, under the leadership of German-born Abraham Geiger, Reform Judaism shocked the Jewish world by rejecting not only the Talmud but the belief in a messiah who would lead the Jews back to Palestine. The European Jewish community reacted so strongly that the Reform movement was transplanted to America. Today it has swung away from the principles of Geiger and reintroduced many ceremonies and customs abandoned earlier.

The *vernacular* is the language native to a country or region.

Schecter (1850–1915) became world-famous with his discovery of the last Hebrew original of Ecclesiasticus (Sirach) in a Cairo synagogue.

To answer a need for a middle position between the two extremes, a third form of Judaism appeared: Conservative Judaism, which retains maximal observance of ritual law and custom despite a more liberal theology. In America, the congregations of Conservative Judaism were organized by Solomon Schecter into the United Synagogue of America. Conservative Jews place high priority on the mission of Judaism to bear witness to the true God. "Tradition, with change" is their motto.

Despite these divisions, Jews experienced a profound sense of unity in the sorrow of the Holocaust and the joy of their own homeland. These three religious positions reveal Judaism's great flexibility.

How can you identify which branch of Judaism someone professes?

The use of the yarmulke (**yarh**-mul-keh) identifies the religious position of a Jew. In the West, raising the hat is a sign of reverence. To the Jew, reverence, especially to God, is shown by covering the head. Orthodox males wear the skullcap at all times to remind them of God's constant presence and to honor God's name when it comes up in conversation. Other religious males wear it in the synagogue, while studying sacred texts, and while engaged in religious ritual at home. Reform Jews do not wear the yarmulke because they feel that its meaning has disappeared in modern Western society.

What feasts do the Jews celebrate?

The Christian liturgical year owes much to the Jewish "Sacred Round," as the Jews call their annual cycle of feasts. As you study the accompanying table, find parallels with Christian worship.

Sabbath is from the Hebrew "shab-bath," meaning "rest."

Why do the Jews observe the Sabbath on Saturday?

Six days God created; on the seventh, according to the Jewish scribes, he rested. The third commandment required Jews to rest from work on every seventh day. The Sabbath was reckoned from sundown on Friday to

The Sacred Round

CELEBRATION	SIGNIFICANCE	WHEN HELD/ACTIVITY
Sabbath—Seventh day	The Sabbath is the most significant religious celebration besides the Day of Atonement. By setting aside a day every week exclusively for worship and reflection on the meaning of life, the Jews showed their independence of the pagan nature gods that demanded working every day to insure material success. Instead, they honor the God of time and history who (1) is Creator and (2) enters into human history to aid and save his creatures.	From sundown on Friday to sundown on Saturday. Just before sunset every Friday, the wife and mother lights the Sabbath candles. Bread and wine open the evening meal amid the scent of sweet spices. The Sabbath is spent discussing, studying, meditating, and praying over the teachings of the Torah.
Passover (Pesach)— Seder Feast	The anniversary of Israel's liberation from Egypt. The Seder is the Passover meal. *Note*: No joyous festivities are permitted, including weddings, for the next forty-nine days after Passover.	Held at home in late March or early April at the full moon.
Shevout or *Shabout* (formerly Pentecost)	The festival of the giving of the Torah, of God revealing himself to Moses on Sinai. It is a day of confirmation (Bar Mitzvah or Bat Mitzvah).	Held on the day of the new moon on the fiftieth day after the day of the Seder.
High Holy Days (1) *Rosh Hashana*	Jewish New Year's Day, which opens a period of repentance that lasts for ten days.	Begins in September or October with the blowing of the ram's horn, the shofar.
(2) *Yom Kippur*	Day of Atonement, or Sabbath of Sabbaths—a day of strict fasting.	Held ten days after Rosh Hashana.

CELEBRATION	SIGNIFICANCE	WHEN HELD/ACTIVITY
Succot or *Sukkoth*	The Feast of Booths (Tents), which commemorates God's grace and protection during the time when the Israelites lived in the desert.	Held in the fall around Thanksgiving. Many Jewish families and most Jewish congregations erect booths. Originally, the roof was made of tree branches, and fruits, flowers, and greenery were placed inside. Some Jews slept in these booths.
Rejoicing over the Torah or *Simachas Torah*	This is a celebration of another complete reading of the Torah during the preceding year.	Held eight days after Succot. A procession, with song and dance, of the sacred scrolls from the ark in the synagogue.
Hanukkah or *Chanukah*	The Feast of Lights, which commemorates the rededication of the Temple by Judas Maccabeus in 165 B.C.	Held near the time of the Christian celebration of Christmas. Like Christmas, Hannukah features gift-giving and special meals.
Purim	The Feast of Lots associated with the Book of Esther, which celebrates deliverance of the Jews from persecution through Esther's courageous and patriotic action.	Held in late February or March. A joyous celebration with a carnival atmosphere, similar to Mardi Gras.

sundown on Saturday. It became a time for reading the Scriptures, especially with the family. Today the Sabbath still begins at home on Friday evening.

The first followers of Jesus observed the Jewish Sabbath faithfully, and then gathered in a believer's home

CALLED BY THE FATHER

on the following day to celebrate the Lord's Supper. The first day of the week (Sunday) was the anniversary of Jesus's resurrection, so it became known as the Lord's Day. When Christians no longer went to the synagogue, they transferred the readings, psalms, hymns, and prayers from that service to the Sunday celebration of the Lord's Supper.

Does Judaism have sacraments?

Like Christians, the Jews consecrate life's greatest moments, but their ceremonies are not sacraments in the Christian sense of visible signs that bring about an inward change. Their ceremonies represent a remembering of God's saving events of the past for the purpose of experiencing his presence and power at the time of the celebration. The festival then becomes a pledge of God's fidelity in the future. See the chart, "Jewish Life Sanctified," for the more important rituals.

- What similarities do you see between the practices of Judaism and Christianity? What major Christian feasts or rituals are not observed?
- Research and report any of the following ritual objects used by Jewish people in their religious practices: mezuzah, embroidered cloth to cover the bread, silver goblets, Hanukkah menorah, booths, Seder plate, matzo, yarmulke, siddur, milchig and fleishig, kosher, shehitah, wedding glass.

Is the Jewish Bible different from the Christian Bible?

Before Christ, the Jews did not have a canon, or official list, of books they regarded as inspired, only a collection of sacred writings. The Greek version, called the Septuagint, had been translated between 250 and 100 B.C. With the early Christians using this version and proclaiming the twenty-seven New Testament books canonical, the Jews settled on their own canon in Jamnia in A.D. 90. This list excluded from the Septuagint six books and some other passages that had not always been held as inspired in the Jewish tradition.

The Septuagint ("seventy") is said to have been translated by Jewish scholars in Alexandria, Egypt.

The Council of Florence in 1441 and the Council of Trent in 1545 confirmed the present Catholic Canon.

Jewish Life Sanctified

EVENT	CEREMONY	PURPOSE
Birth	Circumcision	Incorporates the child into the covenant of Abraham. (A child born of a Jewish mother is automatically a Jew.)
31 days after birth of male firstborn	Presentation (redemption of firstborn son)	Releases the firstborn from service to God, to whom all firstborn were to be dedicated.
Puberty (Age 13)	Bar Mitzvah (boys) Bat Mitzvah (girls)	Calls the male Jew to observance of the Law and marks the individual's commitment. From this time on he may don the phylacteries (*tefillin*) at prayer. Reform and Conservative Jews have a Bat Mitzvah ceremony for girls. Bar Mitzvah means "son of the commandment"—that is, one who is obligated to observe the commandments.
Age 15, 16	Confirmation	Marks group commitment to the Law after graduation from nine or ten days of religious elementary training in Jewish history, law, customs, and traditions.

Have the Jews added anything to their Scriptures?

Christians added the New Testament to the Hebrew Scriptures, but the Jews have not added any books to those they share in common with Christians. By A.D. 550, however, they had completed an additional collection of oral tradition called the Talmud. The Talmud ("to learn") is an encyclopedic book of rabbinical teachings and interpretations of the Torah. It was worked on in the rabbinical schools after the destruction of Jeru-

EVENT	CEREMONY	PURPOSE
Marriage	Kiddushin (sanctification)	Standing under a canopy, which represents the home the married couple will establish, and drinking wine, a sign of the goodness of life, the couple are married in the presence of the rabbi.
Death	Viddui	The dying person makes a faith confession (the final act of acceptance of death), prays to God to protect those left behind, and recites the Shema. After burial, there are seven days of mourning. Kaddish is the Jewish prayer recited by mourners after the death of a relative. For one year, children recite special prayers of thanks each month in the synagogue on the anniversary of the death.

salem so that no scrap of Jewish learning might be lost. It has two parts.

The first part is known as Hallakah ("which way to walk"). It consists of Israel's oral law and was codified and arranged into a system between A.D. 70 and 200. The second part, called Mishnah, is a collection of stories (haggadah), sayings, and discussions commenting on the oral law. They were gathered over a period of a thousand years (400 B.C.–A.D. 500). When the hagga-dah stories interpret the spiritual meaning of the Scrip-tures, they are known as midrash ("to seek out"). Parts of the New Testment are written in this form.

Although the Jews differ in their belief concerning divine Revelation, Orthodox and Conservative Jews are bound by both the oral Talmudic tradition and the writ-ten Torah. The most widely used commentary is that of Rashi, an eleventh-century French scholar.

The name of Rashi (1040–1105) was made up of the Hebrew initials of Rabbi Solomon, son of Isaac.

Although burned in the marketplace and strewn page by page upon the waters during times of persecution, the Talmud has served to protect the observance of the Torah and to preserve the high religious and moral char-acter of the Jewish people from the corruption of worldly morality. The holy and learned rabbis who study and teach it are still the great leaders of Judaism.

■ Following are short wise sayings from the Talmud. Which do you recognize? Which do you like?

"Give everyone the benefit of the doubt."
"Look at the contents, not the bottle."
"When in a city, follow its customs."
"All's well that ends well."
"One good deed leads to another."
"Going backward is still a form of travel."
"If you travel slower, you'll arrive a little sooner."
"If all pulled together, the world would fall over."

■ Name any Jewish rabbis who are respected in your community. What leadership do they exercise?

Do all Jews speak Hebrew?

Just as Latin was used for Catholic worship, Hebrew is still the holy language of worship for Orthodox and Conservative Jews. Although in daily affairs Jews speak the language of their country, many also learn Hebrew. During the Middle Ages, the Jews developed in two geographical divisions: the Spanish Jews, called Se-phardim; and the German-speaking Jews, called Ash-kenazim.

Boys and, with the exception of the Orthodox, girls are expected to chant the prophetic portion of the Scriptures in Hebrew at their Bar/Bat Mitzvah.

CALLED BY THE FATHER

The Sephardim spoke an old dialect of Spanish called Ladino. The pronunciation of the official Hebrew of modern Israel today is Sephardic. During the medieval persecutions, the Jews from Germany (the Ashkenazim) formed their own language, blending medieval German with Hebrew. Today it is known as Yiddish. Most Jews today are Ashkenazim.

You may become familiar with the wonderful humor of the Ashkenazi Jews through Leo Rosen's book, *The Joys of Yiddish*.

Do the Jews, like Christians, have creeds that sum up their beliefs?

Judaism transmits its faith mainly through the study of the Torah in the home, school, and synagogue. It has no official creed or catechism besides the belief in the one living God, as expressed in the Shema. Nearest to a fully developed creed are the Thirteen Articles of Jewish Faith drawn up by a philosopher of the Middle Ages, Moses Maimonides.

The Articles are summarized in the book *Judaism*, by Arthur Hertzberg, as follows:

> I believe with perfect faith that God is the creator of all things and he alone; that he is one with a unique unity; that he is without body or any form whatsoever; that he is eternal; that to him alone is it proper to pray; that all the words of the prophets are true; that Moses is the chief of the prophets; that the law will never be changed and no other will be given; that God knows all the thoughts and actions of men; that he rewards the obedient and punishes transgressors; that the Messiah will come; that there will be a resurrection of the dead.

Although not accepted by every Jew and in no way binding, these Articles appear in the Jewish Daily Prayer Book as an introduction to the morning service.

JEWISH SACRED OBJECTS

Mezuzah

A small box which is the receptacle for pieces of parchment containing key biblical texts called the Shema, for the first words of Deuteronomy 6:4–9 and 11:13–21. It is fixed to the right doorpost and touched reverently on entering or leaving the house. It is the sign of an Orthodox Jewish household.

Menorah

A seven-branch candelabrum originally used in the Tabernacle of the Temple to commemorate the seven days of creation. Today eight- and nine-branch candelabra are used for the celebration of Hanukkah, the Feast of Lights.

Sacred Scrolls

Handwritten by scribes who worked as long as a year on each, according to very strict rules of accuracy, the scrolls of the Torah are kept wrapped in beautiful silk or velvet mantles in the ark. Ornamental silver crowns adorn the wooden rollers.

Shofar

A ram's horn. It sounds the call to repentance at the New Year (Rosh Hashana).

Siddur

The book containing the prayers for daily and Sabbath worship compiled over thousands of years and put together in the tenth century. It contains many scriptural texts and uses the Psalms extensively.

EXTENDING YOUR INTEREST

1. Words and events to know:

Dispersion/Diaspora	May 14, 1948	confirmation
Pharisees	Palestinians	kiddushin
rabbinical school	messianism	Hebrew Scriptures
synagogue	Orthodox Judaism	Septuagint
holocaust	Reform Judaism	Talmud
master race	Conservative	midrash
anti-Semitism	Judaism	Thirteen Articles of
ghetto	yarmulke	Jewish Faith
shtetle	"Sacred Round"	Hebrew
pogrom	Sabbath	Sephardim
Spanish Inquisition	Pesach	Ashkenazim
Enlightenment	Rosh Hashana	Yiddish
golden age	Yom Kippur	shofar
Moses Maimonides	Sukkot	menorah
Cabbala	Hanukkah	sacred scrolls
Hasidim	circumcision	mezuzah
Zionism	bar/bat mitzvah	siddur

2. Read Articles 4 and 5 of the Vatican II document, *Declaration on the Relation of the Church to Non-Christian Religions*. Which part do you agree with most? If you had been a Council Father, would you have voted to include in the document some sort of admission of guilt or apology on behalf of Christians toward the Jews, who had been mistreated for so long? Why or why not? In your own words, write a brief declaration of how Catholics and Jews should feel toward one another.

3. Compare the Vatican II statement on Jewish-Christian relations with that of the World Council of Churches made in Delhi in 1961. Comment on the similarities and differences. Which do you prefer?

4. Compose a prayer for the improvement of Jewish-Christian relations.

5. Interview a rabbi or another Jewish person about his or her understanding of and feelings toward Christianity.

6. Report on the origin and aims of these organizations: (a) Institute of Judaeo-Christian Studies; (b) National Conference of Catholic Bishops: Secretariat for Catholic-Jewish Relations; (c) National Conference of Christians and Jews.

7. Contact the following Jewish organizations for materials put out by the Jewish people to promote better relations with other religions:

> The American Jewish Committee
> 165 East 56 Street
> New York, NY 10022

> Anti-Defamation League of B'nai B'rith
> 315 Lexington Avenue
> New York, NY 10016

> Union of American Hebrew Congregations
> Department of Audiovisual Aids
> 838 Fifth Avenue
> New York, NY 10021

8. Find out the purpose of three of the following Jewish organizations and look up three more that are not listed here: B'nai B'rith (rhymes with Renée Smith); B'nai Zion; Jewish Conciliation Board of America; American Zionist Youth Foundation, Inc.; Women's League for Israel; B'rith Abraham; United Hias Service, Inc.; National Council for Young Israel.

9. Investigate and report or write on the lives of any of these Jewish converts to Christianity: Saint Paul, Karl Stern, Edith Stein, Lillian Roth, Monica Hellwig, Marie Alphonse Ratisbonne, Marie Theodore Ratisbonne, venerable Francis Liebermann.

10. How has the study of Jewish history changed your attitude toward the Jewish people?

11. What insights into Christianity and modern changes in the Church did you gain from your study of Judaism? Write them in your journal or in a paper to be submitted to the class. What practical resolutions have you arrived at? Note them in your journal as well.

Bible Handbook

A lamp unto my feet is your word, a light to my path.

PSALM 119:105

What is the world's best-seller? What was the first book published in 1456 after Johann Gutenberg's invention of the printing press? What book covering two thousand years of history is among the oldest manuscripts in existence? The answer to all three questions is the Bible.

What the Bible Is

The Bible is the Word of God. It is a major way God communicates with humankind, and thus it is a sacred book. The Bible is also like a library, because it is actually a collection of seventy-three books. *Bible* is from the Greek word *biblia*, which means "the books."

The Bible is *revelation*, God's unveiling himself to become available for our salvation. He reveals *mysteries*—that is, truths that cannot be exhausted by human explanations. These mysteries include God's infinite self, his breaking into history to save us, and his inviting us to a fuller life.

Scripture and tradition form the Deposit of Faith, everything we need to know to be saved. *Tradition* is the sum of teachings of the Catholic Church—her dogmas, declarations, encyclicals, sermons, and writings. Revelation is presented in the Bible and is interpreted through tradition.

The message of the Bible is that God is a loving Father who has entered into a covenant with us in order to save us.

The Purpose of the Bible

- "From your infancy you have known the sacred Scriptures, the source of the wisdom which through faith in Jesus Christ leads to salvation." (2 Timothy 3:15)

The Bible is God's Word, living and active. Human words inform, reassure, bind, heal, wound, build, and destroy. The words of God have the power to create, to give life, and to save. Thus the Bible puts you into contact with God. Through his words you

CALLED BY THE FATHER

can experience the Christ event, take on the mind and heart of Christ, and respond to his invitation to a fuller life. In this way, we speak of the Bible as the eighth sacrament.

The Holy Spirit makes Christ's saving power available to the Church in the Bible when it is read in public or in private. The first part of the Mass (the Liturgy of the Word) celebrates Scripture. Passages from both the Old and New Testaments are read and form the basis for the homily.

■ Look up these references in God's Word about God's Word, and copy your favorite three: Ps. 119:72, Ps. 119:89, Ps. 119:103, Jer. 15:16, Rev. 19:13, 1 Jn. 5:13, Lk. 1:1-4, 2 Tim. 3:15–17.

The Bible can be compared to several objects.

The Bible is like *a picture of a loved one.* It reveals what God, our loving Father, is like.

The Bible is like *a mirror.* Looking into its pages, you can see yourself in the story of the Israelites, the story of Jesus, and the story of the early church.

The Bible is like *a roadmap.* The Bible directs you to the surest route to heaven: faith, love, and obedience. Moreover, in revealing the meaning of history by showing you where you have come from, it gives meaning to life.

The Bible is like *a letter.* God communicates to you through its words.

To discover what God repeats in different ways, look up these verses, copy them, and read them through prayerfully: 1 Jn. 4:19, Is. 43:1, Jer. 31:3, Ps. 36:6, Ps. 63:4, Jl. 2:13, Deut. 1:31, Hos. 11:4, Jon. 3:11, Is. 54:10, Ps. 36:8, Mt. 22:37, Jn. 14:23, Jn. 15:9, Eph. 5:2, Wis. 11:24–12:1.

Divisions of the Bible

The Bible has two parts, the Old and New Testaments. *Testament* means agreement or covenant.

The *Old Testament*, or Hebrew Scriptures, covers Jewish history from creation to about a hundred years before the birth of Christ and was written between 1900 B.C. and 100 B.C. The Old Testament reveals God's working to prepare the world for the fulfillment of his covenant with them—his coming among them to save them. The books are classified as follows:

Pentateuch (or Law): Genesis, Exodus, Leviticus, Numbers, Deuteronomy

Historical Books: Joshua, Judges, Ruth, 1 and 2 Samuel, 1 and 2 Kings, 1 and 2 Chronicles, Ezra, Nehemiah, Tobit, Judith, Esther, 1 and 2 Maccabees

Writings: Job, Psalms, Proverbs, Ecclesiastes, Song of Songs, Wisdom, Sirach

Prophets: Isaiah, Jeremiah, Lamentations, Baruch, Ezekiel, Daniel, and the twelve minor prophets

The *New Testament* contains the life and teaching of Jesus Christ, the Messiah, and the beginnings of his Church. It covers the years A.D. 6 to 100, and tells of the new, eternal covenant established by Jesus Christ through the Holy Spirit. The New Testament includes the Gospels, the Acts of the Apostles, the Epistles, and the Book of Revelation.

Gospels: The first four New Testament books proclaiming the life, death, and resurrection of Jesus Christ.

Acts of the Apostles: The fifth book of the New Testament narrating the beginnings of the Church.

Epistles: Letters written by the apostles to individuals or Christian communities in the early Church.

The Book of Revelation: The last book in the New Testament, written to exhort the early Christians being persecuted. The book uses visions and symbolic descriptions to make its point.

A device for remembering the order of the first fourteen epistles is RO-CO-CO/GAL-EPH-PHI/COL-THESS-THESS/TIM-TIM-TI/PHIL-HEB.

Locating Verses in the Bible

With practice, reading a reference to Scripture is as easy as reading the address on an envelope. For example, **1 Sm. 3:9–10.**

Sm.: *Sm.* stands for the Book of Samuel. The title of a book is often abbreviated. A list of abbreviations is usually given in the front of the Bible.

1: There are two books of Samuel. The digit before the name indicates which one is referred to.

3: The chapter follows the book title. It is also found at the top of each page like the guide words of a dictionary.

9–10: These are the verses. They are indicated in very small type within each chapter.

■ Answer the following questions:

1. What kind of person says, "There is no God"? (Ps. 53:1)
2. Finish the sentence "God loves us as much as a mother loves . . ." (Is. 49:15)
3. How did God come down to Mount Sinai? (Ex. 19:18)
4. What did David kill? (1 Sm. 17:36)

5. What did Solomon make for God? (2 Chron. 6:18)
6. What will you have if you believe in Christ? (Jn. 6:40)
7. Christ was disappointed when his apostles did not have this. (Mk. 4:40)
8. What must Christ's followers take? (Lk. 9:23)
9. What will Christ bring for each person when he comes at the end of the world? (Rev. 22:12)
10. How many times was Saint Paul scourged for being a Christian? (2 Cor. 11:24)

Attitude Toward the Bible

The Bible should be read as thoroughly as lovers read love letters—that is, several times, always looking for new insights. Lovers also read between the lines and ponder every word.

As the canon or rule of life, the Bible shows you how to live a covenant of love with God. It speaks to you in your present situation. It is said that Saint Francis of Assisi opened the Bible at random three times and found the three principles that shaped his community of Franciscans.

The Bible should be read with a sense of its being God's holy Word. Each passage should be seen as speaking to the present, to you and your friends, to your world. The Bible should be read with openness, faith, and a readiness to be renewed by God's all-powerful Word.

The Bible holds inexhaustible riches. If you meditate on it like Mary, who pondered all things in her heart, you can penetrate more deeply the mystery of God. The reading of the Bible should be a *prayer*, a dialogue between you and God.

■ Find short verses that make good prayers, like the following:

"I do believe, Lord." (Jn. 9:38)

"Speak, Lord, for your servant is listening." (1 Sm. 3:9)

The Bible should be handled with reverence. It should be covered and kept clean, and not be set on the floor. Some people have their Bible blessed, and in some chapels, churches, and homes the Bible is enthroned.

How to Read the Bible

If you establish a routine for reading the Bible, it will become an important part of your everyday life. You should be in a calm and receptive mood, and follow these steps:

1. Set a time for reading the Bible, every day if possible.
2. Begin with a prayer to the Holy Spirit: *O God, our Father, give us your Holy Spirit. Make us read your Word with faith, treasure it in our hearts with hope, experience it in our lives with love so that we may truly know, love, and live your divine Word that leads to salvation through Jesus Christ, your Son, our Lord. Amen.*

3. Read a book at a time.
4. Understand the book's setting: who wrote it and why, who its original readers were, and the conditions under which it was written.
5. Understand the literary form of the book.
6. Keep a notebook for personal insights, questions, or words to look up.
7. Figure out anything you don't understand by using the dictionary, atlas, footnotes, and biblical commentaries.
8. Think about the passages.
9. Act upon the message.

Authorship of the Bible

God is the principal author of the Bible, but he used human beings as instruments.

The direct *inspiration* of the Holy Spirit was involved in all the writing of the Bible; that is, Cod moved the minds and hearts of people to write what he wanted in the form he wanted.

The word *inspiration* is derived from a term that means "to breathe into." God did not dictate every word of the Bible, but he influenced the writers as to what and how to write, allowing them to express it in their own way. Thus, since God used people to express thoughts, his ideas are limited and enriched by their circumstances, talents, and attitudes. But because the Bible is divinely inspired, it has the quality of *inerrancy*, which means "without error."

Tradition ascribes some books to outstanding figures in Jewish history. For instance, Moses is said to be the author of the Pentateuch (the first five books) and David the composer of all the psalms. Scholars believe that groups of writers were responsible for these works.

Origin of the Bible

The Bible passed through three stages of development:

Oral stage: The Israelites kept their history alive by repeating it throughout many generations.

Written stage: Individuals or groups recorded the oral traditions of the Israelites.

Edited stage: Editors combined traditions into an interpreted story of the dealings of God with humankind.

Scholars believe that most Old Testament books were written during Solomon's reign (900 B.C.) and during the Exile (500 B.C.). The books were written on papyrus scrolls. None of the original manuscripts exist today.

Literary Forms in the Bible

There are many forms of writing in the Bible, so to get to the Bible's message, you should consider the wrappings. What form of literature is a particular book? How do the inspired authors use the characteristics of that form to convey truth? Some of the literary forms found in the Bible are parables, short stories, legends, historical ac-

CALLED BY THE FATHER

counts, speeches, letters, prophecy, poetry, and proverbs.

Your science teacher wouldn't have you study a science-fiction novel to get a picture of reality, and you wouldn't read the newspaper to your little sister as a bedtime story. Writing can be understood only when you know its forms, characteristics, and purposes. A historical book of the Bible should not be approached as a fairy tale, nor should a folk legend in the Bible be read as literal truth. Since the Bible is a religious book rather than a scientific or historical book, it conveys religious truths, not necessarily scientific or historical truths.

■ Skim the books in the left-hand column and then match them with the types of writing in the right-hand column.

2 Timothy	comics
Micah	Dear Abby
Psalms	news article
2 Chronicles	feature article
Revelation 1	editorial
Ruth	horoscope
Jonah 2:1–2; 3:8	poetry

Figurative Language in the Bible

My father was a real bear when he found out about the dent in his car. My mom spilled the beans. Then I put my foot in my mouth by mentioning the fine. Hope Dad cools down before Christmas, because I'm dying to ask for my own car.

Imagine how confusing these statements would be to someone unfamiliar with American figures of speech. Similarly, some expressions in Scripture are meant to be taken figuratively, not literally. Also, the meaning of various words and expressions has changed over time. Reading the footnotes and studying biblical commentaries often helps make passages clear.

The Church and the Bible

The Church is the authority on the meaning of the Bible, and her official decisions have the quality of inerrancy.

Out of all the ancient writings, the Church accepted the books of the Bible as authentic, inspired writing at the Council of Trent in A.D. 1546. These books are said to be on the Canon, or officially approved list. There is another group of books the Church does not recognize officially, and a third group that the Church recognizes but that Protestants and Jews do not.

Canonical books are on the Canon.

Apocryphal books are related to the biblical books, but are not designated as divinely inspired. Some of these are the Assumption of Moses, the Life of Adam and Eve, the Book of Enoch, and the Book of Jubilees.

Deuterocanonical books are books the Catholic Church accepts as canonical but which are accepted by neither the Jews nor the Protestants. They include Tobit, Judith, Wisdom, Sirach, Baruch, 1 and 2 Maccabees, and additions to the Book of Esther and the Book of Daniel.

Versions of the Bible

The original books were written in Hebrew, Aramaic, and Greek. Although the original texts are inspired and are free from error, translations do not have this guarantee. Scholars are continually working to make translations that follow the meaning of the original texts as closely as possible.

Through the centuries there have been different versions of the Bible, including the following:

The Septuagint (second or third century B.C.): A translation of the Bible into Greek for the sake of those Jews living in Alexandria, Egypt.

The Vulgate (end of fourth century A.D.): Saint Jerome translated the Bible into Latin, the common language of the world during his time.

King James Version (1611): The Protestant edition of the Bible.

Revised Standard Version (1953): A modern Protestant edition.

Douay-Rheims (1592–1610): A Catholic edition.

Confraternity Edition (1941): A modern Catholic edition.

Other modern translations of the Bible are the Jerusalem Bible, the New American Bible, and the Good News Bible.

■ Find out about the Gideon Bible, the Thumb Bible, the Vinegar Bible, the Devil's Bible, the Reader's Digest Bible, the Caxton Memorial Bible, and other versions.

The People and Lands of the Bible

The Hebrews (Jews) are the descendants of Abraham. They were called Israelites for Israel (Jacob), the father of the twelve tribes. After the Babylonian Exile, they were referred to as Jews, which is derived from the tribe of Judah. The nationality of the Hebrews is Semitic, since they are descended from Shem, Noah's son.

Canaan (or Palestine), the Holy Land, is the bridge between Asia and Africa. This land, about the size of Lake Erie, borders on the Mediterranean Sea. It has a hot, dry climate and only two seasons—winter, which is rainy, and summer, which is dry.

The terrain of Palestine is a pattern of hills and mountains, plains and deserts. The Jordan River cuts through the land, creating a fertile river valley and connecting the Sea of Galilee and the Dead Sea. Because the Dead Sea has no outlet, water settles there and stagnates, leaving chemical deposits. There is no life in it. The Dead Sea, at 1,290 feet below sea level, is the lowest point on the earth's surface.

The Israelites also spent time in Mesopotamia, where they originated, and in Egypt and Babylon.

The Bible in the Twentieth Century

This is the century of a biblical revival, but studying and reading the Bible weren't always encouraged by the Catholic Church. One reaction of the Catholics to the Protestant Reformation of the sixteenth century was to underplay Scripture, and the reading of the Bible was usually done only by priests. This trend began to be reversed when, in his encyclical *Providentissimus Dei* (1893), Pope Leo XIII recommended reading the Bible; he also encouraged the Dominicans to establish a school for the study of the Bible in Jerusalem. Then in 1943, in

CALLED BY THE FATHER

the encyclical *Divino Afflante Spiritu*, Pope Pius XII exhorted everyone to study the Bible and to learn from the language, customs, and culture of the past what the authors of the Bible intended.

The Bible is being studied from historical, religious, and literary aspects. Archaeological research is unlocking the meanings of different passages. The Dead Sea Scrolls, discovered in 1949, and other ancient manuscripts sparked more interest in Scripture study. (See "The Dead Sea Scrolls: Treasure in a Cave," page 95.) The dogmatic *Constitution on Divine Revelation* of Vatican II in 1965 reinforced the biblical movement.

Bible study groups are springing up everywhere. More and more people are making Scripture reading a daily habit. Public schools and colleges have courses in the Bible as literature. Commentaries and aids to discussing Scripture are being published. The Bible is no longer only kept on the shelf as a register of family names and dates.

REVIEWING THE HANDBOOK

Strengthening Your Grasp

1. What is the Bible? Why is it sacred?
2. Define these terms:

revelation	inspiration
mysteries	inerrancy
Deposit of Faith	literary forms
Tradition	canon
Old Testament	apocryphal books
New Testament	deuterocanonical books

3. Use the contents page in your Bible to answer these questions:
   a. How many books are in the Old Testament?
   b. How many books are in the New Testament?
   c. Which books are named after men?
   d. Which books are named after women?
   e. Which books sound like historical books?
   f. Which books suggest what might be in them?
   g. Which books have interesting titles?
   h. Which are the shortest and longest books?
   i. What are the first and last books?
4. What are the first two and last two verses of the Bible?
5. How is the Bible similar to a sacrament?
6. How is the Bible like a picture of a loved one? A mirror? A roadmap? A letter?
7. What are some Christian attitudes toward the Bible?
8. Explain a good method for reading the Bible.
9. How did the Bible come to be?
10. Why is it necessary to know the literary form of a book of the Bible?
11. What is the Church's role in regard to Scripture?
12. Name and identify some versions of the Bible.
13. What has given impetus to the biblical movement of this century?
14. Why do people read the Bible?

Expressing Your Convictions

1. Enthrone the Bible in your classroom or church and plan a ceremony using appropriate Scripture passages and songs.
2. Illustrate your favorite Bible passages.
3. Prepare a three-minute speech on "The Importance of the Bible in My Life."
4. Write and deliver an original sermon based on a Scripture reading.

5. Collect prayers or prayer starters drawn from the Bible.
6. Look up different responses to God's living word: 1 Kgs. 19:9–14, Ps. 27, Ps. 139, Mal. 3:6, Jon. 14:5–21, Heb. 1:1–14, 1 Jn. 1:5–2:11, 1 Jn. 4:7–21, Rev. 21:7–8, Rev. 4:1–11.
7. Agree or disagree with these statements. Discuss your position.
   a. The Bible is not a book.
   b. God inspired certain people to write or to collect and edit what he had revealed. He preserved these people from error.
   c. The true meaning of the Bible is the one intended by the author. We can determine this if we know the author's background, his literary form, and his purpose in writing.
   d. The Bible teaches historical truth.
   e. The Church, like Mary, ponders God's words generation after generation and gains new insights into its meaning.
   f. The Word of God can be compared to the Eucharist because we encounter God every time we read it and it contains the active power of God.
   g. The liturgy is the Bible "prayed" by the Church.

Extending Your Interest

1. Ask ten people what their favorite passages of the Bible are.
2. Research the role of the Bible in the lives of our presidents or other famous people.
3. Read the book *God's Smuggler* by Brother Andrew or *The Hiding Place* by Corrie ten Boom.

Acknowledgments

The authors wish to thank Sister Mary Raphaelita Boeckmann, S.N.D., Superior General, Rome; Sister Mary Christopher Rohner, S.N.D., Provincial Superior of the Sisters of Notre Dame, Chardon, Ohio; and Sister Margaret Mary McGovern, S.N.D., High School Supervisor of the Chardon Province, who supported and encouraged the writing of the Light of the World series.

Humble gratitude is also due to all who in any way helped to create the Light of the World series: parents, teachers, co-workers, students, and friends. The following deserve special mention for their assistance in planning, organizing, testing, or critiquing the series: Notre Dame Sisters Mary Dolores Abood, Ann Baron, Karla Bognar, Peter Brady, Mary Catherine Caine, Virginia Marie Callen, Deborah Carlin, Naomi Cervenka, Reean Coyne, Mary Dowling, Dorothy Fuchs, Margaret Mary Gorman, Jacquelyn Gusdane, Mary Margaret Harig, Joanmarie Harks, Nathan Hess, Sally Huston, Christa Jacobs, Joanne Keppler, Owen Kleinhenz, Jean Korejwo, Leanne Laney, William David Latiano, Aimee Levy, Nadine Lock, Mary Ann McFadden, Inez McHugh, Louismarie Nudo, Donna Marie Paluf, Helen Mary Peter, Phyllis Marie Plummer, Eileen Marie Quinlan, Anne Marie Robinson, Patricia Rickard, Mark Daniel Roscoe, Kathleen Ruddy, Kathleen Scully, Dolores Stanko, Melannie Svoboda, Louise Trivison, Donna Marie Wilhelm; Ms. Laura Wingert; Ms. Meg Bracken; Sister Mary Kay Cmolik, O.F.M.; Mr. Robert Dilonardo; Rev. Mark DiNardo; Ms. Linda Ferrando; Mr. Michael Homza; Sister Kathleen King, H.H.M.; Ms. Patricia Lange; Mr. James Marmion; Mr. Peter Meler; Rev. Herman P. Moman; Rev. Guy Noonan, T.O.P.; Ms. Nancy Power; Ms. Christine Smetana; and Ms. Karen Sorace.

The following high schools piloted materials: Bishop Ireton High School, Alexandria, Virginia; Clearwater Central Catholic High School, Clearwater, Florida; Elyria Catholic High School, Elyria, Ohio; Erieview Catholic High School, Cleveland, Ohio; John F. Kennedy High School, Warren, Ohio; Notre Dame Academy, Chardon, Ohio; Regina High School, South Euclid, Ohio; St. Edward High School, Cleveland, Ohio; St. Matthias High School, Huntington Park, California.

The following parishes piloted the Parish School of Religion lessons: Corpus Christi, Cleveland, Ohio; St. Aselm, Chesterland, Ohio; St. John Nepomucene, Cleveland, Ohio; St. Thomas More, Paducah, Kentucky.

Special appreciation belongs to Sister Mary Roy Romancik, S.N.D., for managing all production and testing as well as for a careful reading of the original draft. Her suggestions resulted in the reworking of many sections.

Deep appreciation to Mrs. Anita Johnson for research; to Sisters of Notre Dame Linda Mary Elliott, Mary Regien Kingsbury, DeXavier Perusek, and Seton Schlather; to Robert Clair Smith for special services; and to typists Sisters Mary Lucie Adamcin and Catherine Rennecker, and Josetta Marie Livignano, Charlain Yomant N.N.D.

Index